Syntactic Analysis

A First Course

Syntactic Analysis

A First Course

Jeong-Seok Kim

SEJIN

Preface

Not everyone wants to be a linguist. I know that not every linguist wants to be a syntactician. But I am convinced that some are crazy about syntax.

This book has two main goals. The first is to offer a comprehensive introduction to generative syntax before the advent of the Minimalist Program. The second is to offer a description of English structure, utilizing a range of generative concepts and assumptions. My discussion is mainly focused on English. This happens to be the style of exposition with which I feel most comfortable.

To achieve this goal, I have opted for a number of strategies. First, the book is written in a reader-friendly style, avoiding an unnecessary tangle of complexity. Second, it provides a reasonable amount of exercises which I expect students will be able to solve. Some exercises are not complicated, but others will make them ponder. Third, I offer a wide variety of tree diagrams which will help students understand the structure of English and develop analytic skills for English syntax.

The target audience for the book is third- or fourth-year undergraduate students, and any background exposure to syntax is not presupposed. This book is organized as follows: Chapter 1 is a substantial introduction to grammatical concepts from descriptive and theoretical perspectives.

Chapter 2 introduces the notion of Lexicon, the mental dictionary. Chapter 3 deals with the English auxiliary system and the classic organization of Transformational Generative Grammar. Chapters 4 and 5 cover the phrase structure of language, which is instantiated as X-bar theory.

The successive chapters then discuss specific properties of English and how the notions and mechanisms introduced in the first five chapters can be applied to them in order to refine an understanding of English structure. Chapter 6 discusses the formation of verbal morphology. Chapter 7 investigates the concept of abstract Case and Case-driven movement. Chapter 8 compares raising and control phenomena, and provides insights into the features of the two different constructions. Chapter 9 deals with passivization and its related phenomena. Particularly, the similarity between raising and passivization is examined. Chapters 10 and 11 explore metaphorical island constraints and certain attempts to generalize them into one principle. Chapter 12 discusses the referential dependency between nominal expressions, which is captured with Binding theory. Chapter 13 outlines the Principles and Parameters theory of Grammar, and motivates the level of representation called Logical Form, which is the syntax-semantics interface with the Conceptual-Intentional system of the mind. Chapter 14 provides a brief synopsis of the current development of the linguistic program called Minimalism. The Appendix illustrates a variety of tree diagrams drawn by the students I have taught. I hope that this special section helps students to broaden and deepen their understanding of the structure of English.

Although the book was written by me, nothing could have happened without the help of my students: Sangceup Yune, Duk-Ho Jung, Hyo-Jin Kim, Da-eun Chang, Soohyun Kwon, among others. I am especially grateful to Sangceup Yune and Duk-Ho Jung for their patience in going over earlier drafts of the manuscript and for enhancing the quality of them. I concede that they have pulled me and pushed me through every stage of the project. My gratitude also goes to undergraduate students at Yeungnam University and Korea University who used the drafts of this book as their class text and raised many thought-provoking questions that helped me revise its organization as well as contents. The usual disclaimers apply.

Finally, I am grateful to my family for their endurance of this obsessive and growing preoccupation throughout the many years of my endeavor. This book is thus dedicated to them: my father, mother, wife, and two daughters.

Jeong-Seok Kim

February 2012

Contents

1 Introduction

Linguistics is the study of language.

Syntax is a branch of linguistics. It systematically studies sentence structures, using the following scientific methods:♣

(1) a. Observe data.
 b. Make generalizations.
 c. Develop hypotheses.
 d. Test those hypotheses against more data.

A sentence is the structurally organized unit of words that relates sound and meaning. It has two distinctive properties: linearity (= precedence) and hierarchy (= structure).

Grammar is a set of rules. The following rules apply for both Informal and Formal English:

(2) Do not use *ain't*.
 e.g. You ain't heard anything yet.

♣ Koopman et al. (2003) define syntax as "the set of rules or principles that govern how words are put together to form phrases, well-formed sequences of words."

(3) Do not use *gone* as the past tense of *go*; use *went*.
e.g. He gone too far this time.

The following is relevant only to Formal English:

(4) Do not start a sentence with a conjunction.
e.g. And I agree with you.

(5) Do not use contractions.
e.g. Let's consider the following example.

(6) Do not use sentence fragments.
e.g. Because I overslept.

(7) Do not end a sentence with a linking verb.
e.g. Ross is not happy. Rachel is.

Prescriptive Grammar is a set of rules about how humans are supposed to use their language. It observes the rules of etiquette and society. The sentences in (8) and (9) may be examples of indecent Grammar, but they are acceptable as English sentences. They are prescriptively deficient.

(8) a. A glance can cause injury to those who it falls on.
→ A glance can cause injury to those on whom it falls.

b. Rachel and him bought the ticket.
→ Rachel and he bought the ticket.

(9) a. He was the man whom I heard bought my house.
→ He was the man who I heard bought my house.

b. My dad gave it to her and I.
→ My dad gave it to her and me.

The examples in (10) are clearly ungrammatical sentences of English.♣

(10) a. *A glance cause can injury to those who it falls on. cf. (8a)
b. *Rachel and him the ticket bought. cf. (8b)
c. *He was whom I heard the man bought my house. cf. (9a)
d. *My dad gave it her and I to. cf. (9b)

Descriptive Grammar is a set of rules about how humans actually use their language. The sentences in (10) violate the rules in (11). They are descriptively deficient. They are prescriptively deficient, too. If a sentence is descriptively deficient, then it is necessarily prescriptively deficient.

(11) a. Modal verbs precede main verbs.
b. Verbs precede their objects.
c. Antecedents precede relative clauses.
d. Prepositions precede their objects.

According to Chomsky (1965), Competence is different from Performance. Competence refers to what we know about language. Performance refers to what we actually produce. We will be interested in both of these, but will primarily focus on Competence.

Learning involves conscious gaining of knowledge. Acquisition involves subconscious gaining of knowledge. In this light, the following can be stated:

(12) a. Linguistics is learned.
b. Language is acquired.

♣ The star indicates that the following string is ungrammatical.

It is true that children acquire some aspects of their native language by imitation. However, they do not simply copy what they hear. Instead, they would rather induct linguistic rules from the Primary Linguistic Data (PLD).

Linguists assume that children have an innate capacity of forming linguistic rules. A piece of evidence for this assumption is that they often overgenerate the past forms of some verbs. It suggests that language acquisition is not the rote learning process.

(13) *comed, *goed, *thinked, etc.

Another piece of evidence comes from the question-formation rule. At some stage of language acquisition, children would create questions by way of copying auxiliaries to the sentence-initial position.

(14) a. The girl is pretty. → Is the girl is pretty?
     b. The big hog can sleep in the barn. → Can the big hog can sleep in the barn?

The questions in (14) are gradually replaced with those in (15) in which auxiliaries are not copied but fronted.

(15) a. Is the girl ___ pretty?
     b. Can the big hog ___ sleep in the barn?

We can imagine two possibilities for children to utter questions. (16a) is structure-dependent, whereas (16b) is structure-independent. Apparently, (16b) is simpler, but it is not desirable.

(16) a. To form a question from a declarative sentence containing an auxiliary element, invert the auxiliary element with the subject

of the sentence.

b. To form a question from a declarative sentence containing an auxiliary element, move the first auxiliary element to the beginning of the sentence.

Let us consider the following complex sentence:

(17) The girl who is texting her friends is sitting on the bench.

If children adopt (16a), they probably produce (18a). If children adopt (16b), they possibly produce (18b). Actually, children never produce (18b). A question is then why.

(18) a. Is the girl who is texting her friends ___ sitting on the bench?

b. *Is the girl who ___ texting her friends is sitting on the bench?

The *structure dependency* principle forces language learners to assign abstract syntactic structure to sentences by grouping words together into some units called *constituents*. We have an intuition that certain words in a sentence belong together. For example, in (19) [*all the dependents*] is a constituent, and [*dependents are*] is not a constituent.

(19) All the dependents are acquitted.

Words can belong together even though they are not adjacent. In (20) [*hit Rachel*] is a constituent, and [*hit who*] WAS a constituent.

(20) a. Ross <u>hit Rachel</u>.

b. <u>Who</u> did Ross <u>hit</u>? cf. Ross hit who?

There is evidence for structure dependency: structural ambiguity. (21) is ambiguous.

(21) Joey hit the man with a flashlight.

In order to disambiguate the structurally ambiguous sentence, we use appropriate paraphrases.

(22) a. Joey hit the man who held a flashlight.
b. Joey hit the man by means of a flashlight.

In contrast to structural ambiguity, the following shows lexical ambiguity. In (23a) *bank* may mean 'money bank' or 'river bank'. In (23b) *bear* may mean 'endure', 'produce', or 'support'.

(23) a. I went to the bank.
b. Courteney cannot bear the children.

It is possible for one sentence to contain another. This property is called *recursion*. Language is recursive; that is, there is no upper bound on the length of sentences in natural human language.

(24) a. She passed away.
b. Robin reported that [she passed away].
c. Ted informed me that [Robin reported that [she passed away]].
d. I recalled that [Ted informed me that [Robin reported that [she passed away]]].

Adjuncts are optional and can appear repeatedly. This is another instance of recursion.

(25) a. Lily slept very soundly in her bed all night dreaming beautiful dreams.

b. I saw the book [on the chair] [in the library] [on the hill].

One of the central research issues in modern linguistics since the mid-1950s is concerned with solving Plato's Problem (i.e., the ease of acquisition), as given below:♣

(26) How are children able to acquire grammatical Competence despite the impoverished nature of the data that is input to this process?

Human beings are born with language faculty. Universal Grammar (UG) is a model or theory of human language faculty. UG is composed of (several) Principles and (several) Parameters. For instance, structure dependency and recursion are UG Principles. UG is not completely fixed, but allows some variation. That is, individual languages differ. So we need to specify the types of variation that UG manifests among different languages. This is called Parameters.

(27) UG is composed of principles with open parameter values that are set by experience, i.e., PLD.

There are two basic facts characterizing language acquisition.

(28) a. It is considerably fast in spite of the very serious deficiency in the data.

b. Languages display an intricate surface variation.

Below, you have five English words.

(29) a, the, boy, girl, kissed

♣
Plato's Problem is the term given by Noam Chomsky to the gap between knowledge and experience. It presents the question of how we account for our knowledge when environmental conditions seem to be an insufficient source of information. It is used in linguistics to refer to the *argument from poverty of the stimulus.* In a more general sense, Plato's Problem refers to the problem of explaining a *lack of input.* Solving Plato's Problem involves explaining the gap between what one knows and the apparent lack of substantive input from experience. [Wikipedia]

Based on (29), you can generate various different orders to form grammatical sentences.

(30) a. A girl kissed the boy.
b. The girl kissed a boy.
c. A boy kissed the girl.
d. The boy kissed a girl.

But you could generate ungrammatical sentences.

(31) a. *A kissed girl the boy.
b. *The kissed a girl boy.
c. *A boy girl kissed the.
d. *The boy girl a kissed.

Generative Grammar spells out an explicit way of determining which sequences of words in a language are grammatical or not.

The following sentences make sense but are (syntactically) ungrammatical:

(32) a. *Me no drink coffee.
b. *He goes not today.
c. *Does matter some of the notes?
d. *Result significant the future of the province.

In syntax, we usually aim to explain the grammaticality (but not acceptability) of linguistic expressions. The following may be acceptable but not grammatical:

(33) a. You ain't seen anything yet.
b. You haven't heard nothing yet.

The following does not make sense but is (syntactically) grammatical. It is semantically (or pragmatically) anomalous:

(34) #Colorless green ideas sleep furiously.♣ (Chomsky 1965)

In contrast to (35), (36) sounds pragmatically anomalous. However, people can still understand the utterance even if they find it funny. This suggests that certain interpretations forced by syntax are assigned to the subject and object positions.

(35) The cow chewed the cud.

(36) #The cud chewed the cow.

Below, noun antecedents are modified with relative clauses. Each sentence is both grammatical and acceptable.

(37) a. The Joker [that the Batman hunted down] ran away.

b. The Batman [that the Catwoman scared] stumbled on the curb.

Notice, however, that (38) is grammatical but not acceptable with many speakers. How do you feel?

(38) The Joker [that the Batman [that the Catwoman scared] hunted down] ran away.

As in various scientific domains, linguistics has been conducted along with several dimensions: elegance, simplicity, naturalness, etc. Yet it could turn out that our language faculty is nothing but ugly, complex, and redundant. Language faculty may have design flaws.

♣ As a convention, the prefixed pound sign indicates semantic or pragmatic anomaly.

Exercise 1

《 1-1 》

Explain the following terms:

(39) a. Linguistics, Syntax, Grammar, Generative Grammar
b. Sentence
c. Prescriptive Grammar, Descriptive Grammar
d. Competence, Performance
e. Learning, Acquisition
f. Structure Dependency
g. Constituent
h. Structural Ambiguity, Lexical Ambiguity
i. Recursion
j. Adjunct
k. Plato's Problem
l. Language Faculty, Universal Grammar
m. Principles, Parameters
n. Pragmatic Anomaly, Semantic Anomaly
o. Grammaticality, Acceptability

《 1-2 》

The following sentences are ungrammatical by many native speakers. First, decide whether the ungrammaticality of each sentence is prescriptive or descriptive. Then, discuss the reason why the sentence is ungrammatical. You might want to revise the original sentence.

(40) Me no go today.

(41) You ain't seen nothing yet.
(42) You are taller than me.
(43) The bolt of lightning killed the rock.
(44) The VP-internal subject raises to Spec of IP.
(45) Joey Rachel loves.
(46) Rachel's brother is not her sibling.
(47) My toothbrush loves sesame.

《 1-3 》

Disambiguate the following ambiguous expressions:

(48) The proprietor of the fish store was the sole owner.
(49) I saw the man with the telescope.
(50) The man put the book in the box on the table.
(51) I killed the king with the knife.
(52) Visiting relatives can be tiresome.
(53) Flying planes can be dangerous.
(54) The shooting of the hunters occurred at dusk.
(55) They took the animal to the small animal hospital.
(56) Wanted: Man to take care of cow that does not smoke or drink
(57) Every man thinks he is lucky.

Noam Chomsky

http://en.wikipedia.org/wiki/Noam_Chomsky

Born: Philadelphia, Pennsylvania in 1928

- Expertise: Generative Linguistics, Psycholinguistics, Cognitive Psychology, Philosophy, Ethics, Intellectual History, International Affairs and U.S. Foreign Policy, Contemporary Issues, etc.
- Institution: MIT (since 1955)
- Degrees: University of Pennsylvania (PhD, MA, BA)
- Doctoral Advisor: Zellig Harris
- Dissertation Title: *Transformational Analysis* (1955; Published under the title of *The Logical Structure of Linguistic Theory* in 1975)
- Known for: Initiator of Modern Linguistics, Principles and Parameters Theory, Minimalist Program, Critiques of U.S. Foreign Policy and Contemporary Capitalism, etc.

2 Lexicon

By way of Phrase Structure Rules (PSRs), we can generate an infinite number of grammatical sentences in English. However, Phrase Structure (PS) trees like (1b) and (2b) show that Grammar may generate ungrammatical sentences.[♣ ♣♣ ♣♣♣]

(1) a. An architect built the house.

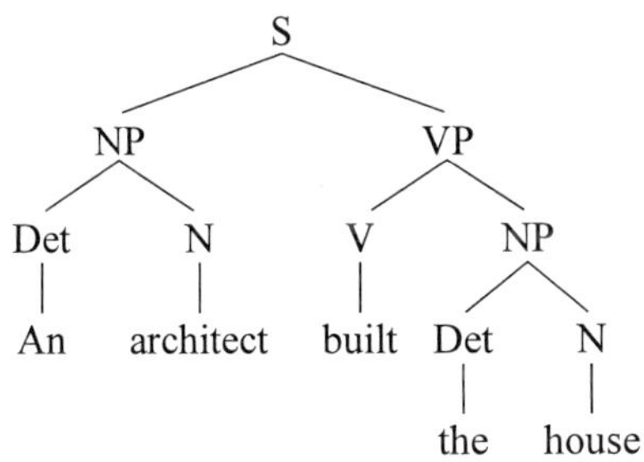

♣
S (Sentence or Clause)
NP (Noun Phrase)
VP (Verb Phrase)
Det (Determiner)
N (Noun)
V (Verb)

♣♣
Phrase Structure Tree = PS Tree = Tree = Phrase Marker = P-marker

♣♣♣
Some of PS rules (= PSRs) are given below:

(i) S → NP VP
[S rewrites as NP and VP.]
(ii) NP → Det N
(iii) NP → N
(iv) VP → V NP
(v) VP → V

Based on PS rules, we generate trees. Conversely, we could say that PS rules can be deducted from trees.

b. *An architect snored Chandler.

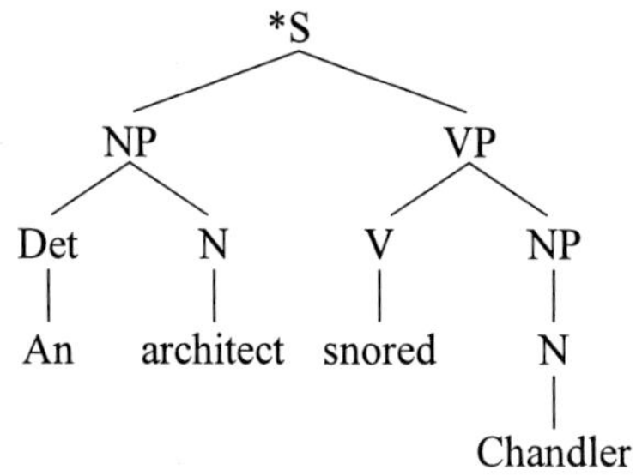

(2) a. Chandler snored.

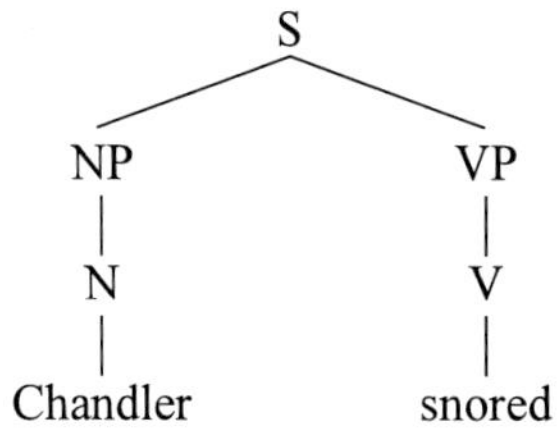

b. *An architect built.

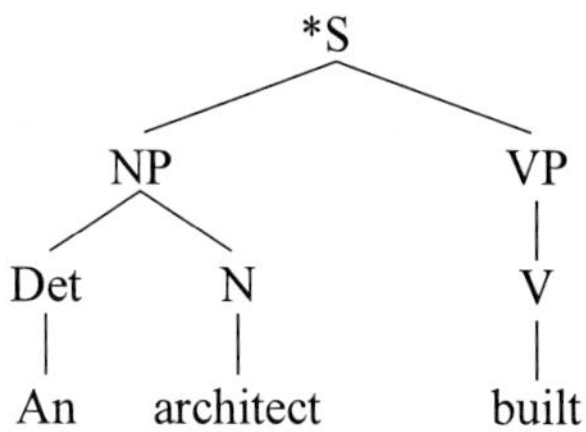

In order to prevent ungrammatical strings from being generated by trees, we should constrain Grammar in various ways. One way is in the Lexicon.

The Lexicon is a mental dictionary. It is the storage of information about particular words. It is composed of lexical items. Each lexical item has a lexical entry in which the following lexical information is provided:

(3) a. Phonological information
b. Syntactic (= Formal) information
c. Semantic information

The *predicate* defines the relation between the individuals being talked about in a sentence or an utterance and the real world. The *arguments* are the individuals who participate in that relation.

(4)	Syntacticians	like	semantics.
	ARGUMENT	PREDICATE	ARGUMENT

Let us consider the lexical entry of the verb *snore*. *Snore* is a 1-place predicate.

(5) Tom snored.

(6) *snore*
Phonological information: /sno:r/
Semantic information: "to breathe noisily while you sleep"
Syntactic information:
Category: V

Build is a 2-place predicate.

(7) a. *An architect built the house that building.
b. An architect built the house.
c. An architect built that building.

Put is a 3-place predicate.

(8) a. *Ross put.
b. *Ross put the book.
c. *Ross put on the table.
d. Ross put the book on the table.

In order to capture the x-place property, we assume that the Lexicon has a Predicate-Argument Structure (PAS). Given this assumption, *snore* has the following fuller lexical entry:

(9) *snore*
Phonological information: /sno:r/
Semantic information: "to breathe noisily while you sleep"
Syntactic information:
Category: V
PAS: <1>

Build has the following PAS:

(10) *build*
Phonological information: /bild/
Semantic information: "to make a large structure by putting its parts together"
Syntactic information:
Category: V
PAS: <1, 2>

Put has the following PAS:

(11) *put*
Phonological information: /put/
Semantic information: "to move something into the stated place"
Syntactic information:

Category: V
PAS: <1, 2, 3>

The following shows 1-place predicates: PAS <1>. But (12a) has an Agent argument, and (12b) a Theme argument.♣ More precisely, the verbs in (12a) are unergative, whereas those in (12b) are ergative (= unaccusative).♣♣

(12) a. unergative verbs: *walk, talk, snore,* etc.
b. ergative (= unaccusative) verbs: *arrive, break, melt,* etc.

Each predicate has a distinct PAS and a distinct S(emantic)-selection.

(13) a. The professor talked.
b. *The rock talked.
c. *The light snored.

(14) a. The train arrived.
b. The base broke.
c. The butter melted.

Terrify and *design* are 2-place predicates: PAS <1, 2>.

(15) a. The zombies terrified me.
b. He designed his own house.

They have the following S-selection grid:♣♣♣

(16) a. *terrify*: <Theme, Experiencer>
b. *design*: <Agent, Theme>

The following examples are ungrammatical because they violate the

♣
Agent is an initiator of an action, which is capable of volition.
(i) Ross hit Joey.

Theme (= Patient) is the entity that undergoes actions or the entity that is moved.
(ii) a. Monica loves cookies.
b. A falling rock hit Chandler.
c. The syntactician bought a semantics monograph.

♣♣
See chapter 9.

♣♣♣
Experiencer is the argument that experiences or perceives an event.
(i) a. Monica saw the eclipse.
b. Syntax frightens Ross.
c. Phoebe loves cookies.
d. A falling rock hit Chandler.

S-selection requirement in (16):

(17) a. *The zombies terrified watermelon.
b. *His pencil designed his own house.

Give and *put* share the following property: PAS <1, 2, 3>. More precisely, however, they are different from each other with respect to thematic roles. In the case of *give*, the third argument should be Goal.♣ In the case of *put*, the third argument should be Location.♣♣ Thus, (18b) and (19b) violate S-selection.

(18) a. Ross gave a book to Rachel.
b. *Ross gave a book on Rachel.

(19) a. Ross put the book on the table.
b. *Ross put the book to the table.

In this light, *terrify* has a fuller lexical entry as follows:

(20) *terrify*
Phonological information: (omitted)
Semantic information: (omitted)
Syntactic information:

Category:	V
PAS:	<1, 2>
S-selection:	<Theme, Experiencer>

Put has a fuller lexical entry as follows:

(21) *put*
Phonological information: (omitted)
Semantic information: (omitted)

♣
Goal is the entity towards which a motion takes place.
(i) a. A falling rock hit Chandler.
b. The syntactician bought a semantics monograph.
c. Rachel went to Chicago.
d. Monica was given a semantics article.

♣♣
Location is the place where an action occurs.
(i) a. Yijun and Yijae live in Kilumdong's finest apartment.
b. We are all at KU.

Syntactic information:

Category: V
PAS: <1, 2, 3>
S-selection: <Agent, Theme, Location>

Claim has a fuller lexical entry as follows:

(22) Ross claimed that it was a conspiracy against him.

(23) *claim*
Phonological information: (omitted)
Semantic information: (omitted)
Syntactic information:

Category: V
PAS: <1, 2>
S-selection: <Agent, Proposition>♣

Convince has a fuller lexical entry as follows:

(24) Lasnik convinced me that I am up to the task.

(25) *convince*
Phonological information: (omitted)
Semantic information: (omitted)
Syntactic information:

Category: V
PAS: <1, 2, 3>
S-selection: <Agent, Theme, Proposition>

C(ategory)-selection has been called *subcategorization*. It restricts the range of arguments. It is said that a lexical item C-selects its

♣ Proposition refers to the unit of a meaningful sentence. It has the property of being either true or false.

complements. Consider the C-selectional property of *dwell*.

(26) *dwell*: PAS: <1, 2>
S-selection: <Agent, Location>
C-selection: [___ PP]

(27) a. Joey dwelt in Chandler's apartment.
b. *Joey dwelt Chandler's apartment.

Consider the C-selectional property of *occupy*.

(28) *occupy*: PAS: <1, 2>
S-selection: <Agent, Location>
C-selection: [___ NP]

(29) a. Joey occupied Chandler's apartment.
b. *Joey occupied in Chandler's apartment.

Let us compare the C-selectional property of *reply* and *answer*.

(30) a. *reply*: PAS: <1, 2>
S-selection: <Agent, Theme>
C-selection: [___ PP]
b. *answer*: PAS: <1, 2>
S-selection: <Agent, Theme>
C-selection: [___ NP]

(31) a. I have not replied to Kim's e-mail yet.
b. I have not answered Kim's e-mail yet.

The following suggests that *ask* and *wonder* may have the same argument structure:♣

♣
S' = CP = clause.
S' → C(omplementizer) S.
S' is bigger than or equals S.

(32) a. Ross asked [$_{S'}$ what that noise was].
b. Ross wondered [$_{S'}$ what that noise was].

(33) a. *ask*: PAS: <1, 2>
S-selection: <Agent, Interrogative Proposition>♣
C-selection: [___ S']
b. *wonder:* PAS: <1, 2>
S-selection: <Agent, Interrogative Proposition>
C-selection: [___ S']

Let us compare the argument structures of *ask* and *wonder*.

(34) a. Ross asked [$_{NP}$ that noise].
b. *Ross wondered that noise.
c. Ross wondered [$_{PP}$ about that noise].

(35) a. *ask*: PAS: <1, 2>
S-selection: <Agent, Interrogative Proposition>
C-selection: [___ {S', NP}]♣♣
b. *wonder*: PAS: <1, 2>
S-selection: <Agent, Interrogative Proposition>
C-selection: [___ {S', PP}]

The following suggests that *tell* and *inform* may have the same argument structure:

(36) a. Any actors will tell you that it is easier to perform than to be themselves.
b. Any actors will inform you that it is easier to perform than to be themselves.

♣
Interrogative Proposition = Question

♣♣
To indicate mutually exclusive choices of elements in a string, we use the convention of curly brackets. For example, {α, β} = α or β. This convention states that if you choose α, you cannot choose β, but you should choose at least one; i.e., either α or β, but not both.

(37) a. *tell*: PAS: <1, 2, 3>
S-selection: <Agent, Goal, Proposition>
C-selection: [___ NP S']

b. *inform*: PAS: <1, 2, 3>
S-selection: <Agent, Goal, Proposition>
C-selection: [___ NP S']

However, this suggestion is deceiving, as compared below:

(38) a. They would tell him any progress they had made.
b. *They would tell him of any progress they had made.

(39) a. *They would inform him any progress they had made.
b. They would inform him of any progress they had made.

(40) a. *tell*: PAS: <1, 2, 3>
S-selection: <Agent, Goal, Theme>
C-selection: [___ NP {S', NP}]

b. *inform*: PAS: <1, 2, 3>
S-selection: <Agent, Goal, Theme>
C-selection: [___ NP {S', PP}]

In sum, *put* has the following lexical entry:

(41) *put*
Phonological information: (omitted)
Semantic information: (omitted)
Syntactic information:
Category: V
PAS: <1, 2, 3>
S-selection: <Agent, Theme, Location>
C-selection: [___ NP PP]

Claim has the following lexical entry:

(42) *claim*

Phonological information: (omitted)

Semantic information: (omitted)

Syntactic information:

Category:	V
PAS:	<1, 2>
S-selection:	<Agent, Proposition>
C-selection:	[___ S']

Ask has the following lexical entry:

(43) *ask*

Phonological information: (omitted)

Semantic information: (omitted)

Syntactic information:

Category:	V
PAS:	<1, 2>
S-selection:	<Agent, Interrogative Proposition>
C-selection:	[___ {NP, S'}]

Wonder has the following lexical entry:

(44) *wonder*

Phonological information: (omitted)

Semantic information: (omitted)

Syntactic information:

Category:	V
PAS:	<1, 2>
S-selection:	<Agent, Interrogative Proposition>
C-selection:	[___ {PP, S'}]

In short, lexical items may be further subclassified according to their PAS, S-selection, and C-selection.

◀ Question & Answer ▶

Are there 0-place predicates? Maybe. In (45) weather *it* is a sort of expletives. Alternatively, weather *it* is classified as a quasi-argument.

(45) a. It rains cats and dogs.
b. It becomes dark.

Expletives are non-thematic subjects such as *it* or *there*. In (46a) *it* is the fake subject, and *to* infinitival clause *to park your car here* is the understood subject (= associate). In (46b) *there* is the fake subject, and the nominal *a man* is the understood subject.

(46) a. It is illegal to park your car here.
b. There is a man in the garden.

The VP PS rule states that VP contains V obligatorily as its head, and one or more optional elements.♣

(47) VP → V (NP) ({NP, PP, S'}) cf. (69)

The PSR in (47) may rewrite as 7 VP rules.

(48) a. Ross [$_{VP}$ snored]. VP → V
b. Ross [$_{VP}$ hit Joey]. VP → V NP
c. Ross [$_{VP}$ resides in New York]. VP → V PP
d. Ross [$_{VP}$ knows that I like him]. VP → V S'
e. Ross [$_{VP}$ gave Rachel a present]. VP → V NP NP
f. Ross [$_{VP}$ put a book on the table]. VP → V NP PP
g. Ross [$_{VP}$ persuaded Joey that he should leave]. VP → V NP S'

♣ The parenthesis notation indicates that the inside material is optional.

These seven subcategories correspond to certain traditional labels of verbal classification.

(49) a. [____] (intransitives)
snore, walk, laugh, etc.
b. [____ NP] (transitives)
hit, kiss, meet, etc.
c. [____ PP] (incomplete intransitives)
reside, live, lie, etc.
d. [____ S'] (transitives)
think, claim, believe, etc.
e. [____ NP NP] (ditransitives)
give, buy, teach, etc.
f. [____ NP PP] (incomplete transitives)
put, assign, explain, etc.
g. [____ NP S'] (ditransitives or incomplete transitives)
convince, promise, order, etc.

The following constraint is required to solve the overgeneration problem:

(50) Constraint on Lexical Insertion
Lexical items may be inserted under terminal nodes within a tree only if the environments into which they are inserted match the categorical, PAS, S-selection, and C-selection requirements of the lexical items.♣

Let us consider next the lexical entries of adjectives.

(51) a. Ross is aware.
b. Ross is aware of Joey's success.
c. Ross is aware that Joey won the prize.
d. *Ross is aware Joey's success.
e. *The building is aware.

♣ For instance, in (1a) the terminal nodes are the following: Det, N, V, Det, and N.

(52) *aware*

Phonological information: (omitted)

Semantic information: (omitted)

Syntactic information:

Category:	A
PAS:	<1, (2)>
S-selection:	<Experiencer, (Theme)>
C-selection:	[____ ({PP, S'})]

Let us consider next the lexical entries of prepositions.

(53) of the man vs. *of

(54) *of*

Phonological information: (omitted)

Semantic information: (omitted)

Syntactic information:

Category:	P
PAS:	<1>
S-selection:	<Theme>
C-selection:	[____ NP]

(55) at the restaurant vs. *at

(56) *at*

Phonological information: (omitted)

Semantic information: (omitted)

Syntactic information:

Category:	P
PAS:	<1>
S-selection:	<Location>
C-selection:	[____ NP]

(57) into the hole vs. *into

(58) *into*

Phonological information: (omitted)
Semantic information: (omitted)
Syntactic information:

Category:	P
PAS:	<1>
S-selection:	<Location>
C-selection:	[____ NP]

(59) a. He appeared from behind my back.
b. He arrived from Connecticut.

(60) *from*

Phonological information: (omitted)
Semantic information: (omitted)
Syntactic information:

Category:	P
PAS:	<1>
S-selection:	<Source>
C-selection:	[___ {NP, PP}]

(61) He jumped off (the table).

(62) *off*

Phonological information: (omitted)
Semantic information: (omitted)
Syntactic information:

Category:	P
PAS:	<(1)>
S-selection:	<(Source)>
C-selection:	[___ (NP)]

Let us consider next the lexical entries of nouns. The following nouns are called *deverbal* or *derived* nominals:♣

(63)	a.	their destruction of the city	[____ PP]
	b.	his arrival at home	[____ PP]
	c.	our expectation that he will win	[____ S']

Let us compare the notions of adjuncts, complements, and arguments (cf. 68). Below, the bracketed expressions show time relation. They are NP adjuncts.

(64) a. The man snored [$_{NP}$ all night].
b. Ross saw Joey [$_{NP}$ last week].

Time adjuncts may have a variety of parts of speech (cf. 48).

(65) a. Ross snored [$_{NP}$ last night].
b. Ross hit Joey [$_{S'}$ when he came in].
c. Ross resides in New York [$_{NP}$ these days].
d. Ross knows that I like him [$_{NP}$ now].
e. Ross gave Rachel a present [$_{PP}$ in the morning].
f. Ross put a book on the table [$_{PP}$ at 3 p.m].
g. Ross persuaded Joey that he should leave [$_{NP}$ yesterday].

Let us consider place, manner, time, or reason adjuncts.

(66) a. Ross died last year because he had a pneumonia.
[time + reason]
b. Officials reacted there angrily to those charges.
[place + manner]

♣
(i) [$_V$ destruct] → [$_N$ destruction]
(ii) [$_V$ arrive] → [$_N$ arrival]
(iii) [$_V$ expect] → [$_N$ expectation]

In the following, pre-verbal adjuncts are underlined:

(67) a. Ross <u>suddenly</u> left.
b. Ross <u>unexpectedly</u> hit Joey.
c. Ross <u>happily</u> lives in New York.
d. Ross <u>certainly</u> knows that I don't like him.

Let us check the relations of complements vs. adjuncts vs. arguments (cf. 80).

(68) a. Complements help to complete the meaning of a sentence as required by a verb.
b. Adjuncts do not help to complete the meaning of a sentence.
c. Predicates C-select their complements, not their adjuncts.
d. Arguments are the participants—the place holders—of the PAS of a predicate.
e. Adjuncts do not figure in the organization of the Lexicon.

We need to revise the PSR in (47) to allow VPs containing adjuncts to appear in a sentence.

(69) VP → (AdvP) V (NP) ({NP, PP, S'}) (XP*)♣

Nouns may have PP complements. It is typical that PP complements are realized as *of* NPs.

(70)

	Det	N	PP
a.	her	destruction	of his plan
b.	their	discussion	of the topic
c.	a	student	of linguistics
d.	the	teacher	of jazz

♣ XP* indicates that XP can be recursive.

Verbs may have complements.

(71)		NP	V	NP
	a.	She	destroyed	his plan.
	b.	They	discussed	the topic.
	c.	Chandler	studies	linguistics.
	d.	Phoebe	teaches	jazz.

Nouns may have adjunct PPs.

(72) a. her arrival <u>on Friday</u>
b. their discussion <u>in the seminar room</u>

(73) a. a student <u>from LA</u>
b. the teacher <u>in a blue skirt</u>

Verbs may have adjunct PPs.

(74) a. She arrived <u>on Friday</u>.
b. They discussed the topic <u>in the seminar room</u>.

In the following, adjunct APs are underlined:

(75) a. a <u>young</u> guy
b. the <u>dangerous</u> lady

In the following, the underlined clauses (S') are complements:

(76) a. I believe <u>that he will leave</u>.
b. The belief <u>that he will leave</u> turned out to be a rumor.

(77) a. Phoebe claims <u>that she never kissed Joey</u>.
b. I don't believe Phoebe's claim <u>that she never kissed Joey</u>.

(78) a. Ross asserted that he settled the argument between Rachel and Monica.

b. Ross's assertion that he settled the argument between Rachel and Monica is not convincing.

Nouns such as *baby* and *toaster* do not take complements (unlike event-denoting nouns like *destruction, discussion, claim*, etc.). In the following, the underlined clauses are adjuncts:

(79) a. The baby that the Gellers adopted a while ago is Vietnamese.

b. The toaster that I bought last month does not heat up.

Consider the following comparison of complements vs. adjuncts (cf. 68):

(80) a. Complements denote elements which help to complete the meaning of a head. Their occurrence is often obligatory in the environment of a verb.

b. Adjuncts provide additional information to modify their heads, but are not required by their heads.

The following illustrates grammatical categories. Both X (head) and XP (maximal projection) are categories:

(81) V, P, N, A, VP, PP, NP, AP, S', Det, etc.

The following shows grammatical relations (GRs) or grammatical functions (GFs):

(82) subject, object, complement, adjunct, head, predicate, etc.

In syntax, subjects, objects, and predicates are not primitive.♣ They can be defined via a dominance/domination relation.

(83) a. The subject is an NP that is immediately dominated by S.
[NP, S]

b. The object is an NP that is immediately dominated by VP.
[NP, VP]

c. The predicate is a VP immediately dominated by S.
[VP, S]

(84)

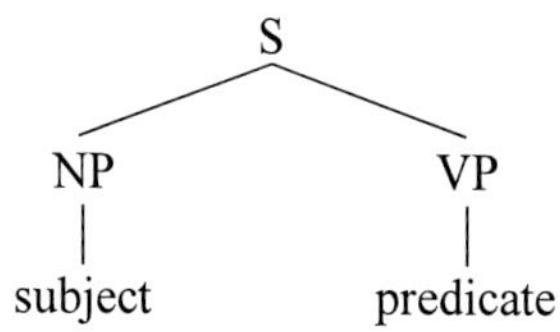

(85)

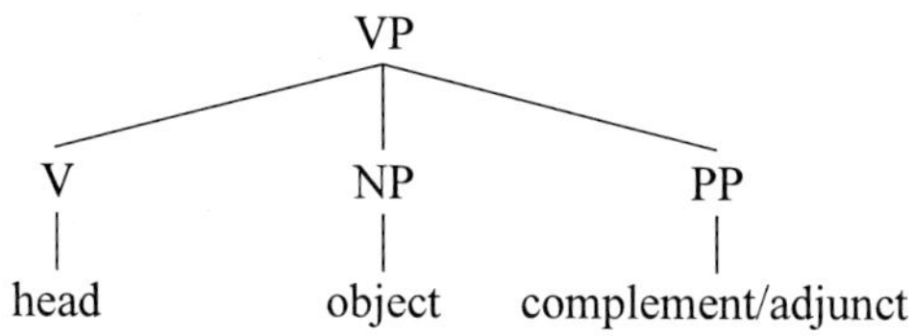

As discussed above, you should encode the thematic relation (or selectional restriction) between a predicate and its arguments in the Lexicon. In order to show the thematic relation, you use terms such as Agent, Theme (= Patient), Experiencer, Goal, Proposition, etc. There are many thematic relations.♣♣

♣
A primitive is the basic form or concept from which a certain form or concept has been derived.

♣♣
Recipient is a special kind of Goal that involves a change of possession.

(i) a. Ross gave Rachel the book.
b. Monica received a book from Chandler.

Source is the entity from which a movement occurs.

(ii) a. Ross gave Rachel an archeology assignment.
b. Phoebe came directly from the semantics class.

Instrument is the entity with which an action occurs.

(iii) a. Chandler hacked the computer with an axe.
b. This key will open the door to the Seokwan building.

Benefactive is the entity for whom an action occurs.

(iv) Monica bought these flowers for Chandler.

For instance, in (86a) *Ross* is an Agent NP subject, *a toy* is a Theme NP complement, and *to the boy* is a Goal PP complement.

(86)	a.	Ross	handed	a toy	to the baby.
		AGENT		THEME	GOAL
		NP		NP	PP
		SUBJECT		COMPLEMENT	COMPLEMENT
	b.	A toy	was handed	to the baby	by Ross.
		THEME		GOAL	AGENT
		NP		PP	PP
		SUBJECT		COMPLEMENT	ADJUNCT
	c.	The baby	was handed	a toy	by Ross.
		GOAL		THEME	AGENT
		NP		NP	PP
		SUBJECT		COMPLEMENT	ADJUNCT

The interpretation of an object remains the same. This suggests that the interpretation of an object is solely determined by the verb itself. The object is an internal argument.

(87)	a.	Ross	broke	the window.
				PATIENT
	b.	The stone	broke	the window.
				PATIENT

The interpretation of the subject is determined not solely by the verb, but also by the choice of the object. The subject is the external argument. For instance, in (88b) *Ross* can be an Agent, a Patient, or an Instrument, depending on the context. However, in (89b) *Ross* can be neither a Patient nor an Instrument due to the word choice of *deliberately*, which forces *Ross* to be an Agent.

(88) a.

Ross	broke	the window.
AGENT		
INSTRUMENT		

b.

Ross	broke	his leg.
AGENT		
PATIENT		
INSTRUMENT		

(89) a.

Ross	deliberately	broke	the window. (Gruber 1976)
AGENT			
*INSTRUMENT			

b.

Ross	deliberately	broke	his leg.
AGENT			
*PATIENT			
*INSTRUMENT			

θ-role (theta-role) is a bundle of thematic relations associated with a particular argument. An argument may have many thematic relations, but only one θ-role.

(90)

Ross	gave	the book	to Rachel.
AGENT/SOURCE		THEME	RECIPIENT/GOAL
θ-ROLE		θ-ROLE	θ-ROLE

Exercise 2

《 2-1 》

Explain the following terms:

(91) a. PS Rule, PS Tree, Phrase Marker, P-marker, Tree
b. Lexicon, Lexical Item, Lexical Entry, Lexical Information
c. Predicate, Argument, Internal Argument, External Argument
d. Predicate-Argument Structure (PAS), S-selection, C-selection, Subcategorization
e. Unergative Verb, Ergative Verb, Unaccusative Verb
f. Complement, Adjunct, Object, Adverbial
g. Grammatical Relation (GR), Grammatical Function (GF)
h. Dominance, Domination
i. Thematic Relation, Selectional Restriction, θ-role

《 2-2 》

Identify the usage of the underlined adjuncts in the following:

(92) Ross resides in Boston happily these days.
(93) Ross knows that I like him because it is obvious.
(94) Ross gave Joey a present in the classroom.
(95) Ross put a book on the table with a loud noise.
(96) Ross told Joey the story yesterday because of my request.

《 2-3 》

Identify the thematic role of each argument in the following examples:

(97) Pete drank a pint of milk.

(98) The government banned speeches fomenting terrorism.

(99) Ross sent a letter to Rachel.

(100) Rachel received a letter from Ross.

(101) It seems that Ross likes Rachel.

(102) The dog chewed the slipper.

(103) The dog saw the slipper.

《 2-4 》

For each of the following PS rules, write out the possible sequences that each rule generates:

(104) A → B (C D) E

Answer: A → B E

A → B C D E

(105) A → B (C) (D) (E)

(106) A → {B, C} {D, E}

(107) A → B {C, D, E} {F, G} I

(108) A → B (C) ({D, E, F, G}) I

《 2-5 》

Provide the lexical entry of the following words, illustrating relevant examples:

(109) declare

(110) persuade

(111) sneeze

(112) reside

(113) inhabit

(114) arrive

(115) reach

3 Auxiliaries

3.1 Auxiliary System

The auxiliary (Aux) is an optional helping verb. The following is a PS rule which rewrites an Aux. Note that *to* as in *to* infinitive clauses is treated as an Aux:♣

(1) Aux → ({Infinitive, Modal}) (Perfective) (Progressive)

Let us consider the infinitival Aux. As shown below, the clause with the infinitival particle *to* does not contain any marking for tense.

(2) a. I didn't mean to offend her.
b. I was hoping to have finished by now.
c. They just wanted us to be happy.
d. To buy things cheaply from a poor country is to connive in its poverty.

If a clause or sentence is not infinitival, it is necessarily marked for either present or past tense.

♣
Infinitive → to
Perfective → have -en
Progressive → be -ing

(3) a. Ross {dances, danced}.
b. Ross {will, would} dance.
c. Ross {has, had} danced.
d. Ross {is, was} dancing.

Question

Why is the following ungrammatical?

Answer

There are two or more tense markers in one sentence. Each sentence should contain one and only one tense marker.

(4) a. *Ross will dances.
b. *Ross is dances.
c. *Ross will had been dancing.
d. *Ross will have was dancing.

(5) a. *Ross would danced.
b. *Ross would dances.
c. *Ross has is dancing.
d. *Ross would had was dancing.

Phrase Structure Rules (PSRs) are a set of rewriting rules for each single constituent. The Aux in finite clauses may have the following PS rule. Note that tense should appear on the leftmost element in the verb group.

(6) Aux → (Modal) (Perfective) (Progressive)

Let us assume that a PS rule marks each Aux with the [tense] feature.

(7) a. Aux → Progressive
[tense]

b.	Aux	→	Perfective [tense]	(Progressive)	
c.	Aux	→	Modal [tense]	(Perfective)	(Progressive)

Obviously, the three PS rules in (7) cannot be generalized as (8). The latter incorrectly permits the case of more than one tense marker in a string.

(8)	Aux	→	(Modal) [tense]	(Perfective) [tense]	(Progressive) [tense]

In addition, (9) does not grasp the fact that V carries tense only if VP does not follow an Aux. Hence, (7) and (9) lose generality.

(9)	VP	→	V ... [tense]

3.2 Affix Hopping

Chomsky (1965) proposes that Grammar consists of two types of rules: PS rules and Transformations. In this proposal, tense (Tns) is treated as an independent category.

(10) Aux → Tns (Modal) (Perfective) (Progressive)

Tense rewrites as either the present or past morpheme, which further rewrites as the suffix *-es* or *-ed*, respectively.

(11) Tns → {Present, Past}

(12) a. Present → -es
b. Past → -ed

According to Chomsky (1965), the tree diagram of (13) may be represented as (14):

(13) Ross would be dancing.

(14) [tentative]

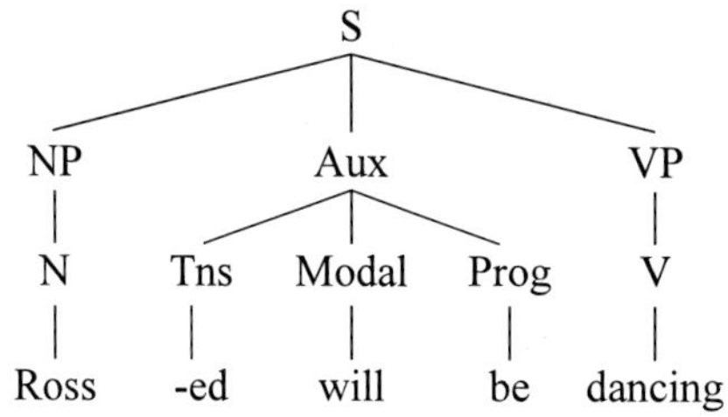

The tree diagram of (15) may be represented as (16):♣

(15) Rachel left suddenly yesterday.

(16)

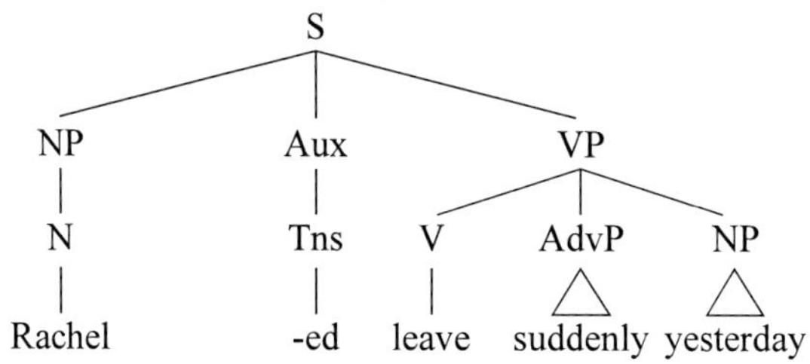

Consider also the following terminal strings prior to the application of Affix Hopping:

(17) a. Chandler *-es have* driven all night.
b. Monica *-es be* cooking in the kitchen.

♣ The dummy symbol (△) is used to simplify an internal structure.

c. Phoebe *-es will* have been singing.

d. Joey *-ed believe* that I *-ed shall* kiss Rene.

By way of Affix Hopping, a verbal affix hops onto the immediately following verb within a verb group. The following shows the results of Affix Hopping:

(18) a. Ross *will+ed* be dancing.

b. Rachel *leave+ed* suddenly yesterday.

c. Chandler *have+es* driven all night.

d. Monica *be+es* cooking in the kitchen.

e. Phoebe *will+es* have been singing.

f. Joey *believe+ed* that I *shall+ed* kiss Rene.

The following shows the results after the application of appropriate morphophonemic rules:

(19) a. Ross *would* be dancing.

b. Rachel *left* suddenly yesterday.

c. Chandler *has* driven all night.

d. Monica *is* cooking in the kitchen.

e. Phoebe *will* have been singing.

f. Joey *believed* that I *should* kiss Rene.

Aspect is a grammatical term which encodes the length of time that an action, event, or situation has gone on. There are two kinds of aspect in English: Perfective and Progressive.

(20) a. Perfective → have -en

b. Progressive → be -ing

Under these assumptions, the tree for (13) should be revised as (21), prior to the application of Affix Hopping.

(21)

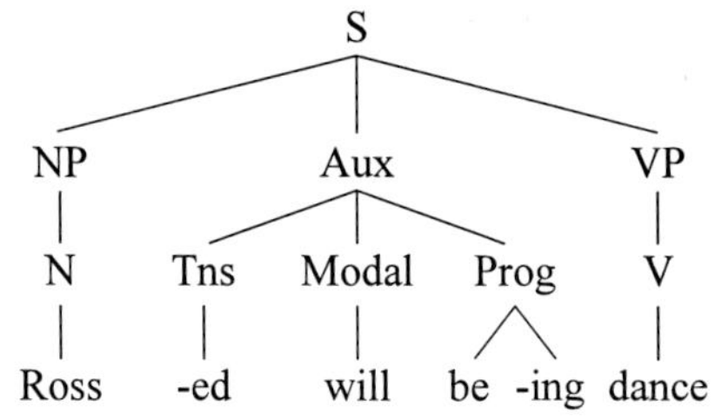

The tree for (19e) would be drawn as (22), prior to the application of Affix Hopping.

(22)

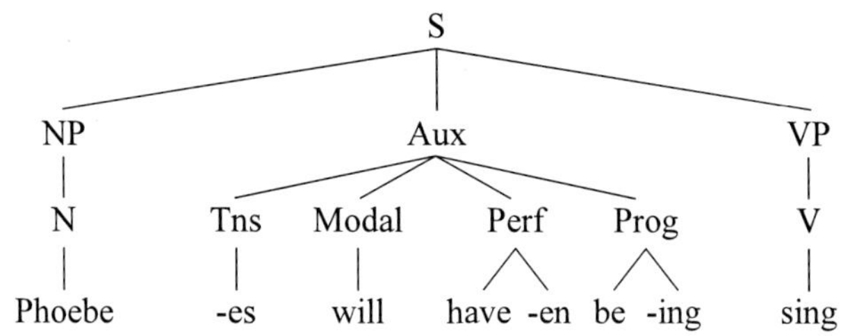

The result of applying Affix Hopping to these structures will derive the following:

(23) a. Ross will+ed be dance+ing.

b. Phoebe will+es have be+en sing+ing.

3.3 Deep Structure, Surface Structure, and Transformation

At an initial stage of modern linguistics, it was believed that Grammar consists of Lexicon and two types of syntactic rules: Phrase Structure Rules (PSRs) and Transformations (Trs).

(24) Grammar = Lexicon + PSRs + Trs

Syntax has two different structures: deep structure (DS) and surface structure (SS).

(25) a. DS is the P-marker generated by the PSRs and Lexical Insertion.

b. SS is the P-marker generated by Transformations which operate on DS.

The organization of the *Transformational Generative Grammar* is as follows: DS is an output of the Base Component. SS is an output of the Transformational Component.

(26) Grammar = Base Component + Transformational Component

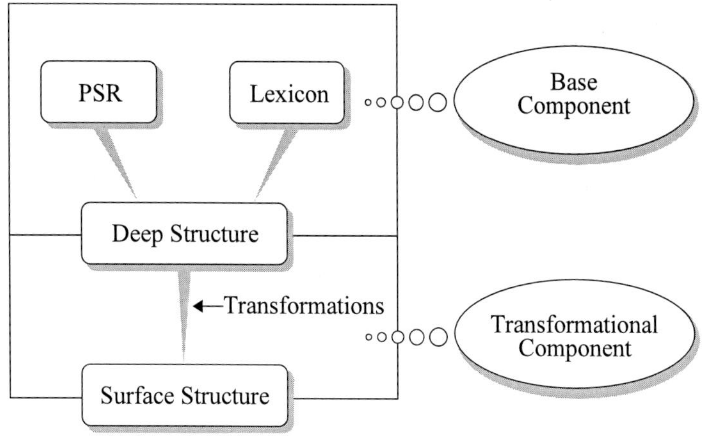

A PSR is context-free. If you have an element X, you can rewrite it irrespective of the context.

(27) X → Y Z W

However, a transformation is context-sensitive. As formulated in (28), Affix Hopping is applied only if a verbal element immediately follows an affix. The immediately following verbal element X thus constitutes the relevant context:

(28) Aff X ⇒ X+Aff
[+V] [+V]

3.4 Subject-Aux Inversion

Let us consider the following in which Aux verbs are fronted in order to convert declarative sentences into interrogative equivalents:

(29) a. You will give my best wishes to Helen.
b. You would have helped me right there.
c. He has forgotten the appointment again.
d. You have been here all along.
e. Keith was driving my Ferrari yesterday.
f. That will be covered in the policy you purchased.

(30) a. Will you give my best wishes to Helen?
b. Would you have helped me right there?
c. Has he forgotten the appointment again?
d. Have you been here all along?
e. Was Keith driving my Ferrari yesterday?
f. Will that be covered in the policy you purchased?

A question may arise if we need to revise the PSR as follows:

(31) S' → {COMP, Aux} S

Let us say yes. Then, why is (32) ungrammatical? Recall that utterances like (32) are occasionally produced by children. We generalize that fronted auxiliary verbs can appear before the subject only if they are missing from the original position after the subject, as shown in (30). Auxiliary inversion is thus not a copying but a chopping rule.

(32) a. *Will you will give my best wishes to Helen?
b. *Would you would have helped me right there?
c. *Has he has forgotten the appointment again?
d. *Have you have been here all along?
e. *Was Keith was driving my Ferrari yesterday?
f. *Will that will be covered in the policy you purchased?

The result of Subject-Aux Inversion (SAI) would be the following:

(33) a. Will you ___ give my best wishes to Helen?
b. Would you ___ have helped me right there?

(34) is the DS of (29b).

(34)

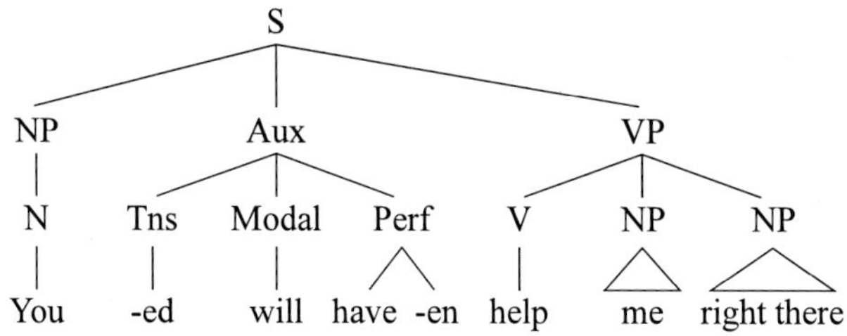

You have two choices at this stage.

Option 1

If you first apply Affix Hopping and then apply SAI in (34), you will derive (35).

(35) Affix Hopping > SAI ('A > B' means that A precedes B.)

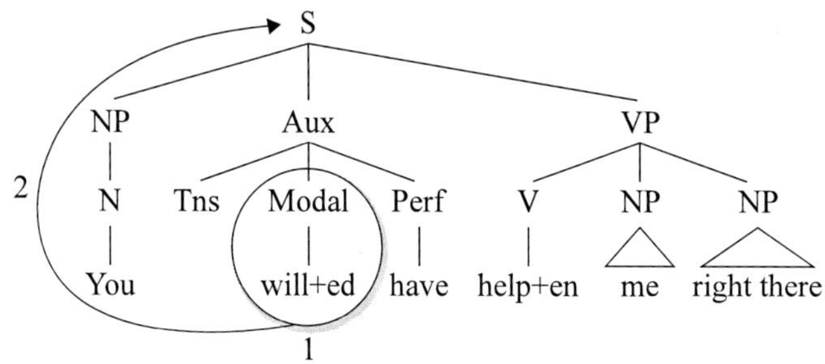

Option 2

If you first apply SAI and then apply Affix Hopping in (34), you will derive (36).

(36) SAI > Affix Hopping

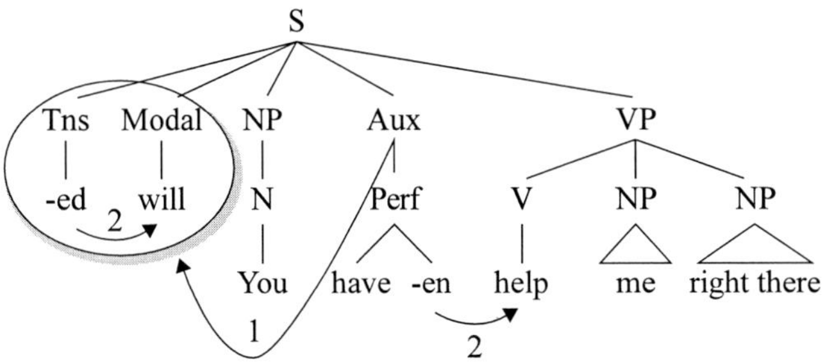

For the moment, either option seems to be fine. In the next section, we will decide which option is better.

3.5 *Do*-support

The following illustrates questions with *do*-support:

(37) a. Do you know that Alicia remarried with Peter?
b. Does she still love him?
c. Did he ask her to divorce him?

Let us now consider the derivations of (37).

The following shows the declarative counterparts of (37):

(38) a. You know that Alicia remarried with Peter.
b. She still loves him.
c. He asked her to divorce him.

The following shows the DS terminal strings of (37). Notice that tense affixes are bound morphemes, and bare verbs are free morphemes.

(39) a. You -es know that Alicia -ed remarry with Peter.
b. She still -es love him.
c. He -ed ask her to divorce him.

The following shows the SAI results of (39). In (40) the tense affixes in matrix clause are stranded. In order to salvage the stranded tense affixes, the pleonastic Aux *do* is inserted in order to play the role of a verbal host.

(40) a. -es you know that Alicia -ed remarry with Peter?
b. -es she still love him?
c. -ed he ask her to divorce him?

The following shows the *do*-support results of (40):

(41) a. -es *do* you know that Alicia -ed remarry with Peter?
b. -es *do* she still love him?
c. -ed *do* he ask her to divorce him?

If you apply Affix Hopping, you can derive (37).

◀ Question ▶

Why are the (b) sentences in (42)-(44) ill-formed?

◀ Answer ▶

Do-support is a last resort operation. In the (a) sentences, tense was not stranded.

(42) a. Zack <u>would</u> seek the spotlight in any case. [Tns will]
b. *Zack did will seek the spotlight in any case.

(43) a. They <u>are</u> attending the flashmob. [Tns be]
b. *They do be attending the flashmob.

(44) a. Alan <u>has</u> burned his bridges with this company. [Tns have]
b. *Alan does have burned his bridges with this company.

◀ Question ▶

Why are the sentences in (45) ill-formed?

◀ Answer ▶

Do-support is a last resort operation. Tense was not stranded.♣

(45) a. *You do know that Alicia remarried with Peter. [Tns know]
b. *She does still love him. [Tns (still) love]
c. *He did ask her to divorce him. [Tns ask]

The following shows the Affix Hopping results of (41):

(46) a. *do+es* you know that Alicia *remarry+ed* with Peter?
b. *do+es* she still love him?
c. *do+ed* he ask her to divorce him?

♣ Let us set aside the emphatic reading.

We thus conclude that *do*-support is a last resort operation, and that SAI precedes *do*-support which precedes Affix Hopping.

(47) SAI > *Do*-support > Affix Hopping
cf. *Affix Hopping > SAI

Exercise 3

⟨ 3-1 ⟩

Explain the following terms:

(48) a. Tense
b. PS Rule, Transformation
c. Terminal String
d. Affix Hopping
e. Aspect
f. Deep Structure, Surface Structure
g. Base Component, Transformational Component
h. Subject-Aux Inversion
i. *Do*-support, Last Resort

⟨ 3-2 ⟩

Draw the DS trees of the following, according to Chomsky (1965):

(49) You should have done that.

(50) Kim's Syntax Textbook must have been being written.

⟨ 3-3 ⟩

Draw the SS trees of (49) and (50).

⟨ 3-4 ⟩

If Affix Hopping is applied prior to SAI, ill-formed sentences may be derived. Explain why this is so, illustrating relevant examples.

❰ 3-5 ❱

Discuss the difference of context-free rules and context-sensitive rules, illustrating relevant examples.

4 X-bar Structures

4.1 Constituents

Phrase structure is a formal means of representing constituency. In this section, we will study a variety of notions with respect to phrase structure and constituency.

Physicists use molecules and atoms as theoretical constructs in order to account for the nature of matter (Radford 2004). What do you think linguists need in order to explicate the nature of language?

Certain words belong together. The elements which belong together and behave independently are called *constituents*. Syntactically, a constituent is a node itself or a set of nodes exhaustively dominated by a single node. In (1) there is intuition that *the* and *man* are more closely related than *her* and *jealous*. This intuition is captured with constituency.

(1) The man is only talking to her to make you jealous.

There are several tests which are used to determine constituency: replacement test, pro-form test, fragment test, movement test, focus test, coordination test, adverb test, etc.

◀ Replacement Test ▶

If you can replace something with a constituent, that could be a constituent.

(2) a. *Phoebe* can't carry a tune.
b. *His girlfriend* can't carry a tune.
c. *That skinny hippie* can't carry a tune.
d. *The odd skinny hippie* can't carry a tune.

(3) a. I've always been concerned about *the woman in a red skirt.*
b. I've always been concerned about *Rachel.*

◀ Pro-form Test ▶

Only a constituent can be replaced with a pro-form.

(4) A: What is {*Phoebe, his girlfriend, that skinny hippie, the odd skinny hippie*} up to these days?
B: *She* tries to learn how to carry a tune.

(5) A: Monica *bought a German sedan with chrome garnish.*
B: Phoebe *did so* too.

◀ Fragment Test ▶

If you can reply with a sentence fragment to a question, that sentence fragment could be a constituent.

(6) A: Who can't carry a tune?
B: {*Phoebe, his girlfriend, that skinny hippie, the odd skinny hippie*}.

(7) A: Who were you talking to?
B: To the cable guy.

(8) A: What exactly do you expect me to look up?
B: *Up anything relevant.

(9) A: What has Steve resigned from?
B: {The chairman of the board, From the chairman of the board}.

Movement Test

Only a constituent (usually, an XP) can be moved.

(10) a. Tommy likes cupcakes with icing snowflakes.
b. *Cupcakes with icing snowflakes*, Tommy likes. [Topicalization]♣

(11) a. My pretty daughter hugged *the drooling puppy*.
b. *The drooling puppy* was hugged by my pretty daughter. [Passivization]

Focus Test

Only a constituent (usually, an XP) can be clefted.

(12) It is {*Phoebe, his girlfriend, that skinny hippie, the odd skinny hippie*} that would go out on a limb and file a complaint.

(13) a. It was *the pool in the backyard* that Rachel didn't like. [*It* clefting]
b. What Rachel didn't like was *the pool in the backyard*. [Wh-clefting]

♣ See section 10.4.

Coordination Test

Only constituents of the same type can be coordinated.

(14) a. [fond of syntax] *and* [indifferent to phonetics]
b. [slowly] *but* [certainly]
c. [to take] *or* [to leave]

(15) A: What does he do to keep in shape?
B: Run *on the treadmill* and *on the elliptical trainer.*

(16) A: What exactly do you expect me to look up?
B: *Look *up the Britannica* and *up anything relevant*.

The coordination test has to be used with care. What are conjoined in (17)? If a PP and an AP are conjoined as in (18a), (17) is predicted to be ruled out. The well-formedness of (17) suggests that two predicates are conjoined as in (18b).

(17) The economy is in the doldrums as yet but likely to bottom out.

(18) a. The economy is [$_{PP}$ in the doldrums as yet] but [$_{AP}$ likely to bottom out].
b. The economy is [$_{PRED}$ in the doldrums as yet] but [$_{PRED}$ likely to bottom out].

Adverb Test

Only a constituent can be modified with an adverb. In the following, the underlined elements are modal adverbs (e.g., *possibly, perhaps, maybe, probably, conceivably, definitely, certainly*):♣

(19) a. Perhaps *the senator has come up with a stronger regulation.*
b. The senator definitely *has come up with a stronger regulation.*
c. The senator has certainly *come up with a stronger regulation.*
d. *The probably *senator has come up with a stronger regulation.*

♣ Modality is the qualification in a proposition that indicates that what is affirmed or denied is possible, impossible, necessary, contingent, etc.

◀ Caution ▶

In order to determine the constituency of a string of words, it is better to perform two or more constituency tests, which are sometimes misleading.

◀ Question ▶

Why are the sentences in (20) ungrammatical?

◀ Answer ▶

Modal adverbs in English cannot generally appear within a VP.

(20) a. *The senator has come up conceivably with a stronger regulation.
b. *The senator has come up with a stronger maybe regulation.
c. *The senator has come up with possibly a stronger regulation.

◀ Misnomer ▶

The term *pronoun* is potentially deceptive. In fact, pronouns replace noun phrases (NPs) instead of just nouns. Hence, they have a good reason to be called pro-NPs.

(21) a. *Phoebe* wrote the lyric of the song.
b. *His girlfriend* wrote the lyric of the song.
c. *That skinny hippie* wrote the lyric of the song.
d. *The odd skinny hippie* wrote the lyric of the song.

(22) a. She wrote the lyric of the song.
b. *His she* wrote the lyric of the song.
c. *That skinny she* wrote the lyric of the song.
d. *The odd skinny she* wrote the lyric of the song.

Constituents need not be NPs. For instance, the italicized sequences in (23) are constituents on the basis of the evidence in (24).

(23) It happened {*very recently, an hour ago, during the day, on Monday*}.

(24) a. Question-Answer Pairs
A: *When* did it happen?
B: {*Very recently, An hour ago, During the day, On Monday*}.

b. *It* clefting
It is {*very recently, an hour ago, during the day, on Monday*} that it happened.

c. Substitution of pro-form
It happened *then*.

4.2 Projecting Syntactic Structures

The lexical item *formulate* is a verb.

(25) a. VERB They *formulated* a successful approach.
b. ADJECTIVE *They *formulable* a successful approach.
c. NOUN *They *formulation* a successful approach.

It combines with two NPs.

(26) a. *They *formulated*.
b. They *formulated* a successful approach.
c. *They *formulated* the syntacticians a successful approach.

We can imagine two basic trees of *formulate*. For the moment, let us assume that the subject NP originates within VP.

(27) a.

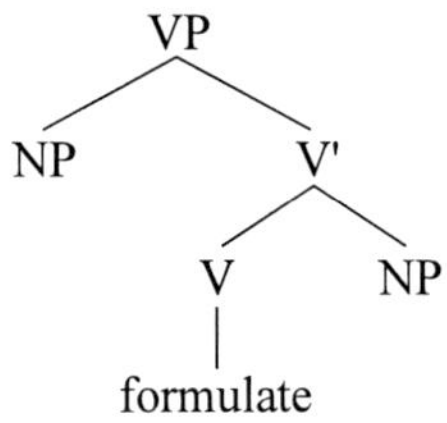

b.

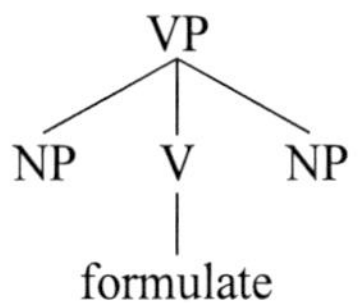

There is evidence that (27a) is better than (27b); V' is a constituent. In the following, *formulated a new approach* is a constituent since it can be replaced with the pro-form *do so*:

(28) a. In the first place, the syntacticians *formulated a new approach*.
b. And then the phoneticians *did so*.

(29) shows X-bar schema (X'-schema). X is a head. ZP is a specifier. YP is a complement.

(29)

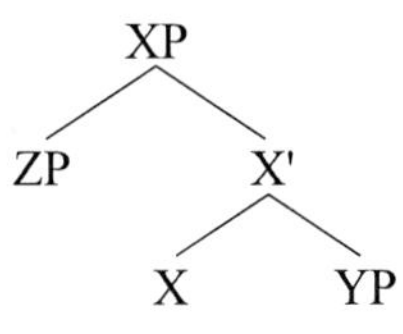

The three projections (X, X', XP) have the bar levels as in (30).

(30)

PROJECTION	BAR LEVEL	EXAMPLE
MAXIMAL	2	VP
INTERMEDIATE	1	V'
MINIMAL	0	V

In the following, you have intransitive verbs:

(31) a. Bush lied.
b. Da Vinci sneezed.

In the following, you have transitive verbs:

(32) a. The tsunami devastated the region.
b. The accidents traumatized the child.

In the following, you have ditransitive verbs:

(33) a. I gave them a good impression.
b. Dan would not loan me money.

Transitivity is a syntactic concept, whereas valency (or adicity) is a semantic concept. Semantically speaking, verbs like *read, eat,* and *write* are always two-place predicates. Syntactically speaking, however, they can be realized as transitive verbs or intransitive verbs. When they are transitive, they require two overt arguments: a subject and an object. When they are intransitive, they require only one overt argument, which is the subject of a sentence.

(34) a. transitive *read*: [___ NP] <Agent, Patient>
Ross is reading the morning paper.

b. intransitive *read*: [___] <Agent, ~~Patient~~>
Rachel is reading. (= Rachel is reading a written material.)

Devastate and *traumatize* are dyadic verbs.

(35) a. *The hurricane devastated.
b. The hurricane devastated the whole residential area.
c. *The hurricane devastated Boston the whole residential area.

(36) a. *The accident traumatized.
b. The accident traumatized the child.
c. *The accident traumatized her the child.

Some of the dyadic verbs can be used both transitively and intransitively.

(37)

		TRANSITIVE	INTRANSITIVE
a.	*eat*	She ate a pizza.	He is eating.
b.	*read*	She is reading a book at home.	He is reading at home.
c.	*write*	She wrote a thesis on minimalism.	He writes twice a week.

Certain monadic (= one-place) verbs can be used transitively with the cognate (= etymologically related) object.♣ ♣♣

(38) a. Achilles fought. [unergative]
b. Achilles fought a heroic fight.

(39) a. She slept. [unergative]
b. She slept the sleep of the just.

(40) a. He sighed. [unergative]
b. He sighed a weary sigh.

♣
Only unergatives can take cognate objects. Ergatives and transitives cannot take cognate objects:
(i) a. *Ross arrived an arrival. [ergative]
b. *The Romans destroyed a destruction. [transitive]

♣♣
See chapter 9.

Triadic (= three-place) verbs can be ditransitive, transitive, or intransitive.

(41) a. John gave my nephew a stuffed bear.
John gave every single detail about fixing my Beamer.
John gave (generously).
b. Kim teaches college students syntax.
Kim teaches college students.
Kim teaches syntax.
Kim teaches (for a living).
c. She cooked me a square meal.
She cooked a square meal.
She cooked.

The following dyadic verbs are transitive or ditransitive:

(42) a. I offered a spousal companionship for my wife.
I offered my wife a spousal companionship.
b. I owe 20 bucks.
I owe him 20 bucks.
c. The county will grant a subsidiary.
The county will grant the immigrants a subsidiary.

The basic tree for transitive *read* is given in (43).

(43)

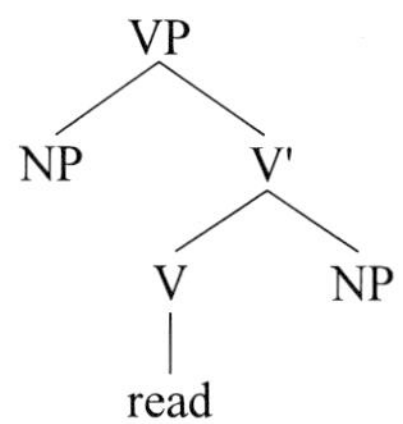

For intransitive *read*, you have two options.

(44) a.

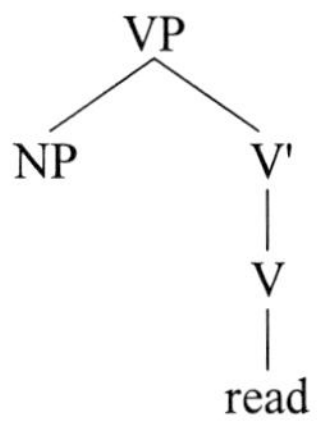

b.

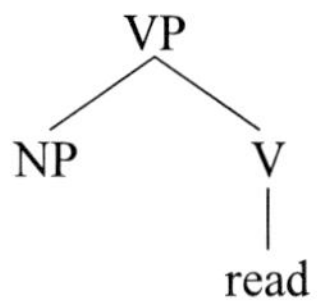

There is evidence for (44a).

Evidence 1

The pro-form *do so* can substitute for the verb and its complement, but not for the verb alone.

(45) a. Ann read one chapter, and then Maggie *did so*.

b. *Ann read one chapter, and then Maggie *did so* two chapters.

With intransitive verbs, *do so* substitution gives the results in (46).

(46) The teacher read, and then the kids *did so*.

Given (44a), the restriction can be stated as follows:

(47) *Do so* substitutes for instances of V'.

Given (44b), the restriction is less intuitive as follows:

(48) *Do so* substitutes for instances of V' or of V without a complement.

◀ Evidence 2 ▶

(44a) permits the concise definition of specifiers as in (49a). Given (44b), you need to define specifiers as in (49b). Which one is better?

(49) a. Specifiers are sisters of intermediate projections.
b. Specifiers are sisters of intermediate projections or of minimal projections without a complement.

In English, the present tense and the past tense are expressed with a bound morpheme.

(50) a. The light blink<u>s</u>.
b. The light blink<u>ed</u>.

The future tense is expressed with a free morpheme.

(51) The light <u>will</u> blink.

The present and past tense in English may be expressed as a bound morpheme affixed to the auxiliary *do* in *do*-support contexts.

(52) a. NEGATION: The light {doesn't, didn't} blink.
b. QUESTION: {Does, Did} the light blink?

The basic trees for *will* and auxiliary *did* are shown in (53).♣

(53) a. b.

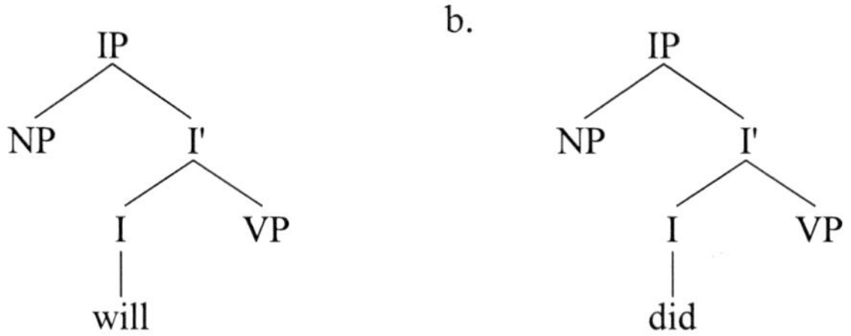

The following shows the structure of (51). We adopt the Predicate-internal Subject Hypothesis (PISH) according to which the subject originates in Spec of VP and moves to Spec of IP.♣♣ ♣♣♣

(54)

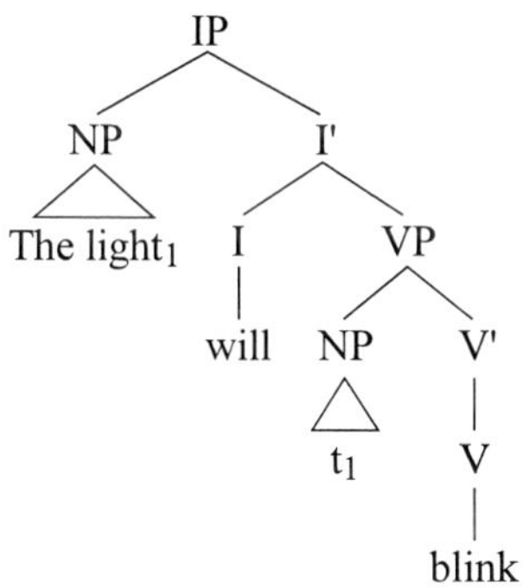

If a linguistic object moves, it takes more than one syntactic position although it is pronounced only once in a particular position.

(55) a. The scholarship$_1$ was granted t_1 to Rachel (by the college).
THEME BENEFICIARY AGENT

♣
IP = Inflection Phrase = S
I = INFL = Inflection

♣♣
When an element moves in syntax, it leaves behind its trace; *t* is short for trace.

♣♣♣
The identical subscript number as in *the light*$_1$ and t_1 indicates that t_1 is the trace of *the light*$_1$.

b. Rachel$_1$ was granted t_1 the scholarship (by the college).♣
BENEFICIARY THEME AGENT

We assume that tense affixes are generated in INFL.

(56) a.

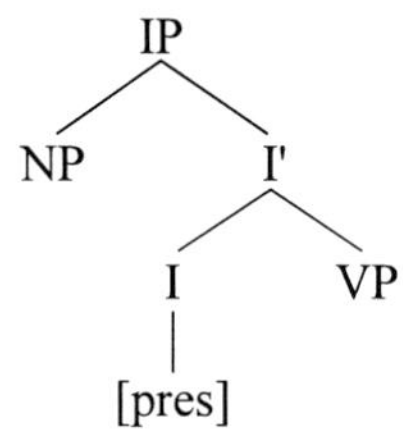

b.

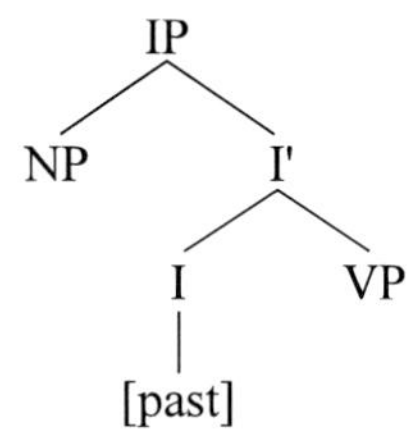

The following shows the structure of (50a):

(57)

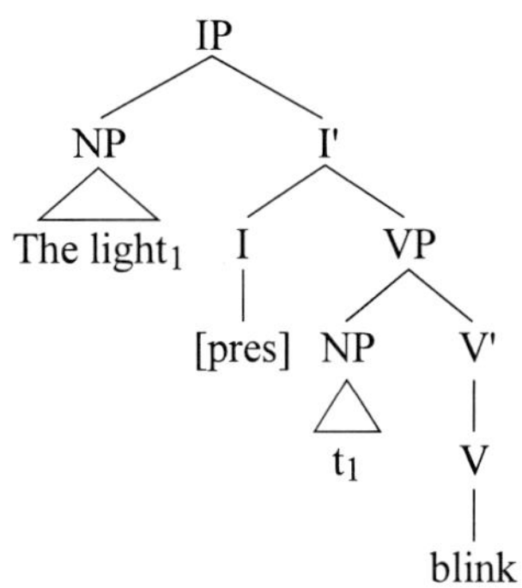

In the following, the underlined clauses are complement clauses (= clausal complements):

(58) a. Kids will ask if chimps talk.
b. They believe that chimps talk.
c. That little boy is wondering whether chimps talk.

♣ Beneficiary ≈ Recipient ≈ Goal

If, that, or *whether* is a complementizer (= COMP = C). It converts an independent clause into a dependent one which could be the complement of a higher verb.♣

(59)

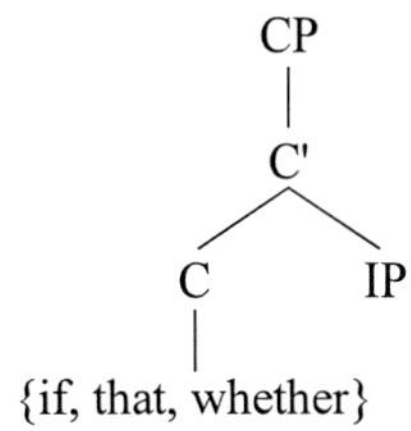

The following is the tree of (58a).

(60)

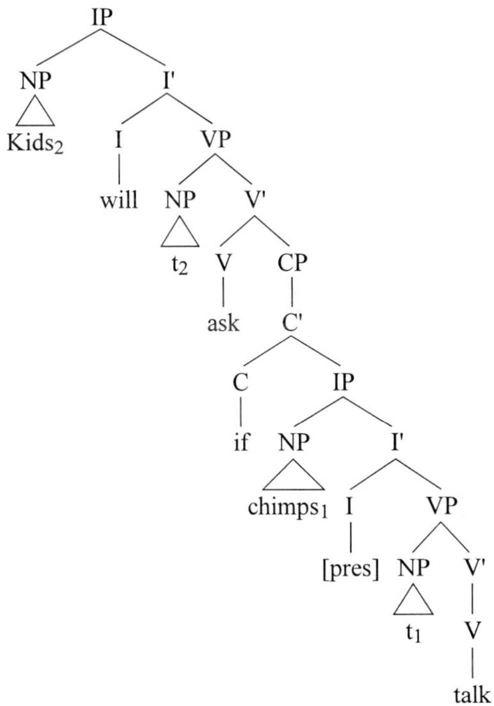

♣ More precisely, complementizers encode something about the nature of the IP (e.g., finiteness) as well as encoding the force of the sentence (whether it is a declarative, exclamative, interrogative, and so on).

4.3 Adjuncts

Arguments refer to central participants in the event denoted by a verb. Adjuncts modify the event by specifying the time at which or the frequency with which it takes place.

(61) a. They take a postprandial walk after meal. [Time]

b. They take a postprandial walk habitually. [Frequency]

Arguments undergo substitution into an empty position. Adjuncts are adjoined to a position via adjunction. In the following, PP is adjoined to V':

(62)

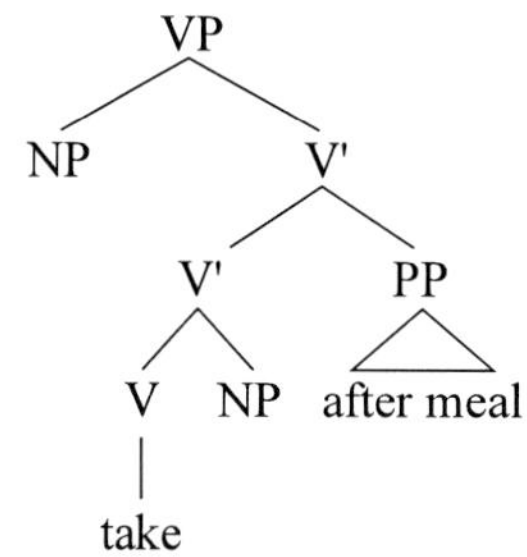

The following shows the structure of (61a):

(63)

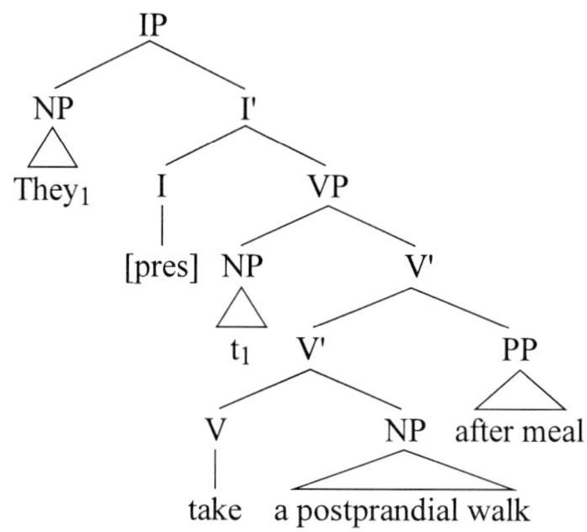

An intermediate projection can be recursive. A piece of evidence comes from *do so* anaphora. As shown in (64), *do so* can replace a verb, its complement, and its adjuncts, suggesting that all the three elements form a constituent.

(64) We *take a postprandial walk {after meal, rarely, in spring}*, and they *do so*, too.

In addition, *do so* can substitute for a verb and its complement excluding adjuncts, as shown in (65).

(65) a. We *take a postprandial walk* after the sunset, and they *do so* around midday.

b. We *take a postprandial walk* rarely, but they *do so* quite regularly.

c. We *take a postprandial walk* in spring, and they *do so* all year around.

What if you have two verbal adjuncts?

(66)

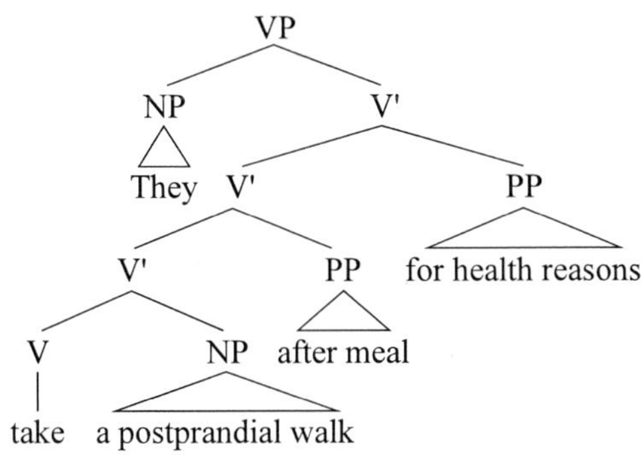

There is no fixed word order between adjuncts.

(67)

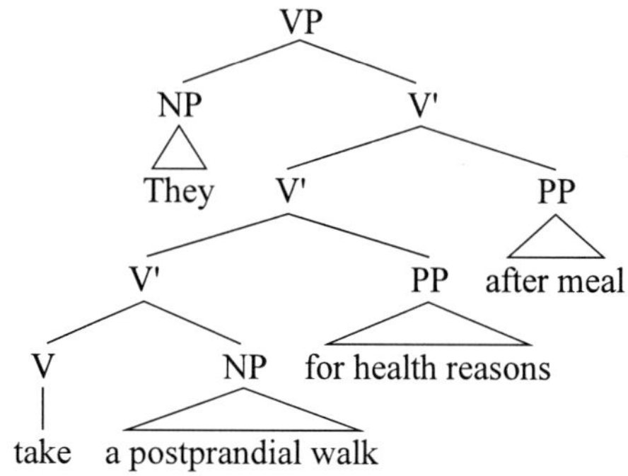

There are three types of syntactic dependents: complement, specifier, and adjunct.

(68) a. A complement is the sister of a head X and a daughter of an X'.
b. A specifier is the sister of an X' and the daughter of an XP.
c. An adjunct is the sister of an X' and the daughter of an X'.

It is not always straightforward whether a phrase is a complement or an adjunct. Usually, the phrases indicating rationale, duration, location, or manner are adjuncts. One reliable test is *do so* anaphora. If a phrase can survive with *do so* anaphora, it is an adjunct. The following illustrates adjuncts:

(69) a. He waited for no compelling reason, but I did so for a good one. [Rationale]
b. He waited for days, but I did so for months. [Duration]
c. He waited in the cafe, but I did so beside the cafe. [Location]
d. He waited calmly, but I did so restlessly. [Manner]

At the moment, the generalization in (70) could be formulated. However, it will be shown shortly that (70b) is false.

(70) a. If a syntactic dependent is obligatory, then it is a complement.
b. *If a syntactic dependent is a complement, then it is obligatory.

(71) shows that the NP *multivitamin pills* is the complement of the verb *take*. (72) confirms that the NP following the verb is a complement. That is, (72b) is ungrammatical because *multimineral tablets* is the complement which should disappear as the result of *do so* anaphora.

(71) a. *Every morning, he takes.
b. Every morning, he takes multivitamin pills.

(72) a. He takes multivitamin pills, and I do so, too.
b. *He takes multivitamin pills, and I do so multimineral tablets.

(73) shows that the phrase *multivitamin pills* is optional. (74c) shows that it is nevertheless a complement.

(73) a. Every time I see him, he's swallowing.
b. Every time I see him, he's swallowing multivitamin pills.

(74) a. He swallowed, and I did so, too.
b. He swallowed multivitamin pills, and I did so, too.
c. *He swallowed multivitamin pills, and I did so multimineral tablets.

Thus, (70b) is false, but it has the consequence in (75).

(75) If a syntactic dependent is not a complement, it is not obligatory.

In short, the following generalization seems to be valid:

(76) a. Obligatory syntactic dependents are complements.
b. Adjuncts are optional.

Let us consider again the syntactic dependency of an element: complement vs. adjunct.

Complements should be string-adjacent to their head.

(77) a. the student of linguistics from Storrs
b. *the student from Storrs of linguistics

(78) a. the passionate determined linguistics student
b. the determined passionate linguistics student
c. *the passionate linguistics determined student
d. *the linguistics passionate determined student

In nominal domains, there is only one complement. But multiple adjuncts are allowed.

(79) a. the *passionate determined* linguistics student
b. *the *passionate determined* philosophy linguistics student

Adjuncts can be reordered without significantly altering the meaning of a string.

(80) a. the student of linguistics from Storrs in a blue hoodie at the cafe
b. the student of linguistics from Storrs at the cafe in a blue hoodie
c. the student of linguistics in a blue hoodie from Storrs at the cafe
d. the student of linguistics in a blue hoodie at the cafe from Storrs
e. the student of linguistics at the cafe in a blue hoodie from Storrs

f. the student of linguistics at the cafe from Storrs in a blue hoodie
g. *the student from Storrs of linguistics in a blue hoodie at the cafe
h. *the student from Storrs in a blue hoodie of linguistics at the cafe
i. *the student from Storrs in a blue hoodie at the cafe of linguistics

Complements can be conjoined with other complements.

(81) the issues [of linguistics and of cognitive science]
(82) the smart [linguistics and psychology] students

Adjuncts can be conjoined with other adjuncts.

(83) the student [in a blue hoodie and with tattoo]
(84) the [passionate and determined] linguistics student

Complements cannot be conjoined with adjuncts.

(85) *the student [of linguistics and in a blue hoodie]
(86) *the [passionate and linguistics] student

Exercise 4

《 4-1 》

Explain the following terms:

(87) a. Constituency, Constituent
b. Domination, Exhaustive Domination
c. Clefting
d. Pro-form
e. Specifier
f. Intermediate Projection
g. Transitivity, Adicity, Valency
h. Cognate
i. Complementizer

《 4-2 》

Using two or more tests, determine whether the underline sequences in the following are constituents or not:

(88) <u>The man</u> ran away.

(89) Appropriate measures will be taken against any student caught cheating on a quiz <u>in this course</u>.

(90) Rachel <u>shops at extremely fancy places</u>.

(91) Rachel <u>shops at extremely</u> fancy places.

《 4-3 》

Draw the trees of the following:

(92) Linguistics students like phonetics tutorials.

(93) the smart linguistics student

(94) the student of linguistics from Storrs with red hair on the bus

(95) Peter built the bridge with Lizzie.

(96) I can lend you some if you need money.

John R. Ross

http://en.wikipedia.org/wiki/John_R._Ross

Born: Boston, Massachusetts in 1938

- Expertise: Generative Syntax, Generative Semantics, History of English, Metaphor, Poetics, etc.
- Institutions: University of North Texas (since 1994), University of Northern British Columbia (1993-1994), National University of Singapore (1992-1993), Universidade Federal de Minas Gerais (1988-1992), MIT (1966-1985)
- Degrees: MIT (PhD), University of Pennsylvania (MA in Linguistics), Yale (BA in Linguistics)
- Doctoral Advisor: Noam Chomsky
- Dissertation Title: *Constraints on Variables in Syntax* (1967; Published under the title of *Infinite Syntax!* in 1986)
- Known for: Crossover, Extraposition, Gapping, Heavy NP Shift, Islands, Pied-piping, Scrambling, Sluicing, etc.

5 Extending X-bar Structures

5.1 Noun Phrases

Sentences and nominals share several properties. Verbs and nouns are semantically central elements of their phrases. In (1) the first argument is an Agent, and the second argument is a Patient.

(1) a. [$_{NP}$ The rumor] *devastated* [$_{NP}$ the celebrity].
AGENT PATIENT
b. [$_{NP}$ the rumor's] *devastation* [$_{PP}$ of the celebrity]
AGENT PATIENT

The passive S and its passive-like NP counterpart are semantically related. In (2) the first argument is a Patient, and the second argument is optionally realized as an Agent.

(2) a. The celebrity was devastated (by the rumor).
PATIENT (AGENT)
b. the celebrity's devastation (by the rumor)
PATIENT (AGENT)

In both sentences and nominals, the semantically central element—the verb and the noun—can be modified in similar ways. In (3) the PP and the AdvP modify the V, respectively. In (4) the PP and the AP modify the N, respectively.

(3) a. She checks the blood pressure [$_{PP}$ on a regular basis].
PP modification

b. She [$_{AdvP}$ regularly] checks the blood pressure.
AdvP modification

(4) a. her checks of the blood pressure [$_{PP}$ on a regular basis]
PP modification

b. her [$_{AP}$ regular] checks of the blood pressure
AP modification

However, sentences and nominals exhibit certain differences.

Difference 1

The first difference is that in (5a) the Agent and the Patient are common NPs, whereas in (5b) the Agent is a possessive NP and the Patient is an *of* NP.

(5)	a.	The rumor	*devastated*	the celebrity.
		AGENT		PATIENT
		COMMON NP		COMMON NP
	b.	the rumor's	*devastation*	of the celebrity
		AGENT		PATIENT
		POSSESSIVE NP		*of* NP

Difference 2

The AdvP which modifies a head V can be used as a premodifier or a postmodifier, as shown in (6). The AP which modifies a head N should be used as a premodifier, as shown in (7).

(6) a. The doctors regularly participate in the charity bazaar.
premodifier

b. The doctors participate in the charity bazaar regularly.
postmodifier

(7) a. the doctors' regular participation in the charity bazaar
premodifier

b. *the doctors' participation in the charity bazaar regular
*postmodifier

Difference 3

Sentences require a subject. In (8) *it* and *there* are expletive subjects.

(8) a. It appears that the document has been redacted all over.
b. There exists censorship.

(9) a. *Appears that the document has been redacted all over.
b. *Exists censorship.

NPs do not require a subject. NPs containing Ns without an Agent argument do not allow an expletive.

(10) a. *{it, its} appearance that the document has been redacted
b. *{there, there's} existence of censorship

NPs do not require an Agent argument.

(11) a. the government's dismissal of the report
AGENT PATIENT

b. the dismissal of the report
PATIENT

Ns must be accompanied by a determiner.

(12) a. *Résumé was not submitted in time.
b. *You should hand in résumé by posting a reply on the designated website.

(13) a. {The, This, That} résumé is not impressive at all.
b. You should hand in {the, this, that} résumé.

NPs are the result of composing two projections: (14a) + (14b) = (14c).

(14) a. b. c.

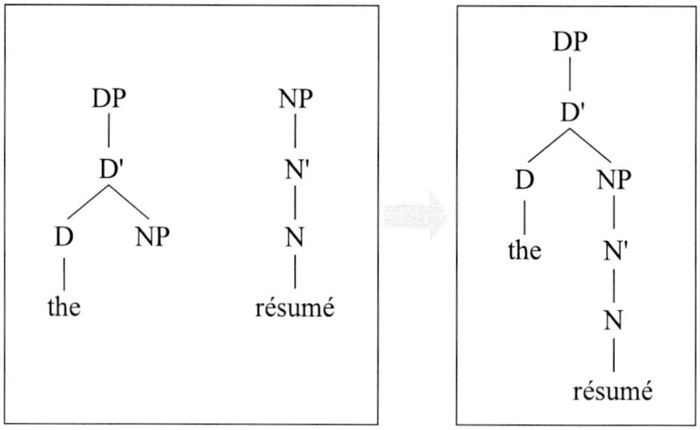

What is the head of the bracketed [ ] material?

(15) a. Dr. Lopez opposed [the assessment].
b. Dr. Lopez opposed [the assessment of the damage].
c. Dr. Lopez opposed [the arbitrator's assessment].
d. Dr. Lopez opposed [the arbitrator's assessment of the damage].

The following shows a partial tree of (15a). In (16) *the* is the head of *the assessment*.

(16)

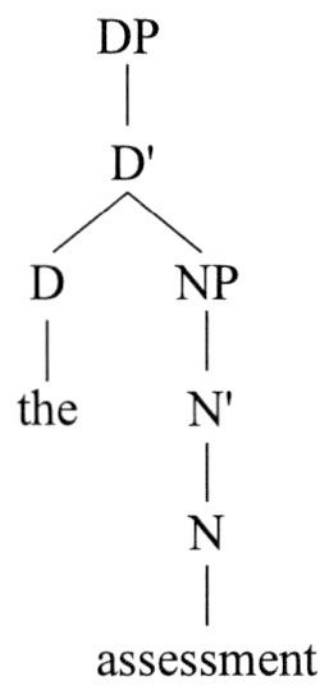

The following shows a partial tree of (15b). In (17) *the* is the head of *the assessment of the damage*, and *assessment* is the head of *assessment of the damage*.

(17)

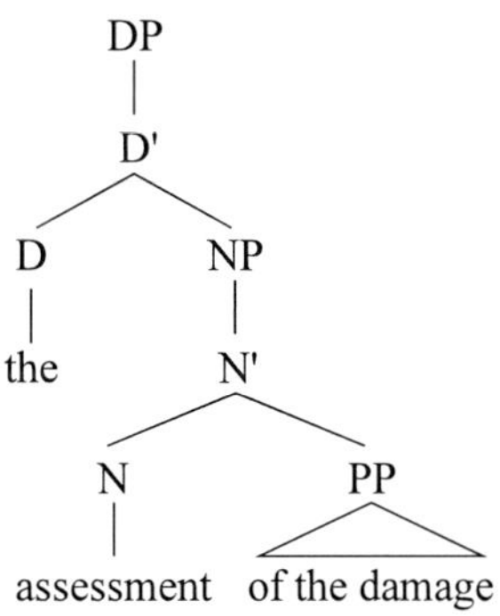

The following shows a partial tree of (15c):

(18)

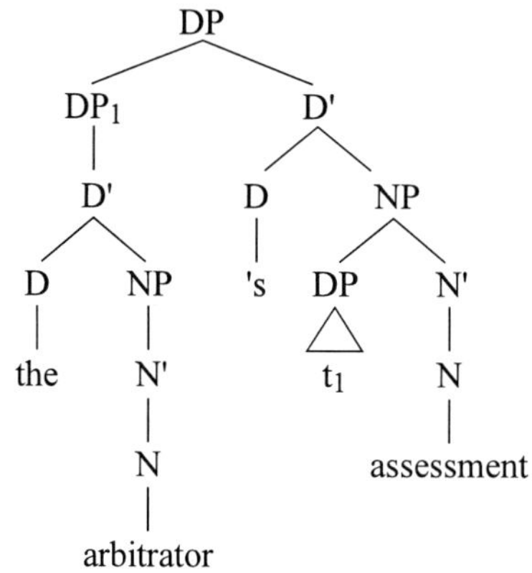

The following shows a partial tree of (15d):

(19)

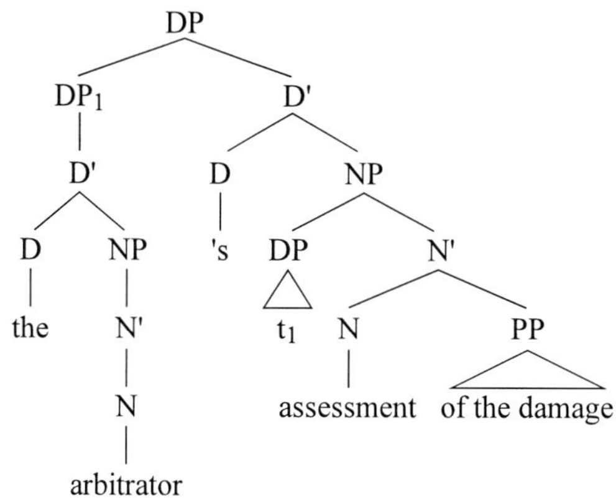

There is some structural affinity between (19) and (20). In (20) the subject is raised from Spec of VP to Spec of IP. In (19) the subject equivalent is raised from Spec of NP to Spec of DP.

(20)

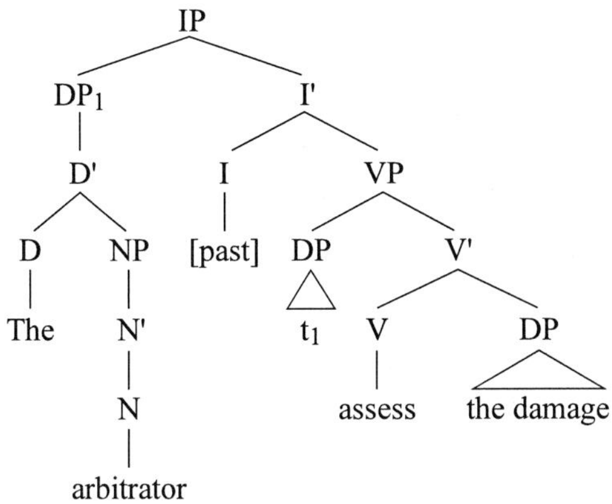

Although articles and demonstratives are classified as determiners, they are different with respect to transitivity. In the following, *the* and *a* always require a complement, whereas *this* and *that* do not need a complement:

(21) a. I'll get {the, a} job.
     b. *I'll get {the, a}.

(22) a. I'll get {this, that} job.
     b. I'll get {this, that}.

Certain common pronouns can be used as transitive determiners.

(23) a. <u>we</u> Californians, <u>you</u> imbecile(s)
     b. we, you

(24) a.

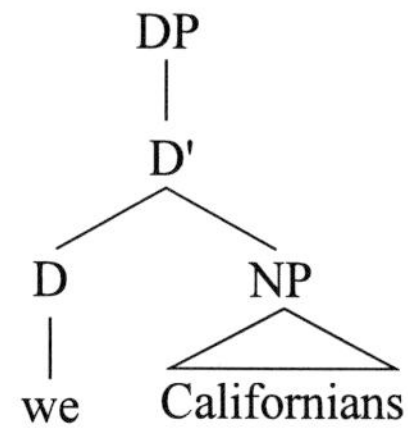

b.

Common pronouns such as *I, he, she, it, they* can be used independently as determiners. They cannot be transitive, as shown in (25).

(25) a. I, he, she, it, they

b. *I fool, *he imbecile, *she psychiatrist, *it piece of rubbish, *they connoisseurs

Misnomer

The term *pronoun* is potentially deceptive. Pronouns behave exactly like complete noun phrases (i.e., DPs). (26) provides evidence for the analysis of pronouns as determiners. Especially, (26b) and (26c) show that determiners and pronouns are mutually exclusive.

(26) a. the conditioner, this guitar, that telephone

b. *the it, *this she, *that you

c. *the these conditioners, *this the guitar, *that the telephone

Basic trees for the various types of determiners are given in (27).

(27) a.

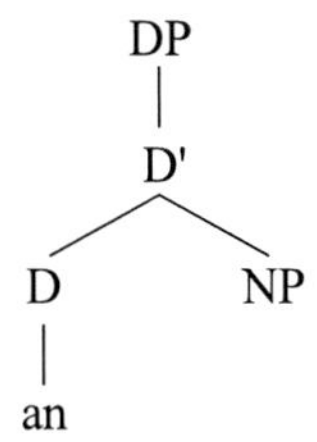

b.

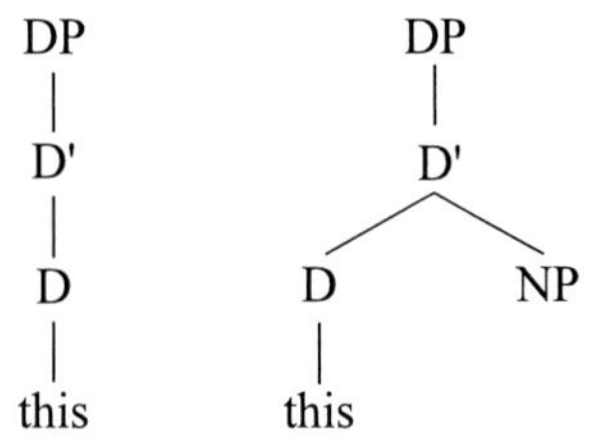

c.

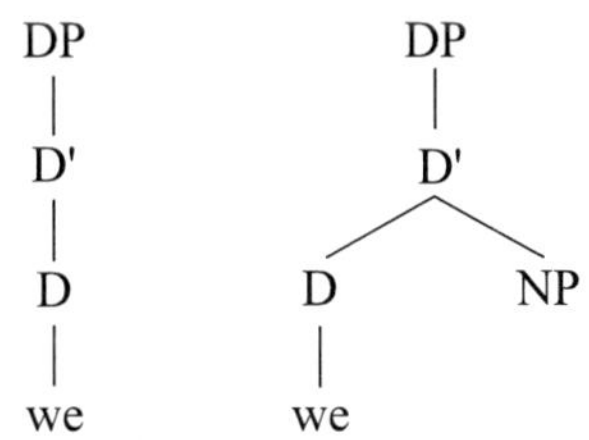

d.

In (28) plural countable nouns and mass uncountable nouns do not have an overt article, unlike their singular and definite forms, respectively.

(28)	a.	automobiles	barley
	b.	an automobile	the barley

We assume that indefinite plural countable nouns and indefinite mass nouns have a null determiner. ∅ indicates a null determiner.

(29)

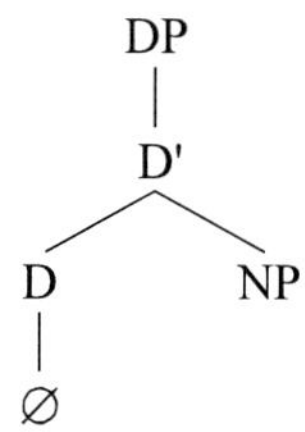

If we assume a null determiner, we can propose a single basic tree of *purchased* for the data in (30), as shown in (31).

(30) a. Some campers purchased some barley.
b. Some campers purchased barley.
c. Campers purchased some barley.
d. Campers purchased barley.

(31)

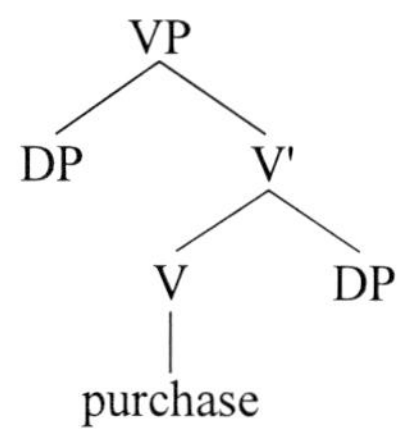

Given a null determiner hypothesis, the following shows the structure of *campers* and *barley*:

(32) a.

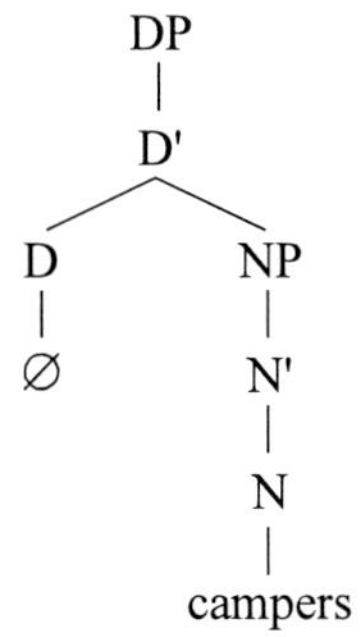

b.

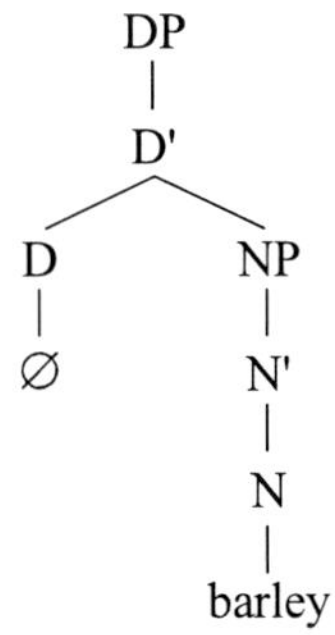

(33) shows the structures of (30).

(33) a.

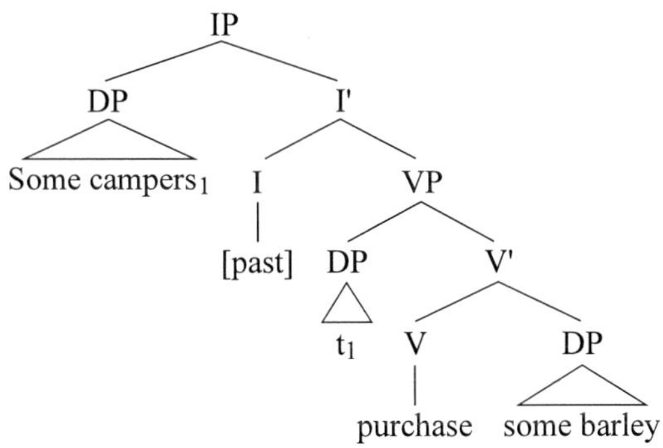

b.

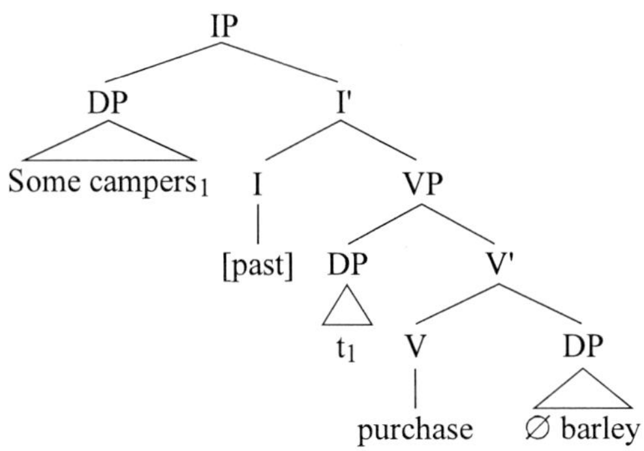

c.

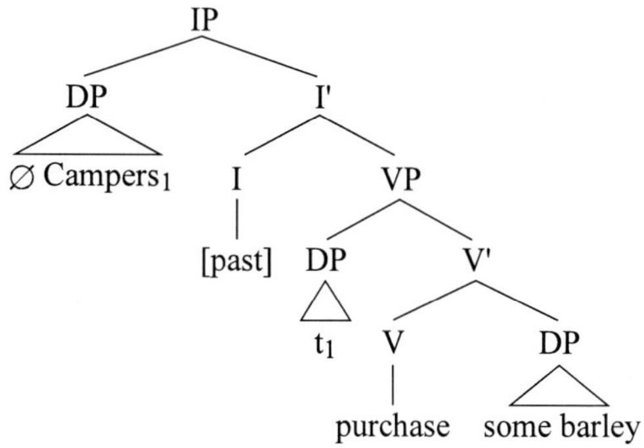

d.

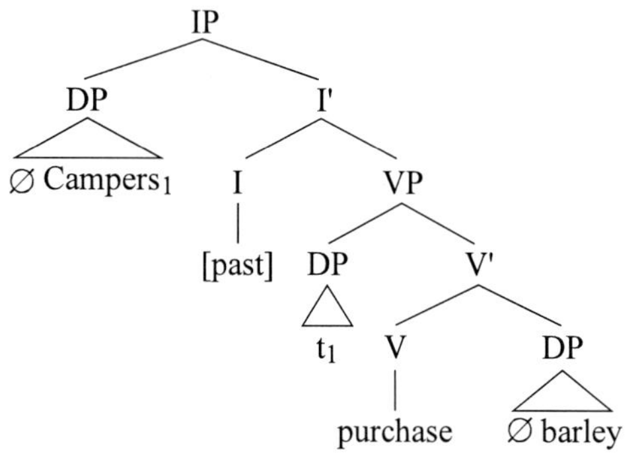

We can imagine an alternative to the null determiner analysis.

(34) a.

b.

Let us compare the following. (35a) is the tree of (30d), given a DP analysis. (35b) is the tree of (30d), given an NP analysis.

(35) a. DP analysis

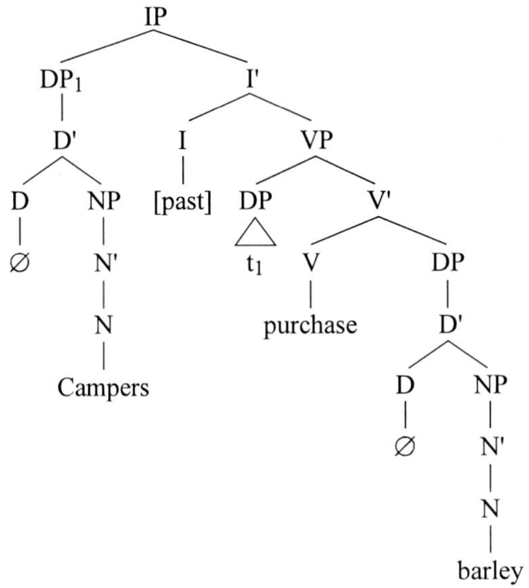

b. NP analysis

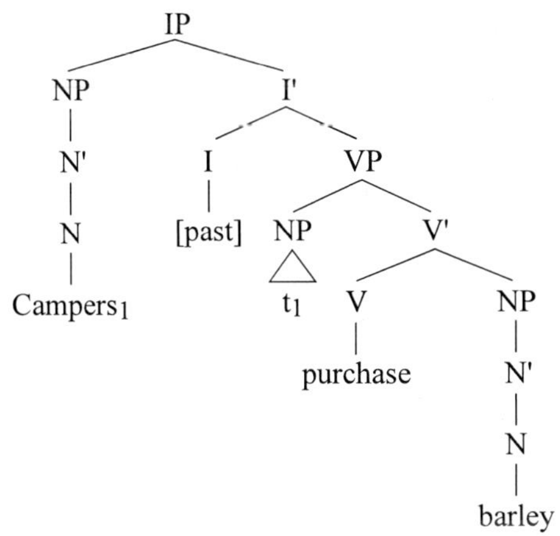

The tree in (35b) is apparently simpler than the equivalent in (35a). However, this simplicity is likely to complicate the nature of basic trees in syntax. At least, the four basic trees in (36) should be postulated.

(36) a. b. c. d.

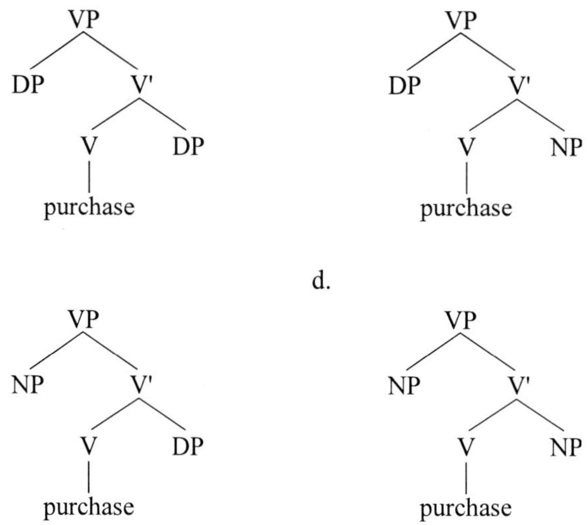

This result seems unappealing on computational grounds. We try to construct the simplest possible Grammar. So we choose a DP analysis (supplemented with a null determiner) for all nominal expressions.

Recall the similarity between sentences and nominals. In (37) the same PP *with the aldermen* modifies a verb and its derived noun, respectively.

(37) a. Lisa cooperated [$_{PP}$ with the aldermen].
b. Lisa's cooperation [$_{PP}$ with the aldermen]

(38) shows the structure of (37a).

(38)

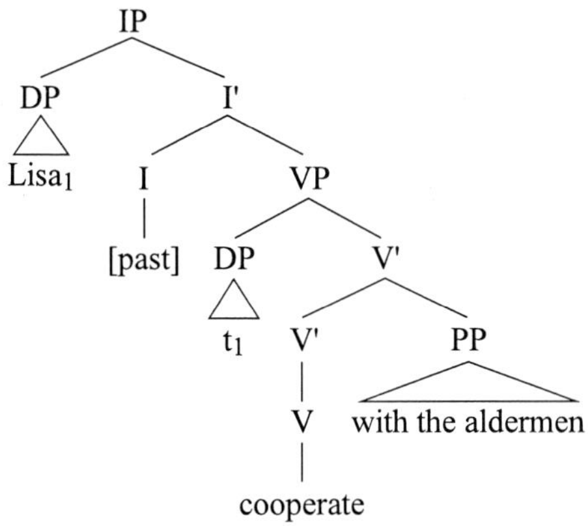

(39) shows the structure of (37b). The structure in (38) is analogous to that in (39).

(39)

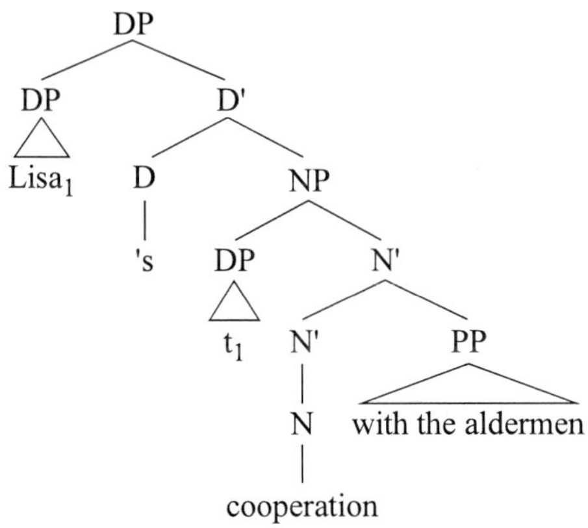

Premodifiers undergo left adjunction.

(40) a. Sarah's sharp scream

b. Sarah sharply screamed.

(41) a. 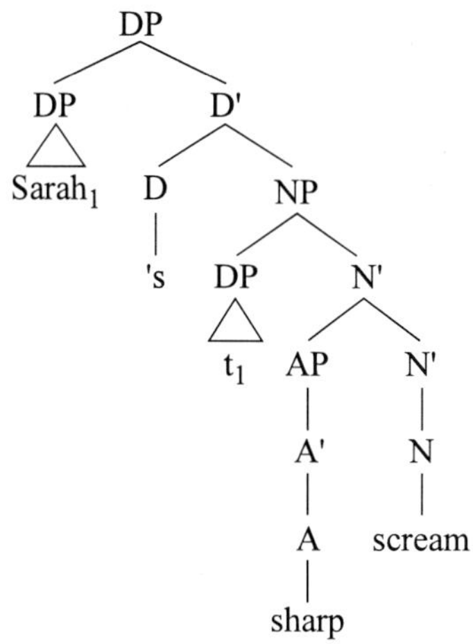

b. 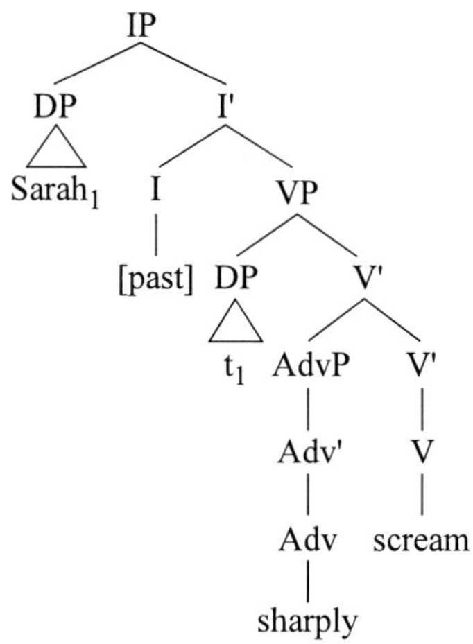

Recall that *do so* anaphora is a test for distinguishing between complements and adjuncts in the verbal system.

One anaphora is a test for distinguishing between complements and adjuncts in the nominal system.

(42) a. this cottage in the woods and that *one*
b. this cottage in the woods and that *one* on the hill

(43) shows the structure of *this cottage in the woods*. *One* is a pro-N'. So you have two targets for *one* replacement, as shown in (44).

(43)

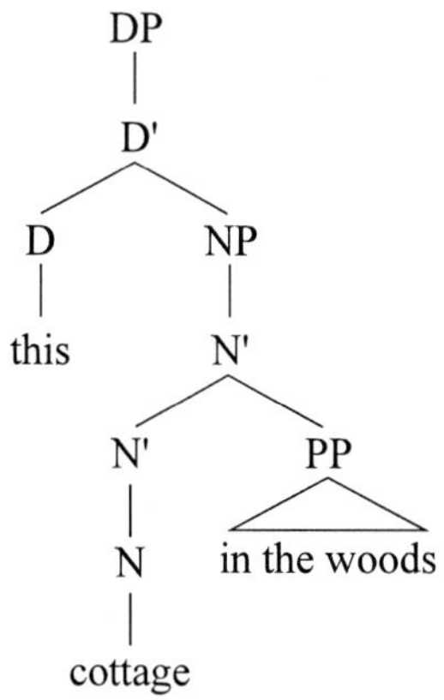

(44) a. this [$_{N'}$ cottage in the woods] and that *one*

b. this [$_{N'}$ cottage] in the woods and that *one* on the hill

As in the case of V', N'-adjunction can be applied repeatedly, creating a multiple adjunction structure. In (45) there are three potential targets for *one* replacement, as shown in (46).

(45)

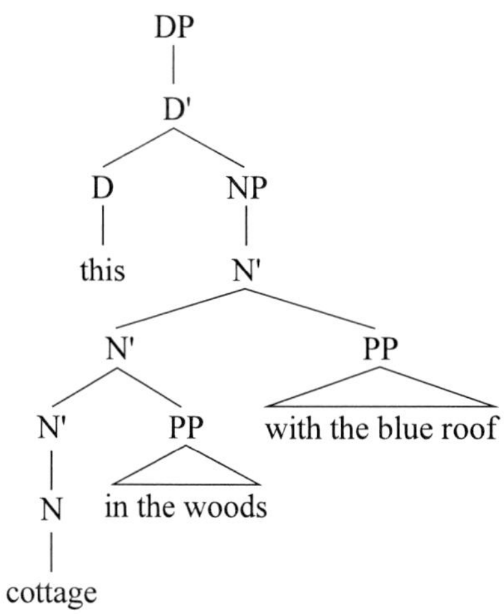

(46) a. this [$_{N'}$ cottage in the woods with the blue roof] and that *one*

b. this [$_{N'}$ cottage in the woods] with the blue roof and that *one* with the red roof

c. this [$_{N'}$ cottage] in the woods with the blue roof and that *one* on the hill with the red roof

Of NP is a typical complement of a head N.

(47) a. This man recommends legal thrillers.

b. this man's recommendation of legal thrillers

(48) shows the structure of (47b).

(48)

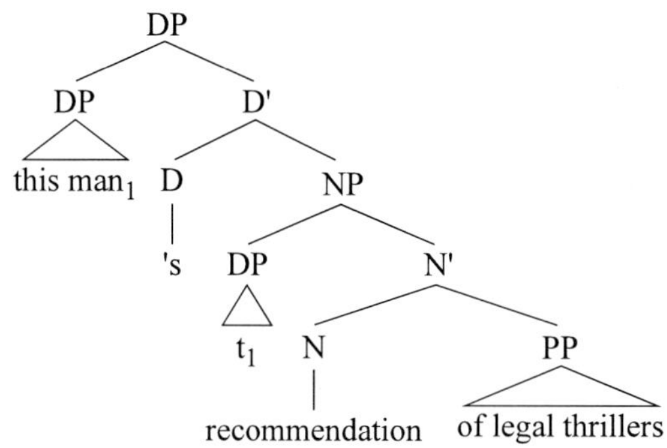

One is similar to *do so* in that both can replace intermediate projections. Note the difference between (49) and (50). *One* and *do so* are pro-X's.

(49) a. This man recommends legal thrillers, and that woman does so, too.

b. this recommendation of legal thrillers and that one

(50) a. *This man recommends legal thrillers, and that woman does so romantic comedy.

b. *this recommendation of legal thrillers and that one of romantic comedy

With the status of intermediate projections in mind, let us return to structural ambiguity. (51) is structurally ambiguous.

(51) Bart spotted an alien on the bicycle.

It has two interpretations, which are paraphrased in (52).

(52) a. It was on the bicycle that Bart spotted an alien.
b. It was an alien on the bicycle that Bart spotted.

(53a) shows one structure of (51), corresponding to the paraphrase in (52a). (53b) shows the other structure of (51), corresponding to the paraphrase in (52b).

(53) a.

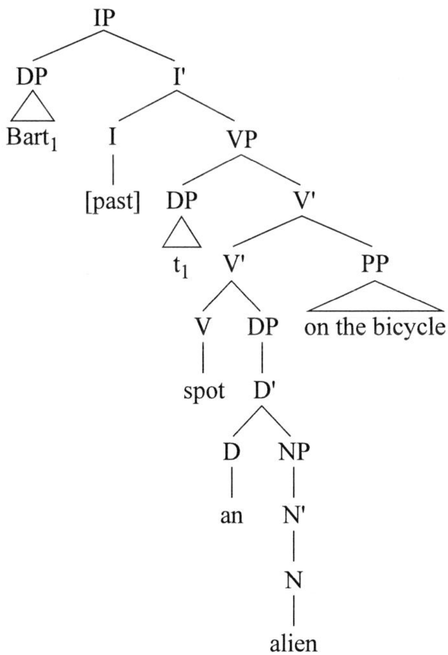

b.

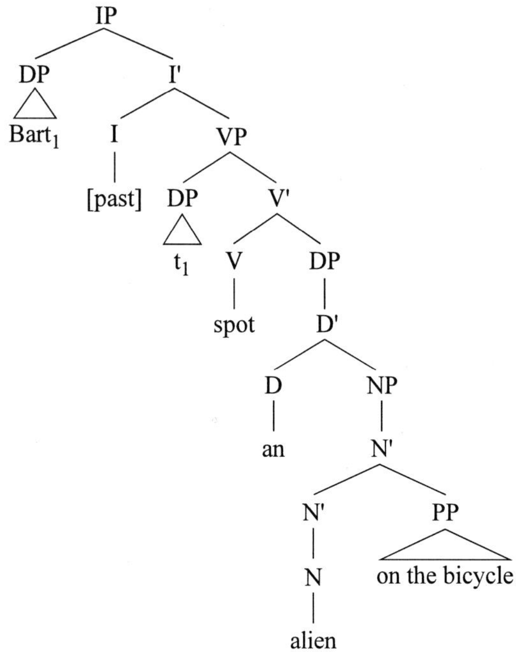

5.2 Adjective Phrases

In (54) and (55) the PP following an A is optional.

(54) a. They are curious.

b. They are curious [$_{PP}$ about her whereabouts].

(55) a. They are delighted.

b. They are delighted [$_{PP}$ with their new coffee brewer].

◀ Test 1 ▶

The pro-form *so* substitution test allows us to examine the inner structure of APs. *So* is a pro-A'.

(56) a. They are *curious*, and we are *so*, too.
b. They are *curious about her whereabouts*, and we are *so*, too.
c. *They are *curious* about her whereabouts, and we are *so* about his, too.

(57) a. They are *delighted*, and we are *so*, too.
b. They are *delighted with their new coffee brewer*, and we are *so*, too.
c. They are *delighted* with their new coffee brewer, and we are *so* with ours.

◀ Test 2 ▶

In the following, *so* is fronted to the clause-initial position, and the clause undergoes the Subject-Aux Inversion (SAI):

(58) a. They are *curious*, and *so* are we.
b. They are *curious about her whereabouts*, and *so* are we.
c. *They are *curious* about her whereabouts, and *so* are we about his.

(59) a. They are *delighted*, and *so* are we.
b. They are *delighted with their new coffee brewer*, and *so* are we.
c. They are *delighted with their new coffee brewer*, and *so* are we with ours.

Result

The *about* phrase is the complement of *curious*, but the *with* phrase is an adjunct of *delighted.* The basic trees for the two adjectives are shown in (60).

(60) a.

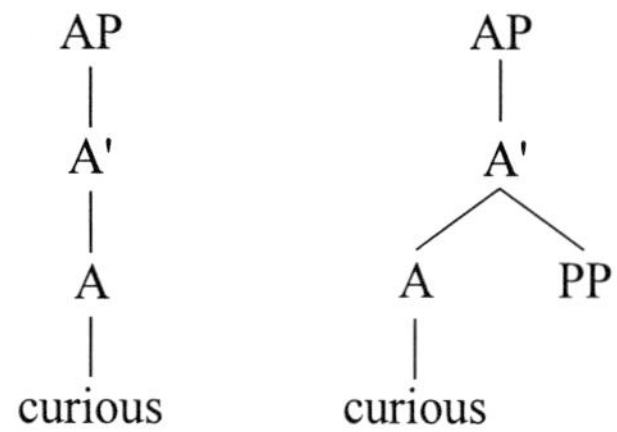

b.

Most adjectives in English can be either intransitive or transitive, but *eager* is always transitive. *For* DP is the complement of *eager*.

(61) a. *They are eager.
 b. They are eager for the dean's approval.

(62) a. They are eager for the dean's approval, and we are so, too.
 b. *They are eager for the dean's approval, and we are so for the professor's approval, too.

(63) a. They are eager for the dean's approval, and so are we.
 b. *They are eager for the dean's approval, and so are we for the professor's approval.

Based on (61)-(63), we conclude that *eager* has the following basic structure:

(64)

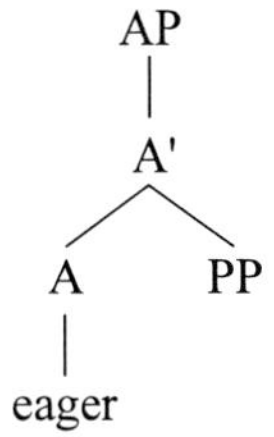

APs may have a specifier. Given the Predicate-internal Subject Hypothesis (PISH), (54a) would be derived as in (65). According to the PISH, the subject may originate in Spec of AP and move to Spec of IP.

(65)

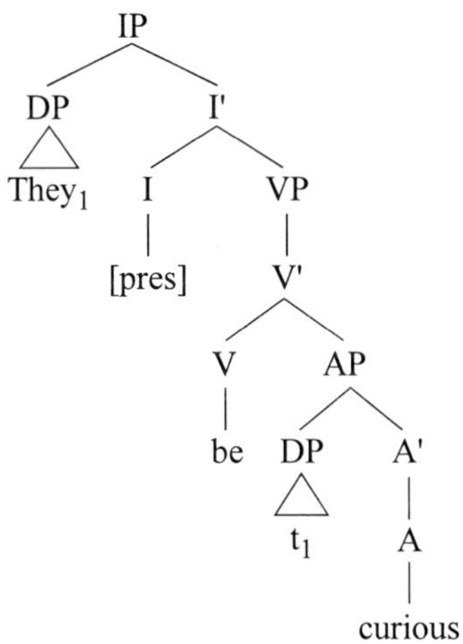

5.3 Prepositional Phrases

According to Traditional Grammar, prepositions (Ps) are always transitive.

(66) a. He came from *(San Francisco).♣
b. The city is located on *(the boundary).
c. She dived into *(her bag) and grabbed the gun.
d. Miguel cares deeply for *(her).

What is interesting is that X'-theory allows intransitive Ps since complements are optional. In fact, intransitive Ps have been called adverbs or particles.

(67) a. They dragged the sled up.
b. Are you in or out?
c. Maggie hopped in.
d. It's time to move on.

We assume that intransitive Ps are allowed in Grammar. The understood complement of Ps is provided in the interpretive component, based on the discourse context.

(68) a. They dragged the sled up (the hill).
b. Are you in (the game) or out (of the game)?
c. Maggie hopped in (my car).
d. It's time to move on (to the next chapter).

♣ The star outside a parenthesis indicates that the parenthetical expression is mandatory.

The basic trees, for instance, for *into* and *in* are shown in (69).

(69) a.

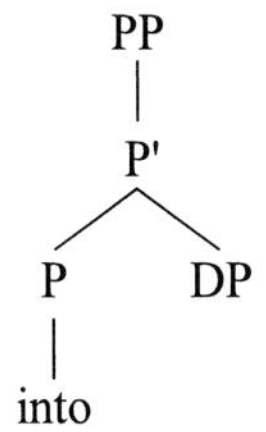

b.

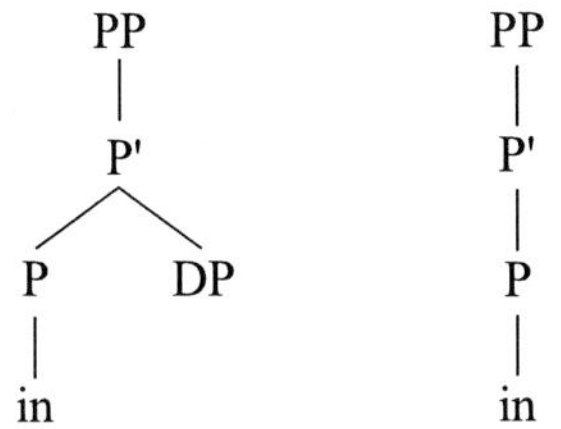

The full structures for the PPs in (66c) and (68c) are shown in (70).♣

(70) a. into her bag

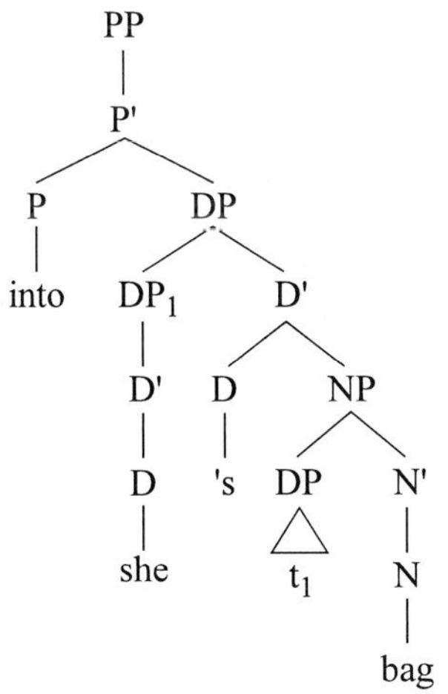

b. in my car

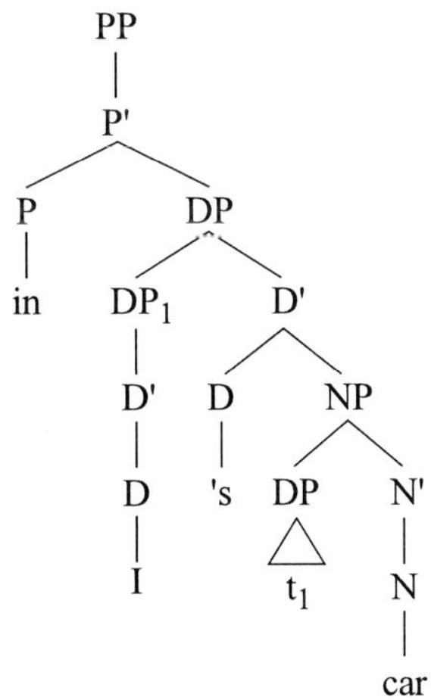

♣
(i) she + 's = her
(ii) I + 's = my

PPs may have a specifier.

(71) right across the street♣

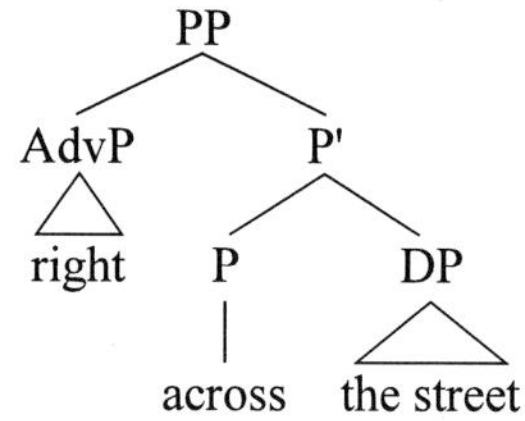

In addition, the PISH predicts that a PP-internal subject may originate in Spec of PP and then move to Spec of IP.

(72) Ross was in the park.

(73) [$_{IP}$ Ross$_1$ [past] [$_{VP}$ be [$_{PP}$ t$_1$ in the park]]].

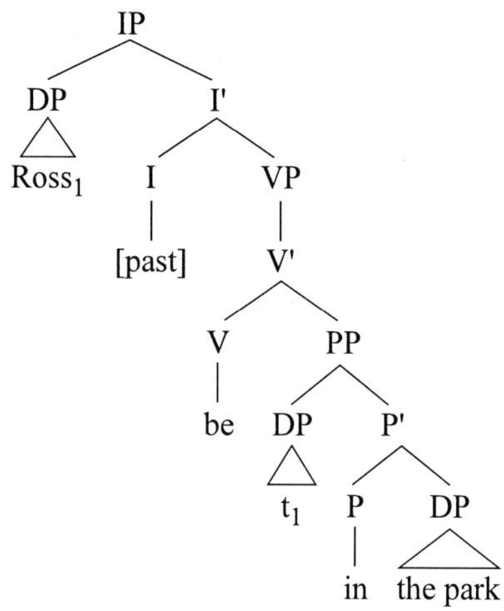

♣ *Right* could be analyzed as a P'-adjunct.

5.4 Head Parameter

Languages tend to be generally head-initial or head-final. This property is captured with Head Parameter.

English is head-initial.

(74) He [$_{V'}$ evaluated [$_{DP}$ the report]].

HEAD COMPLEMENT

Korean is head-final.

(75) 그가 [$_{V'}$ [$_{DP}$ 보고서를] 평가했다].

[Ku-ka	[$_{V'}$ [$_{DP}$ pokose-lul]	phyengkaha]-ess-ta].♣
he-Nom	report-Acc	evaluate-Past-Dec
	COMPLEMENT	HEAD

♣
Nom = Nominative Case marker
Acc = Accusative Case marker
Past = Past morpheme
Dec = Declarative-ending marker

Exercise 5

5-1

Explain the following terms:

(76) a. Expletive
b. Mutually Exclusive
c. Null Determiner
d. *Do So* Anaphora, *On*e Anaphora
e. Pro-form, Pro-X'
f. Adjunction, Substitution
g. Transitivity, Intransitivity
h. Predicate-internal Subject Hypothesis (PISH)

5-2

The following sentences are structurally ambiguous. First, paraphrase two relevant interpretations, and then, draw two different trees for each sentence. Do not forget to indicate which tree goes with which interpretation.

(77) I saw the man with the telescope.
(78) Flying planes can be dangerous.
(79) They took the animal to the small animal hospital.
(80) the Spanish teacher

5-3

Draw the X'-theoretic trees of the following:

(81) Simon is down with flu.

(82) You should stay away from the fire.

(83) Rachel left rather quickly.

(84) Monica often sings beautifully.

(85) The big lazy dog bit a mouthful of food.

(86) I think that Monica mugged the janitor.

(87) That Monica mugged the janitor is obvious.

(88) They differ in that they hold sharply opposing views on educational reform.

(89) I bought the thick book of poems with the red cover.

(90) Phoebe is angry about school violence.

(91) Sara blew it up.

(92) Monica is very in love with her boss.

(93) We often eat parsnips for good health.

(94) Dana considers Sandy a genius.

(95) You prefer hot dogs with ketchup.

(96) from out of town

(97) a tall bearded man with a blue blazer

Richard S. Kayne

http://en.wikipedia.org/wiki/Richard_Kayne

Born: 1944

- Expertise: Generative Syntax, French Syntax, etc.
- Institutions: New York University (since 1997), City University of New York (1988-1997), MIT (1986-1988), University of Paris VIII (1969-1986)
- Degrees: MIT (PhD), Columbia College (AB in Mathematics)
- Doctoral Advisor: John R. Ross
- Dissertation Title: *The Transformational Cycle in French Syntax* (1969; Published under the title of *French Syntax: The Transformational Cycle* in 1975)
- Known for: Binary Branching, Antisymmetry, Alternative Proposals to Chomsky's Ideas, etc.

6 Head Movement

In English, the future tense is realized as a free morpheme, and the past tense as a bound morpheme.

(1) a. The cynics will never believe him.
 b. (Will the cynics believe him?) The cynics will.
 c. *The cynics believe will him.

(2) a. The cynics believe-ed him.
 b. *The cynics -ed never believe him.
 c. *(Did the cynics believe him?) The cynics -ed.

Question

How do a tense morpheme and a verb merge to form a complex word?

Answer

There is a verb movement parameter: either V moves to I (Verb Raising) or I moves to V (Affix Hopping). Both options are instances of head movement.

6.1 V-to-I or I-to-C

According to X-bar theory, nothing may intervene between a head and its complement. However, Irish is a verb-initial language, which exhibits the VSO word order. How can we explain the Irish word order?

(3)

V	S		O
Phóg	Máire	an	lucharachán.
Kissed	Mary	the	leprechaun

'Mary kissed the leprechaun.' (Carnie 2007: 243)

Head movement is an example of transformations. In French, V moves to I overtly.

(4)

	V	Adv		O
[$_{IP}$ Je	mange$_1$	[$_{VP}$ souvent	t_1	des pommes]].
I	eat	often		the apples

'I often eat apples.'

In English, V does not move to I overtly.

(5)

	Adv	V	O
[$_{IP}$ I	[$_{VP}$ often	eat	apples]].
cf.	*I eat often apples.		

Let us consider (6) and (7). In (6a) the verb appears between the subject and the Adv when there is no Aux. In (7a) the verb appears between the Adv and the object when INFL is filled. We conclude that the tensed V in French is in INFL.

(6)	a.	S	V	Adv		O
		Je	mange	souvent	des	pommes.
		I	eat	often		apples
	b.	I	often	eat		apples.

(7)	a.	S	I	Adv	V		O
		J'	ai	souvent	mangé	des	pommes.
		I	have	often	eaten		apples
	b.	I	have	often	eaten		apples.

Let us now compare Negation in English and French. In (8a) the verb appears between the subject and *pas* when there is no Aux.

(8)	a.	S	V	Neg			O
		Je	ne-mange	pas		des	pommes.
		I	eat	not			apples
	b.	I	do	not	eat		apples.

In (9a) the verb appears between Neg and the object when there is an Aux. We thus confirm the conclusion that the tensed V in French is in INFL.

(9)	a.	S	I	Neg	V		O
		Je	n'ai	pas	mangé	des	pommes.
		I	have	not	eaten		apples
	b.	I	have	not	eaten		apples.

(10) [$_{IP}$ I [$_{I'}$ do [$_{NegP}$ not [$_{VP}$ eat apples]]]].

With respect to verbal morphology, there is a Verb Raising parameter by which in English INFL lowers to attach suffixes to the main verb (i.e., Affix Hopping), whereas in French the main verb moves to INFL to pick up suffixes (i.e., Verb Raising).

In order to derive the Irish word order, we need to assume the Predicate-internal Subject Hypothesis (PISH) and Verb Raising as in (12) and (13). The PISH dictates that all θ-roles associated with a head H be assigned within projections of H as in (11).

(11) [$_{VP}$ Mary [$_{V'}$ kiss the leprechaun]]

(12) VSO Word Order

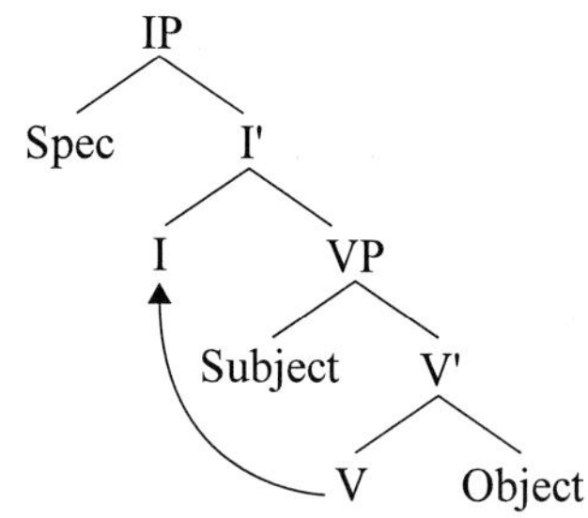

(13)

	V		S			O
[$_{IP}$	Phóg	[$_{VP}$	Máire	__	an	lucharachán]].
	Kissed		Mary		the	leprechaun

'Mary kissed the leprechaun.'

Another instance of head movement is SAI: I-to-C movement.

(14) a. You have taken my travel mug.

b. [$_{CP}$ [$_{C'}$ Have$_1$ [$_{IP}$ you t_1 taken my travel mug]]]?
C I V

In some dialect of English, SAI is allowed in the embedded clause as in (15a). A piece of evidence for I-to-C movement is that even in that dialect, SAI is not allowed with an embedded Q complementizer as in (15c). In the embedded question context, there is a violation of Doubly-filled COMP Filter (i.e., COMP tolerates only one head) if I moves to C.

(15) a. I asked have$_C$ you taken my travel mug.
b. I asked whether$_C$ you have taken my travel mug.
c. *I asked whether$_C$ have$_C$ you taken my travel mug.

In French, both main verbs and auxiliaries are in INFL. Given this, a prediction is that both will undergo I-to-C movement.

(16)	a.	Avez-vous	mangé	des	pommes?
		Have-you	eaten	the	apples
	b.	Mangez	vous	des	pommes?
		Eat	you	the	apples

(17) C ← I ← V

In English, only auxiliaries are in INFL. So only auxiliaries will undergo I-to-C movement.

(18) a. Have you eaten the apples?
b. *Eat you the apples?

(19) C ← I V

6.2 Affix Hopping: I-to-V

In English, frequency adverbs precede main verbs.

(20) a. They {always, never} sang.
b. They will {always, never} sing.
c. They have {always, never} sung.
d. They are {always, never} singing.

(21) a. *They sang {always, never}.
b. *They will sing {always, never}.
c. *They have sung {always, never}.
d. *They are singing {always, never}.

The English verbal morphology is formed via Affix Hopping.

(22) a.

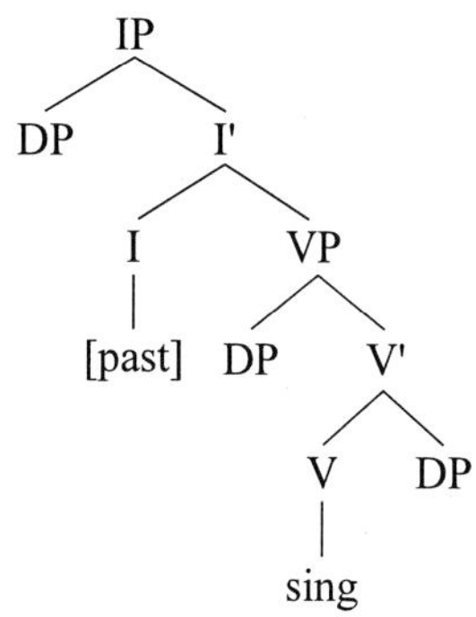

b.

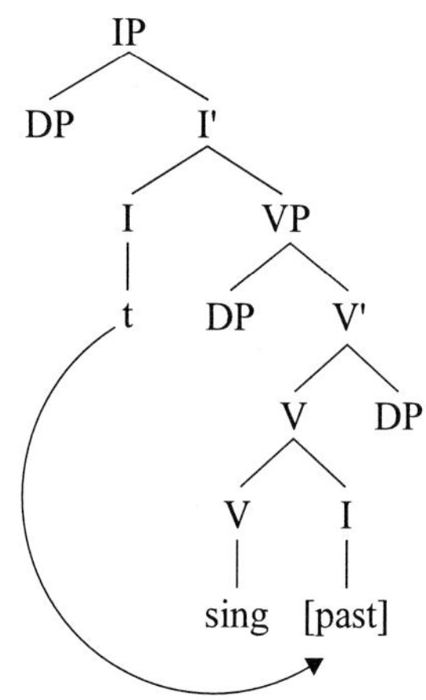

When the structure is delivered to the morphological component, the tensed verb complex is specified following the rules of morphology.

6.3 *Never* vs. *Not*

Never often plays a role of negation.

(23) a. Did you know that David would file a grievance against the layoff?

b. i. Nuh-uh, I never did.

ii. Nuh-uh, I did not.

However, there is a considerable difference between *not* and *never*. *Not* obligatorily triggers *do*-support, whereas *never* does not.

(24) a. *David not replied.

b. David {did not, didn't} reply.

(25) a. David never replied.

b. *David {did, does} never replied.

Never is an XP. *Not* is a head.

(26) a. intransitive *never*

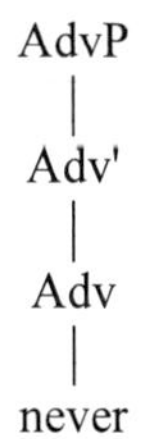

b. transitive *not*

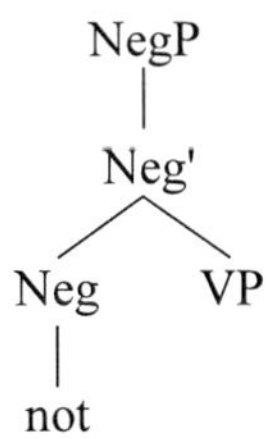

Consider the following. (27a) illustrates a common negative sentence. (27b) illustrates its negative inversion equivalent.

(27) a. Klimt would esteem no subject other than the human body.
b. *No subject* would Klimt esteem other than the human body.

The DP can undergo negative inversion. But the negative determiner *no* cannot be fronted alone without the complement. Note that only XP can undergo negative inversion.

(28) **No* would Klimt esteem subject other than the human body.

Never can undergo negative inversion. That is, *never* is an XP.

(29) a. They will *never* meet the need.
b. *Never* will they meet the need.

The following is the structure of (29a):

(30)

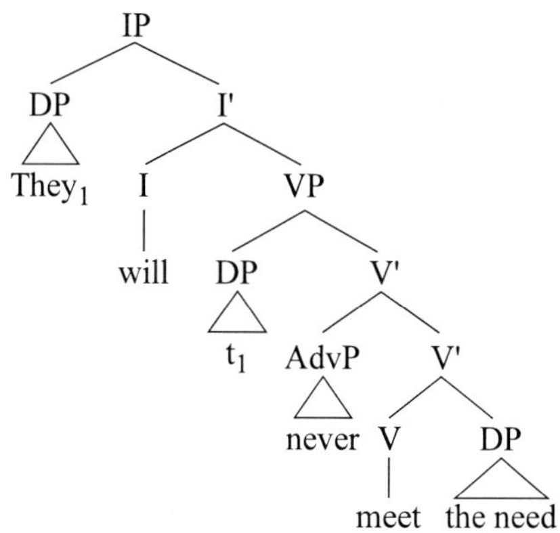

Let us consider the *not* variant of (29a).

(31)

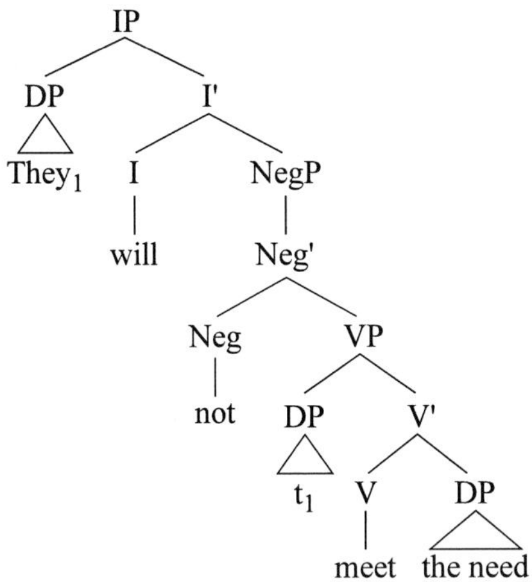

Not is not an XP but a head. It cannot undergo negative inversion.

(32) **Not* will they meet the need.

The head *not* may move to INFL optionally, deriving a contracted complex head.

(33) a. shall-n't → shan't
b. will-n't → won't
c. can-n't → can't
d. dare-n't → daren't

Affix Hopping (though not Verb Raising) is subject to the locality condition in (34). Intervention is defined in terms of structural dominance/domination.

(34) a. When a head α lowers onto a head β, α and β must be in a local relation in the sense that no projection of a head distinct from α and β intervenes on the path of branches that connects α and β.

b. An element γ, γ distinct from α and β, intervenes between two elements α and β iff α (or some projection of α) dominates γ and γ (or some projection of γ) dominates β.♣

Adjoining the adverb *never* to V' results in the adverb being too low in the tree to intervene between I and V.

(35)

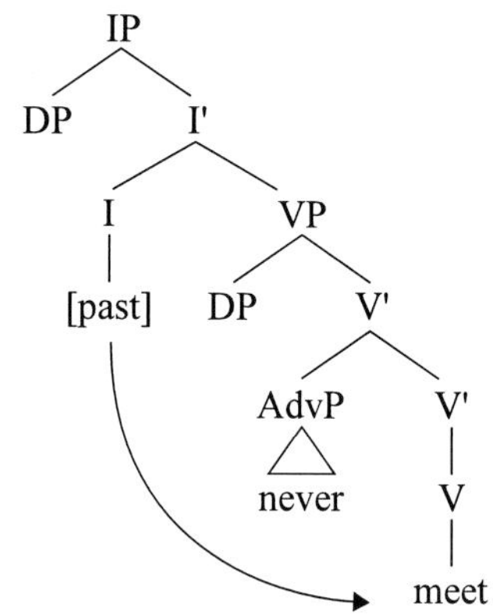

In (36a) Affix Hopping violates the locality condition because the shaded projections of Neg intervene on the path between I and V. Hence, *do*-support is motivated in order to salvage the stranded tense in INFL, as shown in (36b).♣♣

♣
iff = if and only if

♣♣
In (36b) *do* is inserted as an X-zero adjunct.

(36) a. *David not replied.

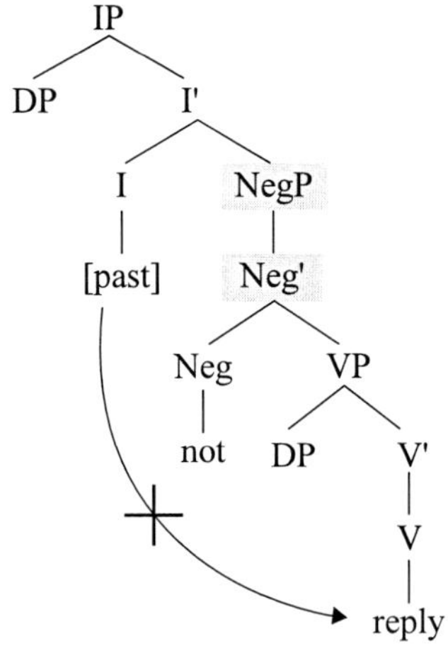

b. David did not reply.

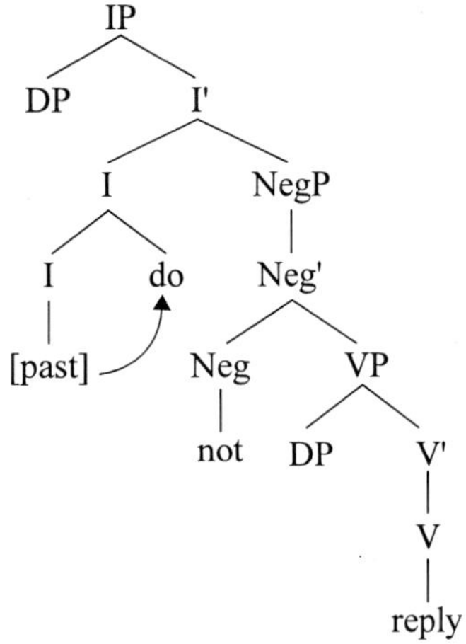

Exercise 6

《 6-1 》

Explain the following terms:

(37) a. Verbal Morphology
b. Verb Raising, Affix Hopping
c. Head Movement
d. Neg
e. Doubly-filled COMP Filter
f. Negative Inversion
g. Locality Condition
h. *Do*-support

《 6-2 》

What do you need to assume in order to derive the VSO word order?

《 6-3 》

Discuss evidence that there is an I-to-C movement in English.

《 6-4 》

Discuss the grammaticality contrast of the following:

(38) a. *No would Jonathan believe in theory more than minimalism.
b. *Not will they spread the word.
c. Never will they be at loggerheads on this.

◀ 6-5 ▶

Explain the ungrammaticality of the following:

(39) a. *Got you the message?
b. *He not backed up.

◀ 6-6 ▶

In Black English Vernacular, the following sentence is acceptable. What do you need to assume in order to derive the word order in the embedded clause?

(40) I know a way that can't nobody fool me.

Howard Lasnik

http://en.wikipedia.org/wiki/Howard_Lasnik

Born: 1945

- Expertise: Generative Syntax, Learnability, etc.
- Institutions: University of Maryland (since 2002), University of Connecticut (1972-2002)
- Degrees: MIT (PhD), Harvard University (MA in English), Carnegie Institute of Technology (BS in Mathematics and English)
- Doctoral Advisor: Noam Chomsky
- Dissertation Title: *Analyses of Negation in English* (1972)
- Known for: Binding, γ-marking, Move-α, Enlightened-Self Interest, Repair-by-Ellipsis, etc.

7 Case

The notion of *Case* is introduced to identify the grammatical function of nominals in a sentence.

7.1 The Case Filter

In English, we have three different configurations for Case realizations.

(1) a. Specifier-Head configuration
    b. Government configuration
    c. Exceptional Case Marking (ECM) configuration

Consider the contrast between (2) and (3). Why are the sentences in (3) ungrammatical?

(2) a. They will find you.
    b. She will find them.

(3) a. *Them will find she.
b. *Her will find they.

The answer is in (4).

(4) a. Subjects of finite clauses take nominative (Nom) Case.
b. Objects take accusative (Acc) Case.

You in (5a) has Nom Case. *You* in (5b) has Acc Case.

(5) a. You will convince her.
b. She will convince you.

My idea in (6a) has Nom Case. *My idea* in (6b) has Acc Case.

(6) a. My idea will be adopted as a working hypothesis.
b. They will adopt my idea as a working hypothesis.

English has three Case values: nominative, accusative, and possessive. What about Korean?

We can represent the values of Case as in (7) and (8).

(7) a. [$_{\text{DP-Nom}}$ They] will take good care of [$_{\text{DP-Acc}}$ her].
b. [$_{\text{DP-Nom}}$ You] will take a shine to [$_{\text{DP-Acc}}$ her].
c. [$_{\text{DP-Nom}}$ My idea] will help [$_{\text{DP-Acc}}$ her].
d. [$_{\text{DP-Nom}}$ It] doesn't hurt to share [$_{\text{DP-Poss}}$ your] view.

(8) a. [$_{\text{DP-Nom}}$ She] will tell [$_{\text{DP-Acc}}$ them].
b. [$_{\text{DP-Nom}}$ She] will drive [$_{\text{DP-Acc}}$ you] up the wall.
c. [$_{\text{DP-Nom}}$ She] will find [$_{\text{DP-Acc}}$ my idea] helpful.

d. [$_{\text{DP-Poss}}$ Her] hipster glasses are out of [$_{\text{DP-Acc}}$ fashion].

Using the concept of Case, we can say that every nominal needs to be associated with a Case as an indication of its function. This requirement, often referred to as the *Case Filter*, is stated in (9).

(9) The Case Filter
Every overt argument DP must have a Case.

7.2 Case Licensing Configurations

We have two basic Case licensing configurations: Specifier-Head configuration and Government configuration.

Consider first the Spec-Head configuration for Case licensing. We assume that Nom Case is assigned by finite INFL.

(10) a. He understands the works of Noam Chomsky.

b. [$_{\text{IP}}$ He$_1$ -s [$_{\text{VP}}$ t$_1$ understand the works of Noam Chomsky]].

The Spec-Head configuration holds between a head and its specifier.

(11)

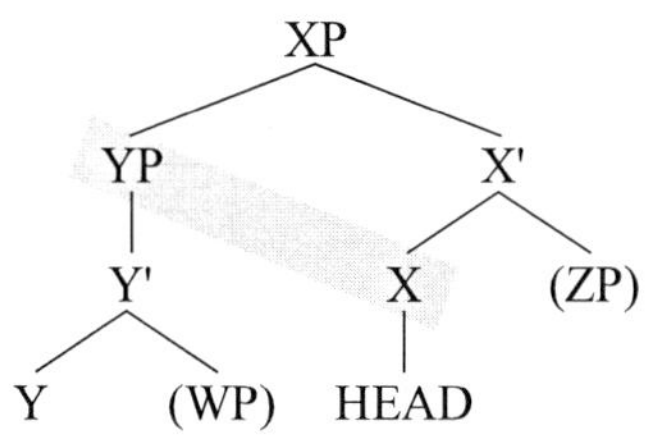

For example, Poss(essive) Case is licensed in a Spec-Head configuration.

(12) the Democrat's campaign

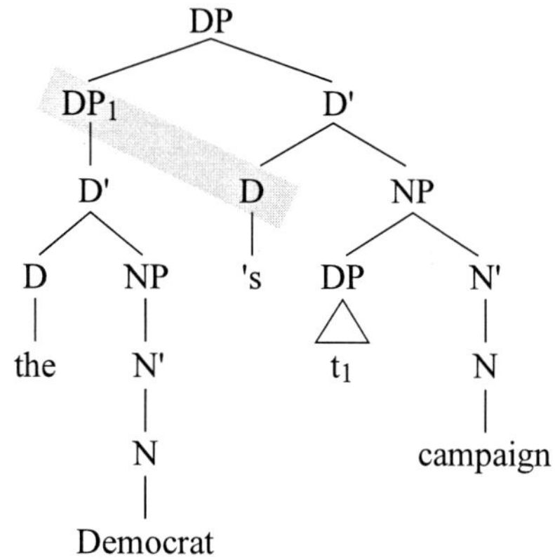

(13) my friend's problem

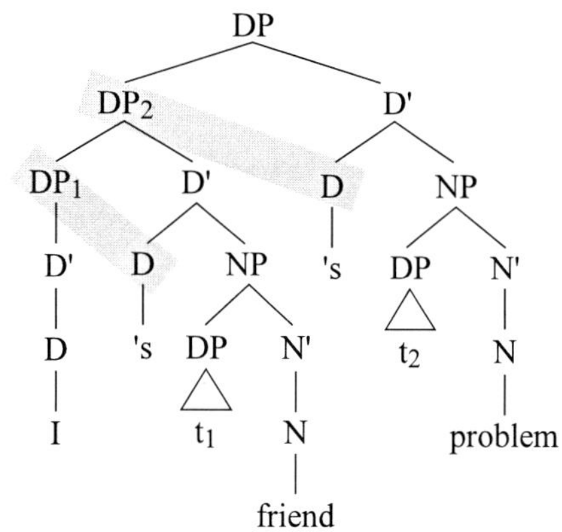

Consider next the Government configuration for Case licensing. The concept of Government is defined as follows:

(14) α governs β iff
 a. α is a head,
 b. β is a maximal projection, and
 c. α and β mutually m(aximal)-command each other.

(15) α m-commands β iff
 a. α and β do not dominate each other, and
 b. the first maximal projection dominating α dominates β.

For example, Vs and Ps license Acc Case via governing their objects.

(16)

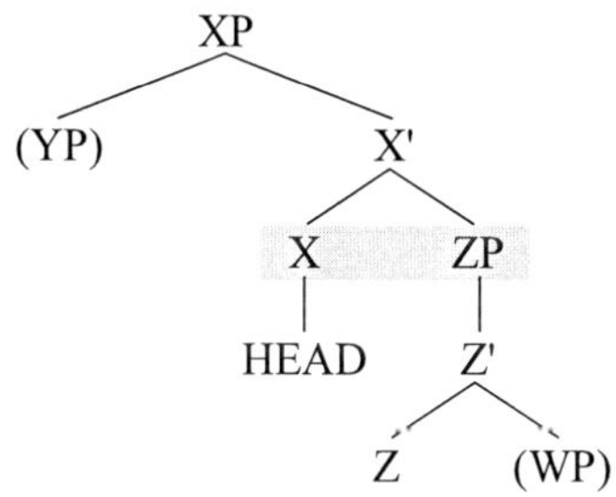

In (17) *required* assigns Acc Case to *me* via government.

(17) He required me.

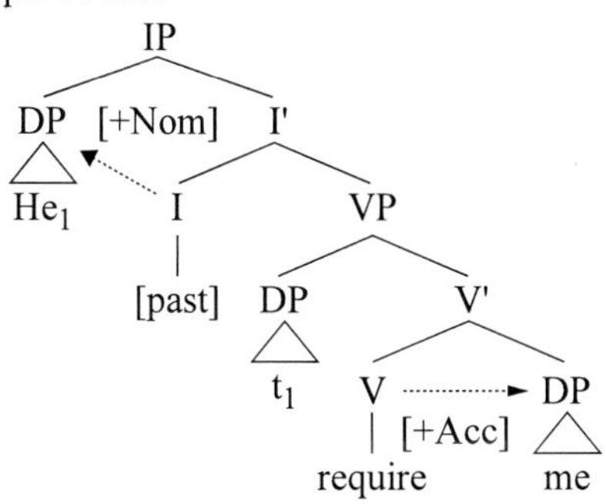

Finally, let us consider the so-called ECM configuration. In (18) the object of *required* is not a person but a state of affairs (= a proposition). (18) means (19).

(18) The supreme court *required* her to reveal the underlying pertinent facts.

(19) The supreme court *required* that she reveal the underlying pertinent facts.

(20) is the structure of (18).

(20)

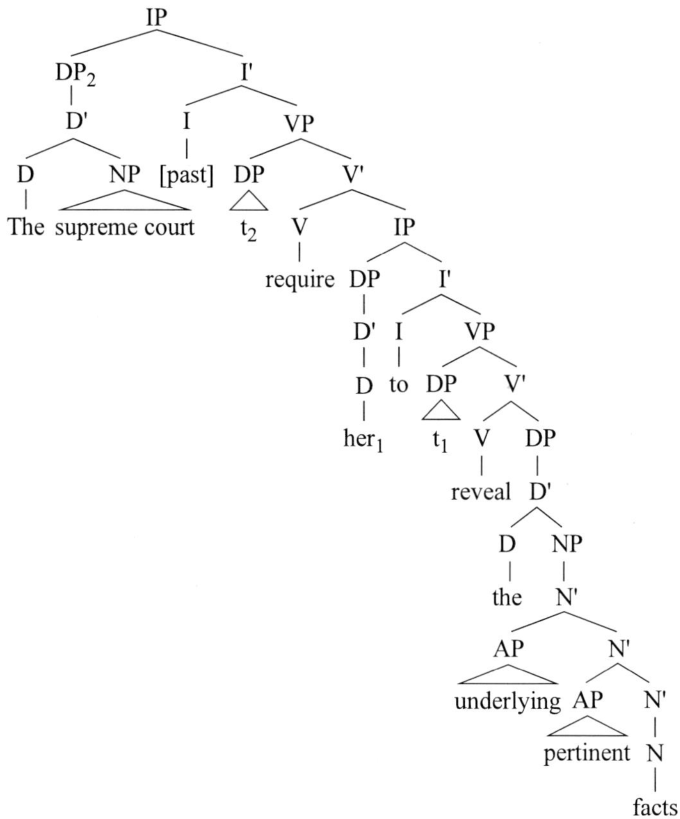

Let us consider evidence for the structure given in (20). Expletive *there* should appear in the subject position.

(21) a. There is a splinter in my spring roll.
b. *I hate there in my spring roll.

(22) indicates that *there* occupies the subject position. (22a) means (23).

(22) a. He required there to be explicit formalism.
b. *He required there.

(23) He required that there be explicit formalism.

Normally, a transitive verb assigns Acc Case to its object. But a verb like *believe*, *expect*, or *require* assigns Acc Case to the subject of its object clause. This looks exceptional. In this light, the term ECM was coined.

(24)

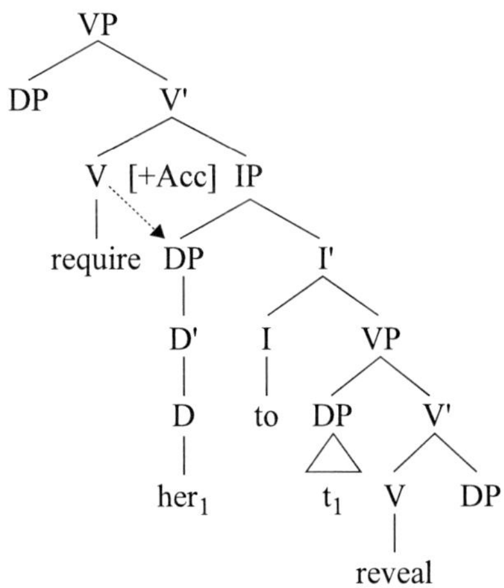

In short, we have the following three Case licensing configurations: Spec-Head, Government, and ECM.

(25)

CASE	CASE-ASSIGNING HEAD	LICENSING CONFIGURATION
NOMINATIVE	Finite I	Spec-Head
POSSESSIVE	Possessive D	Spec-Head
ACCUSATIVE	V, P	Government
ACCUSATIVE	V	ECM

Exercise 7

《 7-1 》

Explain the following terms:

(26) a. Case, Nominative Case, Accusative Case, Possessive Case
b. The Case Filter
c. Spec-Head Agreement
d. Government
e. M-command
f. Exceptional Case Marking (ECM)

《 7-2 》

Draw the trees of the following:

(27) that lady's daughter's sister's pretty doll
(28) The prosecutor will prove you to be guilty.
(29) Ted assumes intelligence to be important.

《 7-3 》

Where does the Case of *Ross* come from? Can you draw a tree of (30)?

(30) For <u>Ross</u> to win the game is not easy.

《 7-4 》

Explain the ungrammaticality of the following:

(31) a. *Rachel to leave would be terrible.

b. *It was seen them.

c. *Ross loves they.

《 7-5 》

Can you collapse three Case licensing configurations in (25) into one? Explore the possibility.

8 Raising vs. Control

Raising and *control* are apparently similar but quite different.

(1) a. Serena seemed to love Dan. [Raising]
 b. Serena decided to love Dan. [Control]

Raising has been distinguished from *control* in Generative Grammar. They display distinct syntactic behaviors including the assignment of thematic roles, selectional restrictions, pleonastic subjects like *it* and *there*, and interpretation of an embedded idiomatic expression. In this chapter, we compare *raising* and *control*.

8.1 Special Subjects

The following DPs are different from common DPs. They must be licensed as the subject of an appropriate predicate.

(2) a. expletive *there*

b. subject idiom chunks

c. weather *it*

First, the expletive *there* subject is special in that it should be selected by verbs of existence.

(3) a. Once upon a time, there *lived* a fisherman and his beautiful wife near the sea.

b. There *is* no assurance that she is eligible for a faculty member.

c. There *began* to be some doubt in my mind as to whether she understood syntax.

d. There *tend* to be indications well before experiencing nervous breakdown.

(4) a. *There *persisted* the same old accusatory tones for weeks.

b. *There *experienced* memory loss, vomit, seizure, and persistent migraine.

c. *There *cleared* a hurdle today.

d. *There *realize* the vagaries of life.

Second, the subject of sentential idioms is special in that it is licensed by being a part of these idioms.

(5) a. <u>The shit</u> hits the fan.

'An extremely unpleasant thing happens.'

b. <u>Jack's goose</u> is cooked.

'All hopes are gone; no chance remains.'

c. <u>The grass</u> is always greener on the other side of the fence.

'Other circumstances seem better than one's own.'

d. <u>Old dogs</u> can't learn new tricks.

'It is hard to change the way they do something when they have been doing it the same way for a long time.'

Third, weather *it* is special in that weather *it* and precipitation verbs license each other. That is why (7) is bad.

(6) It is {raining, drizzling, pouring, hailing}.

(7) *The {air, atmosphere, sky, weather} is {raining, drizzling, pouring, hailing}.

In short, the aforementioned three subjects are special in that they should be locally licensed as the subject of a proper predicate.

8.2 Raising

Under the Predicate-internal Subject Hypothesis (PISH), the VP-internal subject in Spec of VP moves to Spec of IP. Note that the subject remains in its own clause.

In raising constructions, the subject moves out of its clause into a higher one.

Let us consider evidence that there is a raising in English.

◀ Evidence 1 ▶

Below, (8) is ungrammatical because *seem* does not license expletive *there* as in (9). Then, why are the sentences in (10) grammatical?

(8) a. *There seems to persist the same old accusatory tones for weeks.

b. *There seemed to call it a day.

(9) *There seems no way out.

(10) a. There seems to be a serious drawback.
b. There seems to exist a conspiracy.

In (10) *there* is not licensed in the matrix clause. But it WAS licensed in the embedded (nonfinite) clause when it originated. This is evidence of raising.

(11) a. *There seems [to persist the same old accusatory tones for weeks].
b. *There persisted the same old accusatory tones for weeks.

(12) a. *There seemed [to call it a day].
b. *There called it a day.

(13) a. There seems [to be a serious drawback].
b. There is a serious drawback.

(14) a. There seems [to exist a conspiracy].
b. There exists a conspiracy.

◀ Evidence 2 ▶

The examples in (15) are sentential idioms. Note that they have idiomatic interpretations, respectively, although subject idiom chunks and predicate idiom chunks are not local. This is evidence of raising. That is, subject idiom chunks originated in embedded (nonfinite) clauses.

(15) a. <u>The shit</u> seems [to hit the fan].
b. <u>Jack's goose</u> appears [to be cooked].
c. <u>The grass</u> appears [to be always greener on the other side of the fence].
d. <u>Old dogs</u> seem [to be unable to learn new tricks].

◀ Evidence 3 ▶

The contrast between (6) and (7) is parallel to that between (16) and (17). This is another piece of evidence of raising. Recall that weather *it* and precipitation verbs license each other.

(16) a. It was unlikely [to {rain, drizzle, pour, hail}].
b. It seems [to be {raining, drizzling, pouring, hailing}].

(17) a. *The {air, atmosphere, sky, weather} was unlikely [to {rain, drizzle, pour, hail}].
b. *The {air, atmosphere, sky, weather} seems [to be {raining, drizzling, pouring, hailing}].

◀ Misnomer ▶

The matrix verb in raising constructions is called *raising verb*. But this is a sort of misnomer. In fact, the raising verb itself does not move. What it moves is the subject of the nonfinite complement clause of the verb. In this sense, the raising verb is actually a *raising-trigger verb*.

Raising verbs are semantically deficient because they do not select the subjects. Normally, verbs select their subjects as follows:

(18) a. The {penguin, #rock} is swaggering around.
b. Less than a {week, #tooth} has passed before we jazzed it up.
c. The {boy, #sequin} is going through a growth spurt.

The following is the basic tree of a raising verb such as *seem*:

(19)

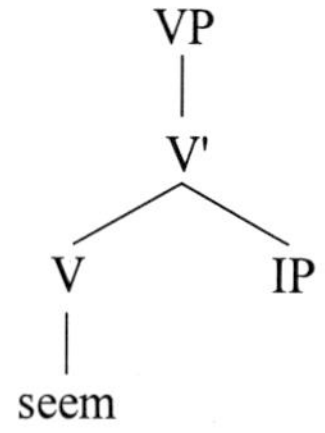

The following shows the deep structure of (10a):♣

(20)

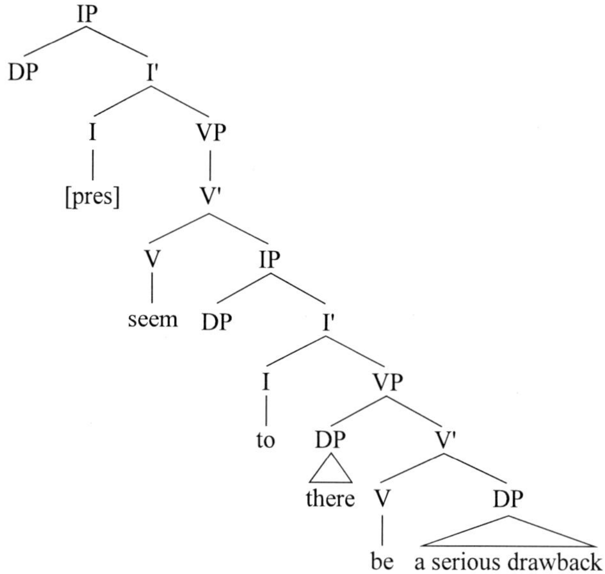

Raising verbs do not license ECM.

(21) He/*Him seems [to spill the beans].

(22) *It$_{expl}$ seems [him to spill the beans].

The following shows the surface structure of (10a):

♣ In the text, it is simply assumed that *there* is inserted in Spec of VP, and then raised to Spec of IP, in compliance with the PISH. Alternatively, however, it could be assumed that *there* is directly inserted into Spec of IP, considering the expletive nature of *there*.

(23)

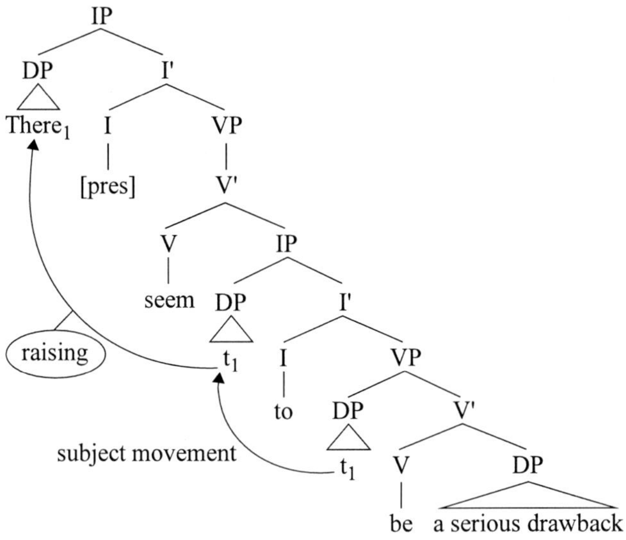

Raising verbs may select finite clauses as their complements. In this case, expletive *it* merges into the subject position of raising verbs.

(24) a. It_{expl} {appears, seems} [that there comes a time in your life].

b. It_{expl} {appears, seems} [that $\text{it}_{\text{weather}}$ is drizzling].

c. It_{expl} {appears, seems} [that the cat got out of the bag].

8.3 Control

There is a similarity between control verbs and raising verbs. Both can select nonfinite clauses headed by *to*.

(25) Kim {attempted, bothered, demanded, expected, hoped, tried} [to move to Storrs].

However, there are differences too.

◀ Difference 1 ▶

Control verbs select their subjects.

(26) #A ream of paper hoped [to dabble their feet in the pool].

Some control verbs can select finite clausal complements.

(27) Kim {decided, expected, hoped} [that he would move to Storrs].

However, the equivalents of (27) with raising verbs are ill-formed.

(28) *Kim {appears, seems} [that he has moved to Storrs].

◀ Difference 2 ▶

Control verbs do not tolerate special subjects. Why? They select their own subjects.

(29) a. *There {attempted, bothered, demanded, hoped} [to be a deadlock].

b. *It$_{weather}$ {attempted, bothered, demanded, hoped} [to rain].

c. #The jig {attempted, bothered, demanded, hoped} [to be up].

The following is the basic tree of a control verb like *choose*:

(30)

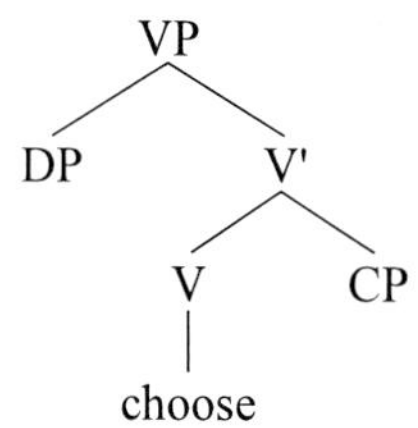

(32) shows the structure of the control construction in (31):♣♣♣

(31) Jung chose to renew his passport.

(32)

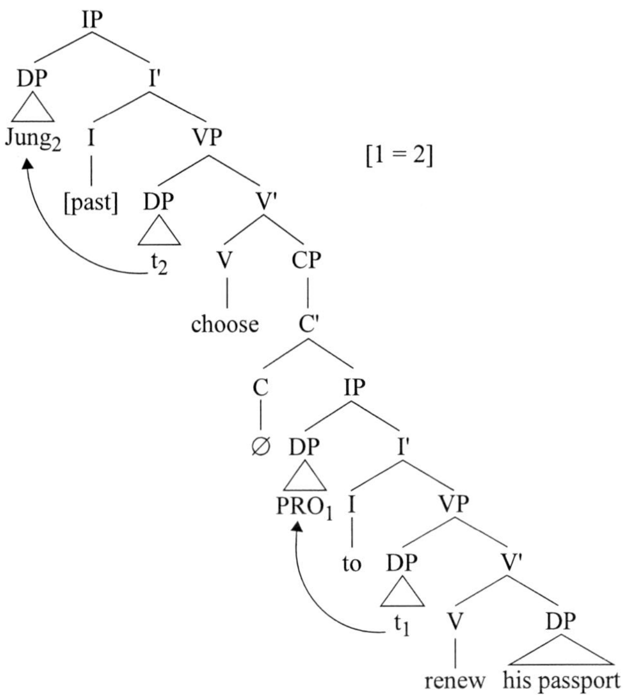

There is evidence that *choose* selects CPs but not IPs. In (33) *whether* is a complementizer.

(33) Jung must choose [whether to renew his passport].

♣
The index 1 and the index 2 in (32) are created by each separate movement. They should refer to the same entity for an interpretive reason.

♣♣
By assumption, PRO is an empty pronoun subject. It lacks phonetic matrix.

(34)

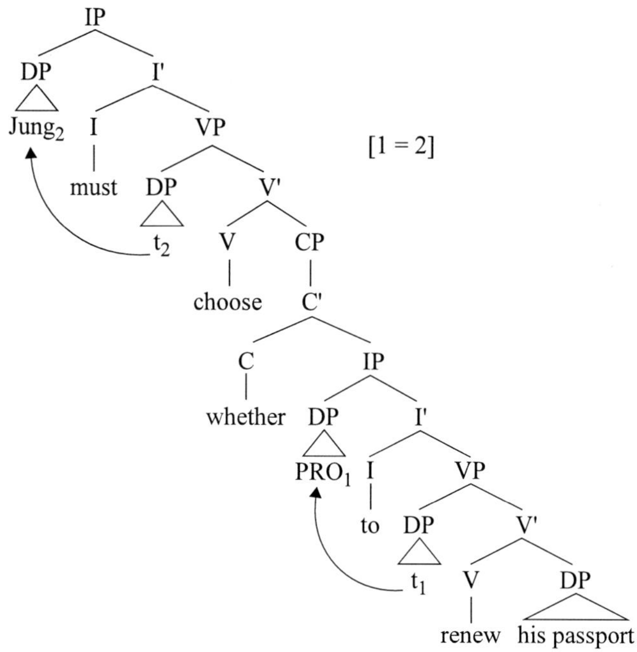

So far, we have considered subject-control verbs like *promise*, *try*, or *attempt*. In English, we have object-control verbs like *persuade*, *order*, *convince*, or *tell*.

(35) a. I_1 promised him [PRO_1 to go].
b. I persuaded him_1 [PRO_1 to go].

Subject-control verbs and object-control verbs are obligatory control verbs. On the other hand, there are non-obligatory control verbs. Below, the reference of PRO is arbitrary; i.e., it is not fixed.

(36) a. PRO to be or not to be, that is the question.
b. PRO to park a car here is prohibited.
c. PRO to leave now would be a mistake.

Exercise 8

⟨ 8-1 ⟩

Explain the following terms:

(37) a. Raising, Control
     b. Subject-Control, Object-Control
     c. Obligatory Control, Non-Obligatory Control

⟨ 8-2 ⟩

Explain the ungrammaticality of the following:

(38) *It seems [him to have a problem].

⟨ 8-3 ⟩

Draw the trees of the following:

(39) Dan ordered Serena to go.
(40) It appears that it is raining.
(41) To fly the plane is dangerous.
(42) There is a cat on the mat.
(43) Serena hoped to kiss Dan.
(44) Serena seemed to kiss Dan.
(45) He seems to be likely to win.

⟨ 8-4 ⟩

In the following, the idiomatic reading is unaffected by the presence of modals, different tenses, different aspects, or negation. Discuss the theoretical implication.

(46) a. The shit {may, should, might, can} hit the fan.
b. The shit {will hit, is hitting, has hit} the fan.
c. The shit did not hit the fan.

9 Passive

9.1 Burzio's Generalization

Unergative verbs are monoargumental. They appear with the subject argument which usually plays the role of an Agent as in (1a). They normally do not choose an object as in (1b). But some of them may tolerate a cognate object (i.e., a noun of the same semantic origin) especially when they are modified as in (2). Some of unergative verbs are illustrated in (3).

(1) a. Serena laughed.
    b. *Serena laughed Dan.

(2) a. dance a tribal dance
    b. die a beautiful death
    c. sleep a troubled sleep
    d. sing a mellow song

(3) *bark, chew, dance, die, dream, jump, laugh, live, run, shout, sing, sleep, talk, walk,* etc.

Ergative (= unaccusative) verbs are also monoargumental in that they appear with the subject argument which usually plays the role of a Theme as in (4a). What is interesting is that they can be transitive as in (4b) although the subject argument in (4a) syntactically turns into the object argument in (4b). Some of ergative verbs are illustrated in (5).

(4) a. The milk froze.
    b. They froze the milk.

(5) *arrive, burn, change, decrease, fall, grow, increase, melt, open, remain, sink, turn,* etc.

On the other hand, a set of ergative verbs has often been called as middle verbs, as illustrated in (6). Middle verbs differ from ergative verbs in that they strongly require an adverbial or the negation *not* as in (7).

(6) *anger, break, bribe, clean, drive, read, scare, sell, start, tease,* etc.

(7) a. Porcelain breaks easily.
    b. This book is a page-turner; it really reads well.
    c. The car starts quickly.
    d. The new model did not sell.

Burzio (1986) observes that verbs which assign a subject θ-role assign accusative (Acc) Case to their objects. Both raising and passivization observe Burzio's generalization in (8).

(8) All and only verbs that can assign θ-roles to the subject can assign Acc Case to an object.

(9)

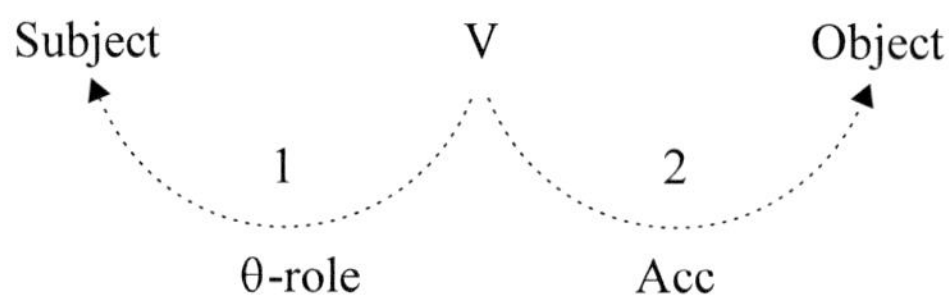

9.2 Properties

In English, active sentences like (10a) have passive counterparts like (10b).

(10)	a.	The council	rejected	the bills.
		AGENT		PATIENT
		SUBJECT		DIRECT OBJECT
	b.	The bills	were rejected	(by the council).
		PATIENT		(AGENT)
		SUBJECT		(ADJUNCT)

Why is (11b) ungrammatical? Past participles cannot assign Case.

(11)	a.	ACTIVE	The council has rejected them.
	b.	PASSIVE	*It_{expl} was rejected them.
			Intended meaning: 'They were rejected.'

English passive morphology is analytically expressed; [Aux *be* + past participle].

Are past participles deverbal adjectives? Well, yes and no. Oh, well, maybe yes.

In English, eventive predicates can appear in the progressive aspect. Why is (13b) ungrammatical? *Know* is a stative predicate.

(12)	a.	They broke their backs proofreading his scripts. [Eventive, Non-progressive]
	b.	They are breaking their backs proofreading his scripts. [Eventive, Progressive]

(13) a. He knows the rules. [Stative, Non-progressive]
b. *He is knowing the rules. [Stative, Progressive]

In (14) past participles show event. That is, they are used in the progressive aspect. In (15) adjectives cannot be eventive.

(14) a. Many Palestinian citizens are persecuted (by Israel).
[Eventive, Non-progressive]
b. Many Palestinian citizens are being persecuted (by Israel).
[Eventive, Progressive]

(15) a. Booster seats for child passengers are mandatory.
[Stative, Non-progressive]
b. *Booster seats for child passengers are being mandatory.
[Stative, Progressive]

However, it is possible for adjectives in English to be eventive. (16a) is synonymous with (16b).

(16) a. We had a quick cup of coffee and caught the early train.
b. We drank coffee quickly and caught the train that was departing early.

Eventive adjectives like *quick, fast, early,* and *late* can appear in connection with the progressive aspect.

(17) a. The flight is being late. [Adjective]
b. The flight is departing/arriving late. [Adverb]

Passive participles can be stative as well as eventive.

(18)

	Aspect	Example	Discourse context
a.	Event	*The line is deleted (by the director).*	The director certainly deletes inappropriate lines.
b.	State	*The line is deleted.*	The director thinks it is an inappropriate line.

Stative past participles cannot be used in the progressive environment.

(19)

	Aspect	Example	Discourse context
a.	Event	*The line is being deleted.*	The director thinks a line is inappropriate so he is deleting it.
b.	State	**The line is being deleted.*	The director thinks it is an inappropriate line.

9.3 Passivization

Only a few special predicates can license object idiom chunks.

(20) a. Barney wouldn't hesitate to take advantage of the situation.

b. They are making some headway on the system architecture process.

c. They will give/pay heed to her warnings.

d. People paid homage to the unknown shoeshine boy who became president.

In (21) the object idiom chunk *heed* makes the sentence unacceptable because it does not have the licensing verb like *give* or *pay*. Much the same point could be made for *headway* in (22). Put briefly, object idiom chunks demand special licensing verbs, while other common objects like *attention* or *progress* do not.

(21) a. My daughter always tries to attract my {attention, *heed}.
b. The child who has ADHD requires a lot of {attention, *heed}.

(22) a. Please be ready to report some {progress, *headway} by Monday.
b. We appreciate your {progress, *headway} in making all the arrangements.

Object idiom chunks are usually unacceptable in the subject position.

(23) a. {Attention, *Heed} facilitates learning.
b. More {attention, *heed} to maintenance would soon pay off in lower repair bills.
c. {Progress, *Headway} is often slower than one expects.
d. {Progress, *Headway} in technology has changed people's lives dramatically.

Of particular interest is that they may stand in the subject position as long as being licensed by passive participles.

(24) a. Huge advantage was taken of Helen's sacrifice.
b. Some headway is being made against his adamant plan.
c. Little heed was paid to his pathological compulsion.
d. Strict tabs were kept on the carbon dioxide emissions.

(25) a. *Huge advantage was attracted of Helen's sacrifice.
b. *Some headway is being reported against his adamant plan.
c. *Little heed was demanded to his pathological compulsion.
d. *Strict tabs were put on the carbon dioxide emissions.

Passivization is an instance of DP/NP movement. Let us consider the basic trees of an active verb vs. a passive verb (i.e., passive participle) in (26). According to Burzio's generalization, *selected* neither assigns Agent θ-role nor Acc Case.

(26) a. Active: [+Acc]

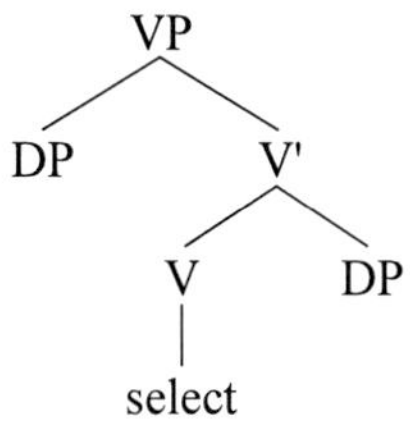

b. Passive: [-Acc]

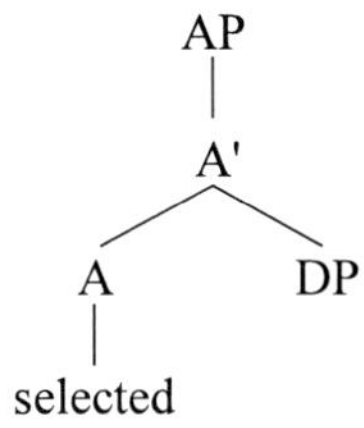

Let us now consider the derivation of (27), as illustrated in (28).♣♣♣

(27) The countermeasure was carefully selected.

(28)

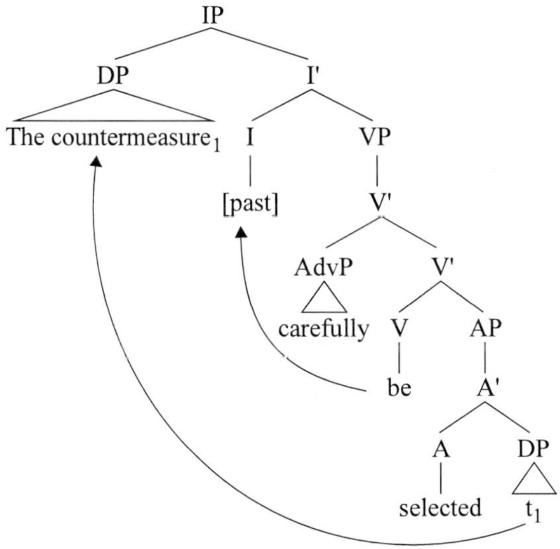

Let us compare raising with passivization. First, raising applies across a clausal boundary, whereas passivization does not. Second, passivization changes the GF of the moved DP, but raising does not.

♣
In (28) *carefully* is generated as a V'-adjunct. It could be an A'-adjunct. It does not matter for the present concern.

♣♣
Unlike main verbs, aspectual Aux verbs (*be* and *have*) in English originate in V and then move to I in order to pick up the tense morpheme. In other words, English aspectual Aux verbs pattern together with French main verbs with respect to Verb Raising Parameter.

(29) a. Raising

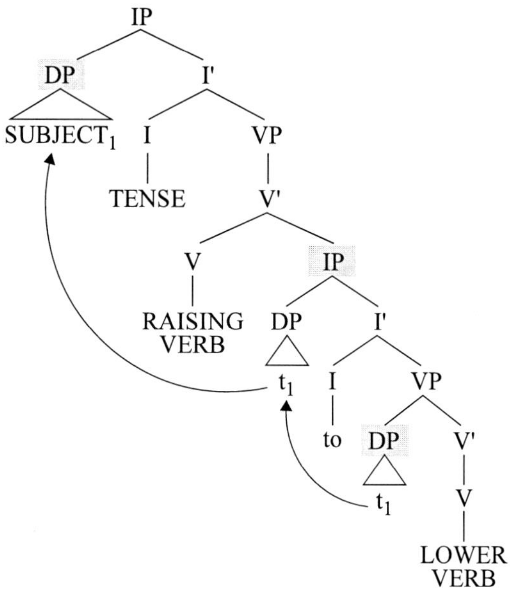

b. Passivization

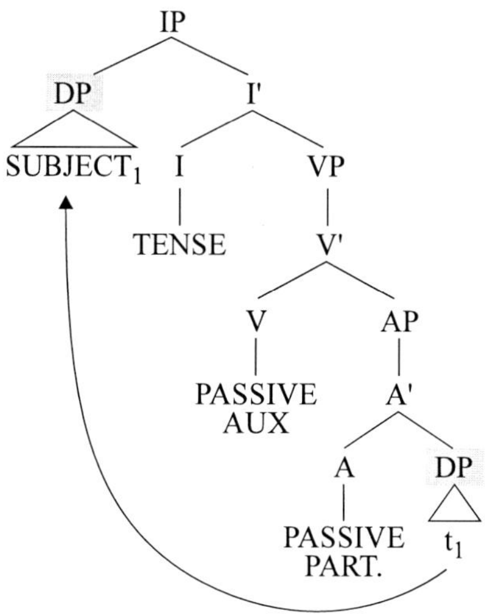

9.4 Nonfinite Complementation

(30a) illustrates ECM, while (30b) illustrates exceptional passivization.

(30) a. The FDA rules require [you to report any relevant adverse effect immediately].

b. You are required [to report any relevant adverse effect immediately] (according to the FDA rules).♣

(31a) is the basic tree of *require*. (31b) is the basic tree of *required*. Compared with (26), the head selects an IP instead of a DP. According to Burzio's generalization, there is no Spec in (31b), and the head does not assign Acc Case.

(31) a. Active: [+Acc]

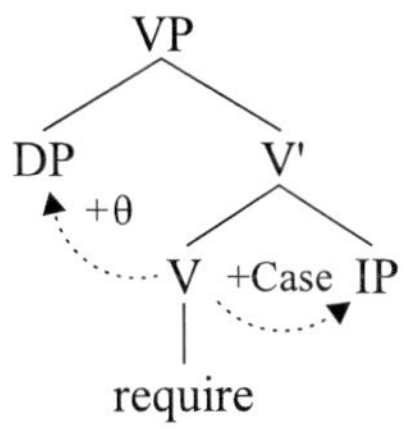

b. Passive: [-Acc]

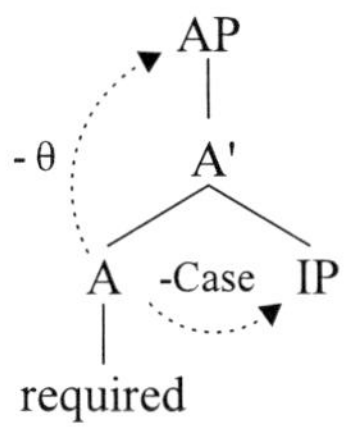

♣ The passivization in (30b) is exceptional in that only the part of the object (i.e., *you*) rather than the bracketed whole object is promoted as the subject.

The following is the structure of (30b):

(32)

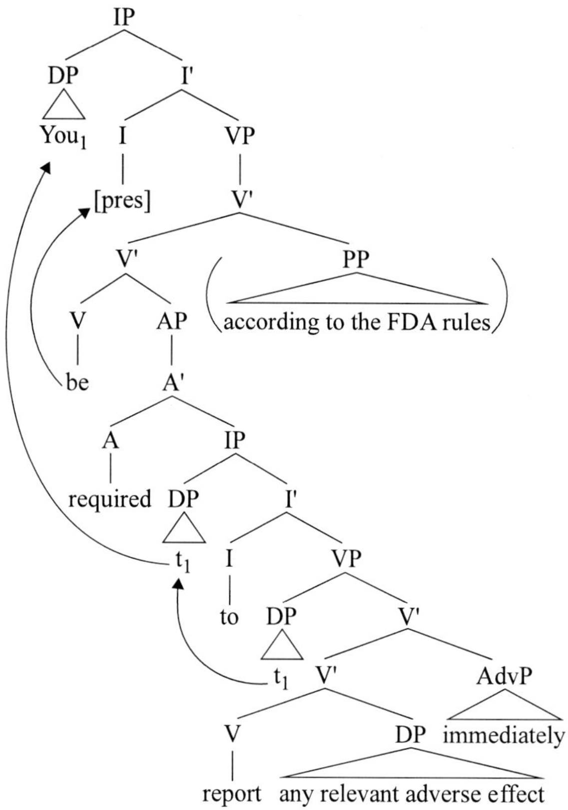

Exceptional passivization chains and raising chains look alike.♣

(33) a. Exceptional passivization chain

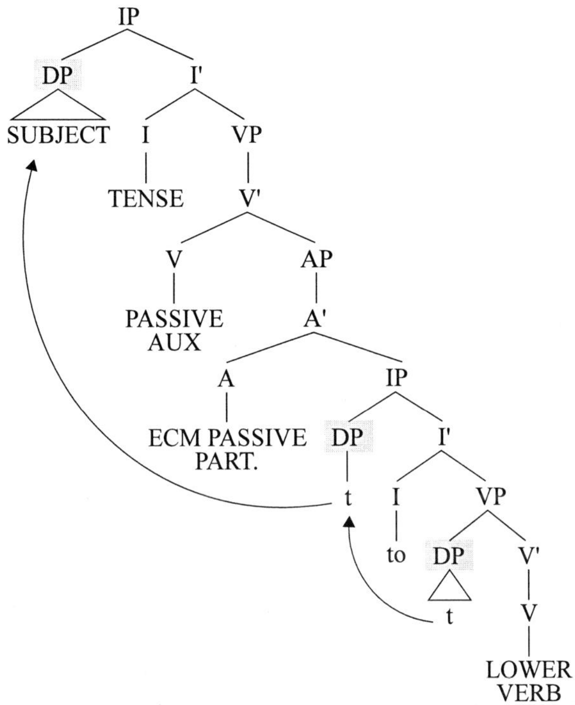

♣
A moved element and its traces form a chain.
(i) Chain = (X_1, ..., t'_1, t_1)

b. Raising chain

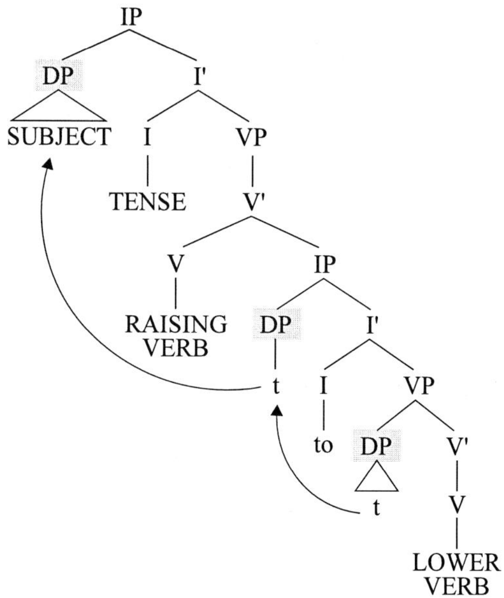

Why are exceptional passive verbs and raising verbs similar? They neither project the Spec position nor license Acc Case.

(34) a.

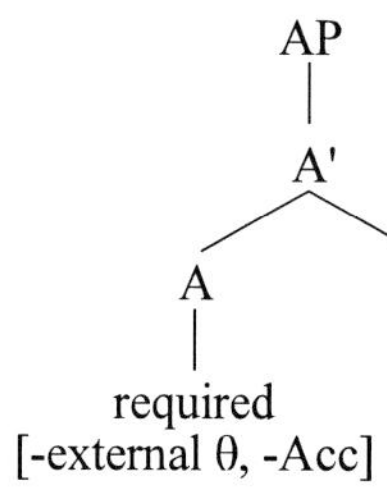

b.

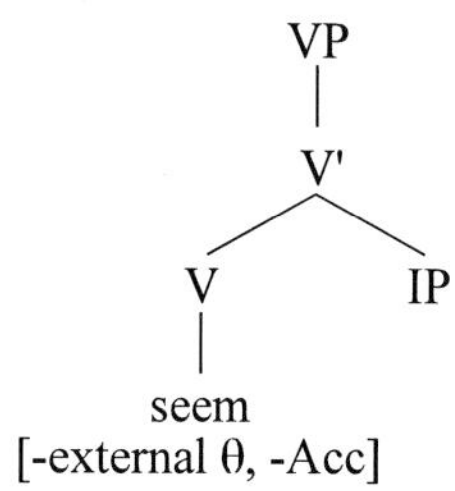

According to Burzio's generalization, (35) is ungrammatical. Why? The head does not assign Acc Case because it cannot assign an external θ-role.

(35) a. *It$_{expl}$ seems [*him* to play badminton].
b. *It$_{expl}$ is expected [*him* to play hockey].
c. *It$_{expl}$ was selected *them*.

Thus far, we have assumed that passive verbs are close to adjectives. But there is evidence that this assumption is questionable. (36) shows an example of passivization. (37) is ungrammatical because the subject is missing, and the object does not receive Case. (38) is still ungrammatical because the object is Caseless.

(36) The film was nominated (for Oscars).
cf. ___ was nominated the film. [at DS]

(37) *Was nominated the film.

(38) *It/There was nominated the film.

Adjectives and passive verbs lack the ability to assign Case to their complement. Why is (40) ungrammatical? *Leslie* is Caseless. We can salvage (40) via the *of*-insertion strategy as in (41).♣

(39) We [$_{VP}$ support Leslie].

(40) *We are [$_{AP}$ supportive Leslie].

(41) We are supportive of Leslie.

The *of*-insertion strategy is not available for passive verbs.

(42) *It/There was nominated of the film.

Thus, we conclude that passive verbs are neither full-fledged verbs nor full-fledged adjectives.

♣ If *of* is a preposition in (41), it is a semantically null preposition. It may be just called as a Case marker.

Normally, Ns do not license Case on their complements.

(43) Howard [$_{VP}$ proved the lemma].

(44) *[$_{DP}$ Howard's proof the lemma]

Of-insertion is allowed for the licensing of the complement.

(45) Howard's proof of the lemma

Movement into the subject position is often allowed.

(46) the lemma's proof

cf. [$_{DP}$ ___ 's [$_{NP}$ proof the lemma]] [at DS]

There are four major lexical categories: V, P, N, and A. With respect to licensing Case on a complement, V and P pattern together. With respect to triggering *of*-insertion, N and A pattern together.

Let us assume that lexical categories are bundles of values for binary features as follows:

(47) a. V [+v, -n] [v] = verbal feature, [n] = nominal feature
b. N [-v, +n]
c. A [+v, +n]
d. P [-v, -n]

Then, we reach to the following generalizations:

(48) Case licensing lexical categories are marked as [-n].

(49) The trigger for *of*-insertion is marked as [+n].

(50) Passivized verbs are marked as [+v].

Exercise 9

⟨9-1⟩

Explain the following terms:

(51) a. Intransitive Verb, Unergative Verb, Ergative Verb, Unaccusative Verb, Middle Verb
b. Burzio's Generalization
c. Deverbal Adjective, Deverbal Noun
d. Eventive Predicate, Stative Predicate
e. Passivization, Exceptional Passivization
f. Object Idiom Chunks, Subject Idiom Chunks
g. *Of*-insertion Strategy

⟨9-2⟩

Draw the trees of the following:

(52) Dan is kissed by Serena.
(53) Study questions for the final exam are being available.
(54) Barney believed Robin to love him.

⟨9-3⟩

It has been argued that passive sentences are not derived from their active counterparts. Discuss the meaning difference of the following pairs:

(55) a. Jimmy Carter has visited KU.
b. KU has been visited by Jimmy Carter.
(56) a. Every student in this classroom speaks two languages.

b. Two languages are spoken by every student in this classroom.

《 9-4 》

Aforementioned, there are two general types of monoargumental verbs in English: unergative verbs and ergative verbs. What is interesting is that only unergative verbs can take cognate objects, as illustrated below. Discuss why.

(57) a. Serena smiled (a beautiful smile).

b. Ted arrived (*an unexpected arrival).

10 Islands

DP movements such as subject movement, raising, and passivization are Case-driven.

Unlike DP movements, wh-movements are not Case-driven but [wh]-driven. They observe island constraints.

10.1 Questions

Wonder requires a CP complement.

(1) They wonder [$_{CP}$ if Ron will make the connection].

The following is the tree of (1):

(2)

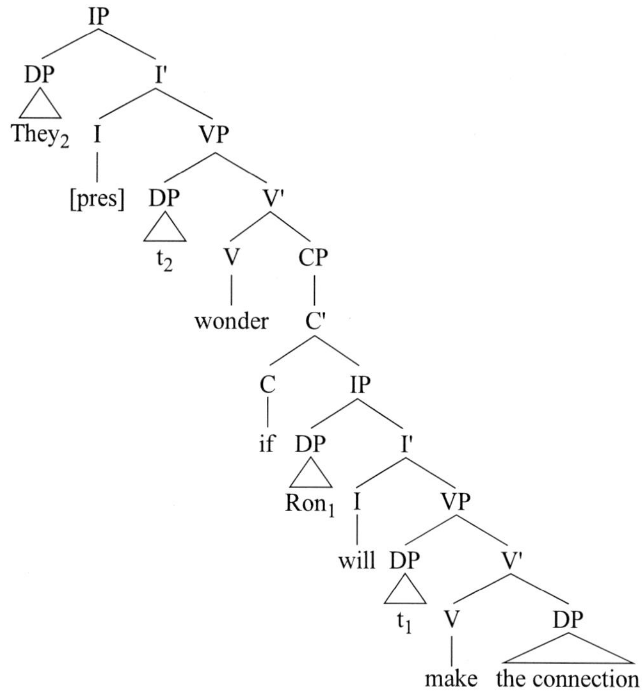

The following is an indirect question.

(3) They wonder what connection he will make.

The following is the tree of (3). There is no overt complementizer. Instead, there is a silent complementizer [wh]. *Make* is a transitive verb.

(4)

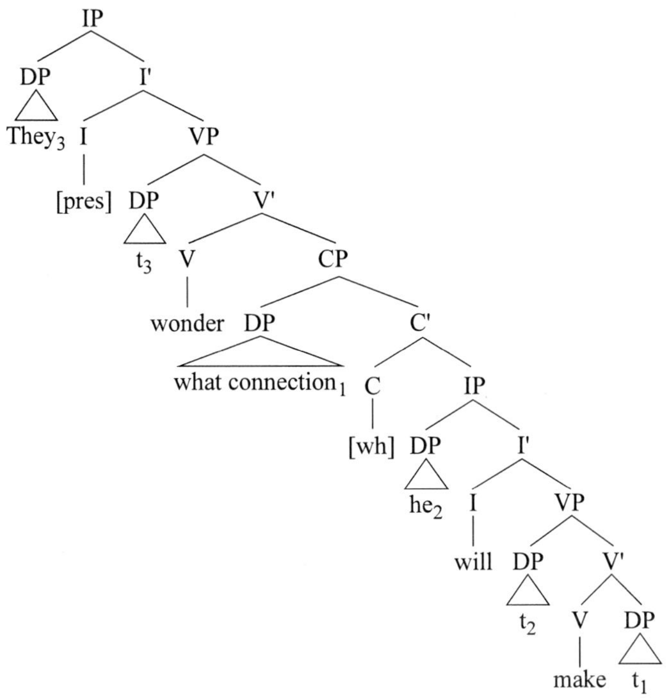

Let us consider the motivations for wh-movement.

Evidence 1

Adverbial modification is evidence of wh-movement. In (5a) *very specifically* adjoins to V' and modifies *make*.

(5) a. Ron will make the connection very specifically.

b. They wonder how specifically Ron will make the connection.

The following is the surface structure (SS) tree of (5b). At DS, *how specifically* WAS generated as a V'-adjunct and modified *make*.

(6)

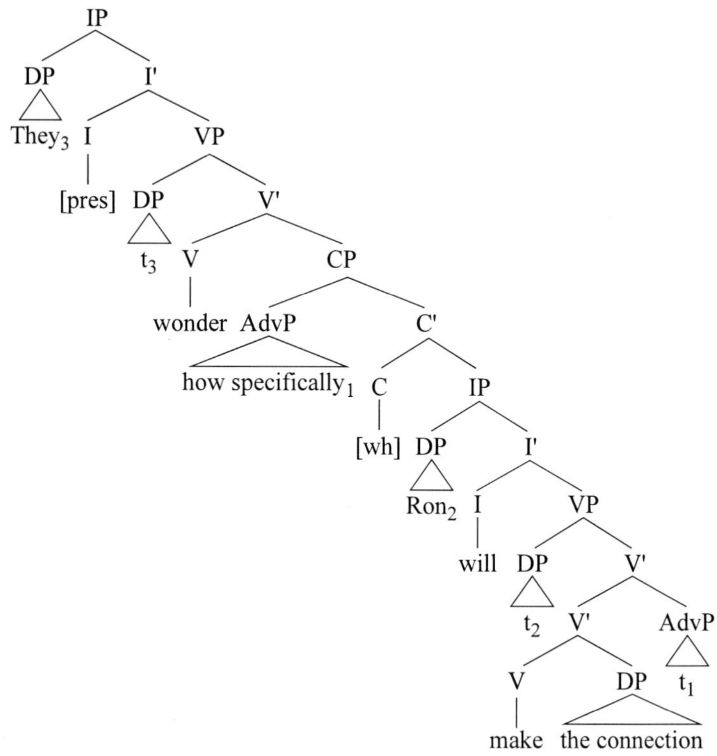

Evidence 2

Case assignment is another piece of evidence of wh-movement. Why is (7b) ungrammatical? The finite INFL of the embedded clause assigns Nom Case, not Acc Case.

(7) a. She believes he will join her for lunch.
b. *She believes him will join her for lunch.

Why is (8b) ungrammatical?

(8) a. I wonder who she believes will join her for lunch.
b. *I wonder whom she believes will join her for lunch.

A plausible answer to this question is to use movement. Given the structure for (8a) in (9), *who* can be assigned Nom Case by *will* before moving to Spec of CP of the *believe* clause.

(9) I wonder [$_{CP}$ who$_1$ [$_{IP}$ she believes [$_{CP}$ [$_{IP}$ t_1 will join her for lunch]]]].

In Case-driven movements, a DP originates in a Caseless position and then moves to a Case-marked position. By contrast, a wh-DP moves from a Case-marked position to a Caseless position (i.e., Spec of CP).

(10)	a.	DP movement:	chain	=	(DP,	trace)
					+Case	-Case
	b.	wh-movement:	chain	=	(wh-DP,	trace)
					-Case	+Case

Note that the filter in (11) is satisfied in a complementary way.

(11) The Case Filter (revised)
Every overt argument DP chain must have a Case.

The wh-movement can move an AP, an AdvP, a PP, or a DP.

(12) a. I wonder [$_{AP}$ how tawdry] the business of politics should be.
b. I wonder [$_{AdvP}$ how quickly] kids grow up these days.
c. I wonder [$_{PP}$ in which jar] Mom hid my Sour Patch Kids.
d. I wonder [$_{DP}$ which method] he will use to provide a seamless solution.

Wh-XPs move to Spec of CP in indirect questions. We also assume that the direct questions in (13) are produced by wh-movement.

(13) a. [$_{AP}$ How tawdry] should the business of politics be?
b. [$_{AdvP}$ How quickly] do kids grow up these days?
c. [$_{PP}$ In which jar] did Mom hide my Sour Patch Kids?
d. [$_{DP}$ Which method] will he use to provide a seamless solution?

The following is the structure of (13c); aforementioned, [wh] is a silent morpheme, expressing interrogative force:

(14)

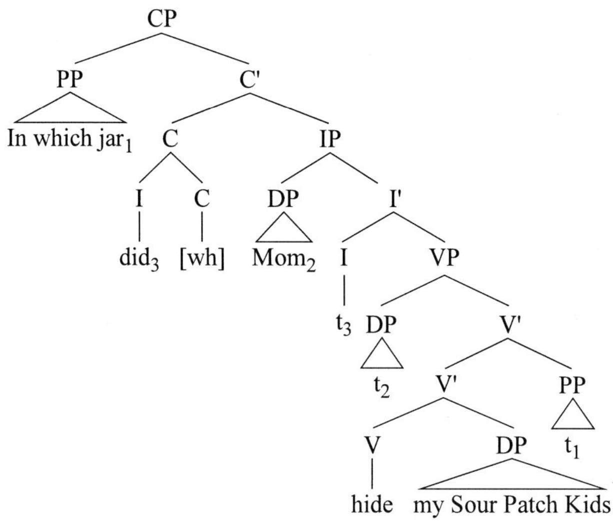

10.2 Island Constraints

Wh-movement is unlimited or unbounded in that wh-phrases may travel across clauses. In (15) three instances of long-distance wh-movement are illustrated.

(15) a. [$_{CP}$ What$_1$ was he stealing t$_1$]?
b. [$_{CP}$ What$_1$ did he say
[$_{CP}$ that he was stealing t$_1$]]?
c. [$_{CP}$ What$_1$ does she claim
[$_{CP}$ that he said
[$_{CP}$ that he was stealing t$_1$]]]?
d. [$_{CP}$ What$_1$ are they assuming
[$_{CP}$ that she claims
[$_{CP}$ that he said
[$_{CP}$ that he was stealing t$_1$]]]]?

Ross (1967), however, suggests that some wh-movement is not unbounded. (16b) is ungrammatical due to the violation of the Wh-island Constraint.♣ ♣♣

(16) a. She has realized [which one$_1$ she could trust t$_1$ in trouble].
b. *When$_2$ has she realized [which one$_1$ she could trust t$_1$ t$_2$]?

(17b) and (18b) are ungrammatical due to the violation of the Complex NP Constraint (CNPC).♣♣♣ ♣♣♣♣ In (17) and (18) the embedded clause is called a noun complement clause.

(17) a. She has been making [the allegation [that Jimmy actually threatened the knucklehead]].
b. *Who$_1$ does she make [the allegation [that Jimmy actually threatened t$_1$]]?

(18) a. He never mentions [the rumor [that he once dated Taylor Momsen]].
b. *Which celebrity$_1$ does he never mention [the rumor [that he once dated t$_1$]]?

♣
(16b) is ungrammatical with the embedded adjunct reading in which *when* modifies the embedded predicate *trust*. It is grammatical with the matrix adjunct reading in which *when* modifies the matrix predicate *realized*. In the latter reading, the movement of *when* does not violate the Wh-island Constraint. You can paraphrase (16b) with the following:
(i) Has she realized which one she could trust and when she could do it?

♣♣
The Wh-island Constraint: Extraction out of an embedded clause introduced by a wh-element is deviant.

♣♣♣
Originally, this constraint was called the CNPC. Given a DP analysis of nominals, it may be called the CDPC.

♣♣♣♣
The CNPC: No extraction is possible out of a complex nominal domain.

Note that the examples in (19) do not violate island constraints. The embedded clause is a verb complement clause.

(19) a. Who$_1$ does she allege [that Jimmy actually threatened t$_1$]?
b. Which celebrity$_1$ does he never mention [that he once dated t$_1$]?

(20b) is ungrammatical due to the violation of the CNPC. The embedded clause is a relative clause.

(20) a. They know [someone [{who, that} would keep Manny in the dark]].
b. *Who$_1$ do they know [someone [{who, that} would keep t$_1$ in the dark]]?

(21b) is ungrammatical due to the violation of the Sentential Subject Constraint (SSC).♣

(21) a. [That Santiago has signed the contract] is extremely unlikely.
b. *What$_1$ is [that Santiago has signed t$_1$] extremely unlikely?

(22b) is ungrammatical due to the violation of the Left Branch Condition (LBC).♣♣

(22) a. She liked Dan's top-siders.
b. *Whose$_1$ did she like [t$_1$ top-siders]?

(23b) and (23c) violate the Coordinate Structure Constraint (CSC). The CSC states that extraction out of coordinate structures is not permitted unless it takes place in an across-the-board (ATB) manner out of all conjuncts (Ross 1967, Williams 1978), as shown in (24).

(23) a. School teachers should avoid [partiality and favoritism].

♣
The SSC: No extraction is possible out of a sentential subject domain.

♣♣
The LBC: The left branch of a nominal expression cannot be extracted.

b. *[What kind of bias]$_1$ should school teachers avoid [t_1 and favoritism]?

c. *[What kind of bias]$_1$ should school teachers avoid [partiality and t_1]?

d. [What kind of bias]$_1$ should school teacher avoid t_1?

(24) a. [$_{IP}$ The boys$_1$ will [$_{VP}$ t_1 write a book] and [$_{VP}$ t_1 be awarded a prize for it]].

b. [$_{IP}$ The policy$_1$ will [$_{VP}$ t_1 wreak havoc] and [$_{VP}$ t_1 be terminated for it]].

c. Here is the prisoner who$_1$ [you saved t_1] and [Lily said t_1 was torched].

d. I know the man who$_1$ [Ted likes t_1] and [we wish t_1 will win the lottery].

In addition to the island constraints discussed above (the Wh-island Constraint, the CNPC, the SSC, the LBC, the CSC), it has been observed that the Subject Condition (SC), the Adjunct Condition (AC), and the Right Roof Constraints (RRC) are operative in English.

(25) *Which student$_1$ did [a picture of t_1] hang on the wall? The SC♣

(26) *What$_1$ did Ross leave [without saying t_1]? The AC♣♣

(27) a. The fact [that Ross gave t_1 to Joey <u>the books which my uncle left to me</u>$_1$] is of no consequence.

b. *The fact [that Ross gave t_1 to Joey] is of no consequence <u>the books which my uncle left to me</u>$_1$. The RRC♣♣♣

♣ The SC: No extraction is possible out of a subject domain.

♣♣ The AC: No extraction is possible out of an adjunct domain.

♣♣♣ The RRC: Rightward extraction out of a clause is banned.

10.3 Relativization

As shown in (28) and (29), wh-interrogative clauses have a remarkable affinity with wh-relative clauses.

(28) a. Who win the lottery?
b. Who(m) do you like?
c. Where did you hear it?
d. Which do you prefer?
e. Whose plan do you support?

(29) a. the people who win the lottery
b. the people who(m) you like
c. the place where you heard it
d. the style which you prefer
e. the senator whose plan you support

It seems that relative wh-movements observe islands.

(30) a. The Wh-island Constraint
*the time $when_2$ she has realized [which one_1 she could trust t_1 t_2]

b. The CNPC: Noun complement clause
*the shoemaker who_1 I don't believe [the claim [that he has threatened t_1]]

c. The CNPC: Relative clause
*the fatalist who_1 I felt antipathetic to [the boss [that cared for t_1 for nothing]]

d. The SSC
*The bribery $which_1$ [{that he admitted, admitting} t_1] endangered his career.

e. The LBC

*the student whose$_1$ you marked [t_1 paper]

f. The CSC

*the prejudice which$_1$ you have [{partiality and t_1, t_1 and favoritism}]

The following shows the structure of (29b):

(31)

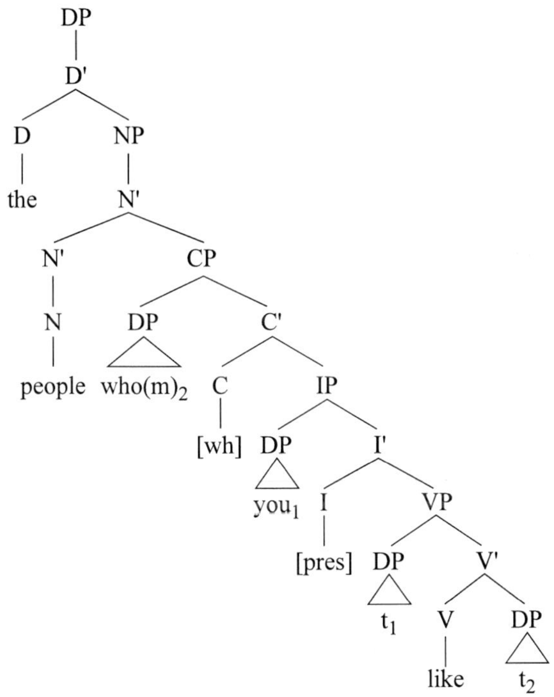

In addition to wh-relative clauses, English has *that*-relative clauses, as illustrated in (32). Apparently, *that*-relative clauses and wh-relative clauses look alike.

(32) a. the people that win the lottery
b. the people that you like
c. the style that you prefer

The following shows the structure of (32b). *That* is an overt complementizer. Op is a null operator, i.e., a silent wh-phrase.

(33)

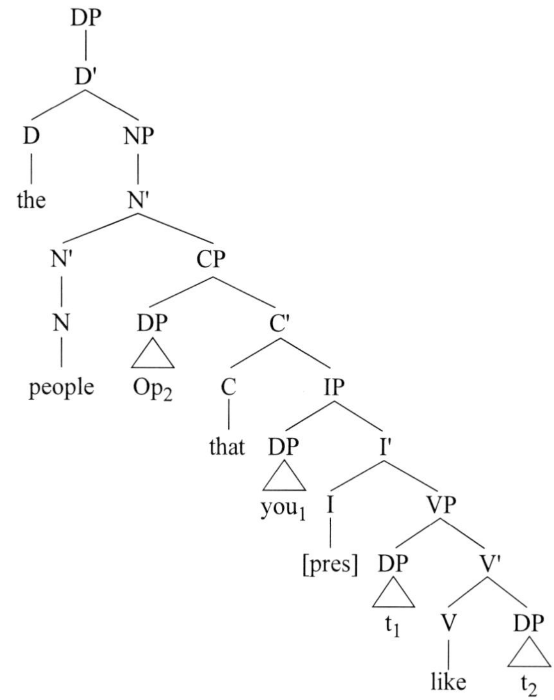

Note that null operators can only be DPs and not PPs.

(34) a. Rachel laughed at [$_{DP}$ the person]$_1$ [$_{CP}$ Op$_1$ Ross was looking at t_1].
b. *Rachel laughed [$_{PP}$ at the person]$_1$ [$_{CP}$ Op$_1$ Ross was looking t_1].

The following illustrates zero-relative clauses in which both wh-element and complementizer are silent. Wh-objects can be missing.

(35) a. the people ___ you like
b. the style ___ you prefer

Wh-subjects cannot be missing. Why? Well...

(36) a. the people who win the lottery (are from Mexico)
b. the people that win the lottery (are from Mexico)
c. *the people ___ win the lottery (are from Mexico)

10.4 Topicalization

Topic is what is being talked about in a sentence. In (37) *apples* is the topic of the sentence.♣ ♣♣

(37) Apples, he likes.
'When it comes to apples, he likes them.'

What is said about the topic is called *comment*. In (37) the constituent *apples* is placed to the left of the clause via an operation called *topicalization*. Topicalization is similar to wh-movement. Let us discuss the nature of topicalization below.

♣
(i) is a normal answer to the question in (ii). (37) is not a normal answer to the question in (ii). However, it sounds natural to the question in (iii).
(i) He likes apples.
(ii) What do you think Ross likes?
(iii) What do you think Ross likes among fruit?

♣♣
Topicalization is uttered with a pause encoded by the comma between a topic and its comment.

The following shows the canonical order:

(38) a. I have recalled that I know the commissioner.
b. The CDC acknowledged that they had made a serious mistake on the vaccine.
c. Lily subbed for Serena's role.
d. The corrupt cops would easily hand him the bum rap like that in a second.

(39) shows a non-canonical order of (38). The clause-initial non-subject becomes a discourse topic. In English, this process is expressed via a movement called topicalization.

(39) a. The commissioner$_1$, I have recalled that I know t_1.
b. A serious mistake on the vaccine$_1$, the CDC acknowledged that they had made t_1.
c. Serena's role$_1$, Lily subbed for t_1.
d. The bum rap like that$_1$, the corrupt cops would easily hand him t_1 in a second.

The clause-initial expression may not be a topic. In (40a) and (40b) the underlined element is a scene-setting expression, i.e., adverbial. In (40c) the underlined element is contrastive.

(40) a. On his way to school, he got robbed again.
b. In such a deepened misery, people tend to take chances.
c. Under oath, she testified that Jimmy had blackmailed her.

In Chomsky (1977), topicalization is analyzed as a case of wh-movement, based on the island effects.

(41) a. The Wh-island Constraint
*From somewhere$_1$, I have recalled [whom I know t_1].

b. The CNPC: Noun complement clause

*A serious mistake on the vaccine$_1$, the CDC acknowledged [the claim [that they had made t_1]].

c. The CNPC: Relative clause

*George Bush$_1$, I loathe [the people of United States [that voted for t_1]].

d. The SSC

*Dependency on narcotics$_1$, [{that he admitted, admitting} t_1] characterizes his schizophrenia.

e. The LBC

*Serena$_1$'s, Lily subbed for [t_1 role].

f. The CSC

*Mango$_1$, my wife loves [{banana and t_1, t_1 and banana}].

Both *wh-movement* and *topicalization* can be unified under the umbrella of *operator movement.*♣ The following shows the structure of (37). Note that the CP is headed by an empty head, [top].

(42)

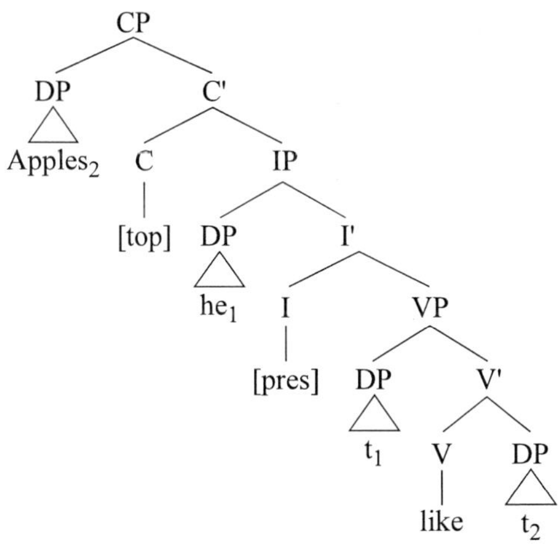

♣

The term *operator* is used in syntax to indicate interrogative, relative, quantificational, or negative expressions which have some syntactic properties, as shown below:

(i) What did you see?
(ii) a. I met the man yesterday who you love.
b. I met the man yesterday *Op* you love.
(iii) Everyone loves someone.
(iv) Nothing can anyone do.

Operators bear a scope relation to some part of their sentence via an overt or covert movement.

Almost equally, topicalization is often analyzed as an adjunction to IP. The alternative structure for (37) is given in (43).

(43)

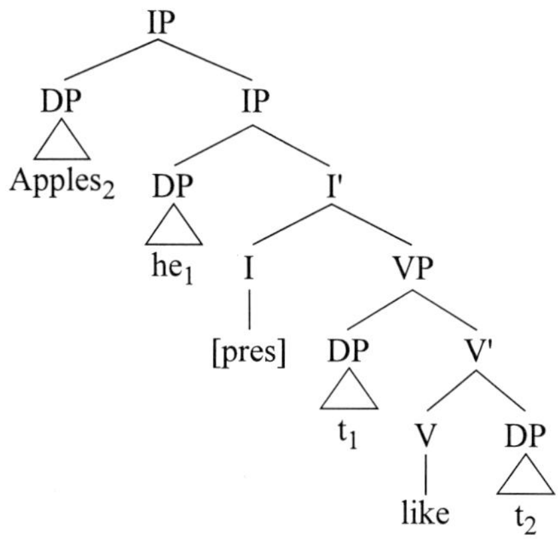

Regarding the linear order of topics and complementizers, it has been pointed out that whenever an overt complementizer co-occurs with a topic, the former must precede the latter:

(44) a. Ross claims that Phoebe, Joey doesn't like.

b. *Ross claims Phoebe, that Joey doesn't like.

The above contrast supports the proposal that embedded topicalization is IP adjunction since the topicalization into the Spec of CP analysis would wrongly predict that the complementizer should follow the topicalized phrase.

Exercise 10

【 10-1 】

Explain the following terms:

(45) a. Island
b. Case-driven, [wh]-driven
c. Silent Complementizer, Overt Complementizer
d. Unlimited Movement, Unbound Movement, Long-distance Movement
e. Wh-island Constraint
f. Complex NP Constraint (CNPC)
g. Sentential Subject Constraint (SSC), Subject Condition (SC)
h. Left Branch Condition (LBC)
i. Coordinate Structure Constraint (CSC)
j. Across-the-board (ATB) Movement
k. Adjunct Condition (AC)
l. Right Roof Constraint (RRC)
m. Wh-relative, *That*-relative, Zero-relative
n. Operator, Null Operator, Operator Movement
o. Topic, Comment, Scene-setting Expression
p. Topicalization

【 10-2 】

Explain the ungrammaticality of the following:

(46) *No would they appreciate present more than another novel by Sheldon.

(47) *These books are hard for Joey to decide when to read.

(48) *Which book did you leave the library without finding?

(49) *Which man do you wonder whether will return?

(50) *Which man did you leave after came in?

10-3

Draw the trees of the following:

(51) I wonder who she thinks will come.

(52) I wonder under which shell he hid the pea.

(53) John wonders who to please.

(54) the movie you prefer

(55) In Brazil, such situations are lamentably frequent.

(56) Which man did you say dislike his boss?

(57) Jack Johnson, I saw on television last night.

10-4

Evaluate the two different approaches in (42) and (43) to English topicalization.

11 Bounding

Every movement must be shortest according to the restrictions on movement by Bounding theory.

11.1 A-over-A Constraint

The A-over-A Constraint is a universal constraint on transformational operations suggested by Chomsky (1964) even before Ross's (1967) discovery of island constraints. The constraint states that if there are two phrases of the same category, both of which are possible targets of a particular operation and if one phrase contains the other, then it is the upper one that the operation applies to, as schematized below:

(1)

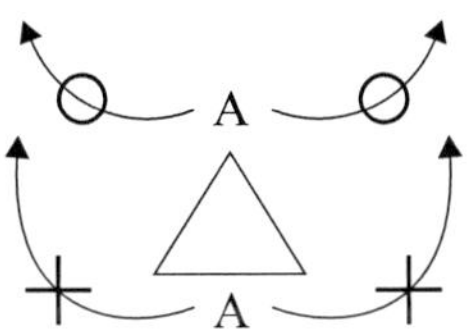

For example, consider the following coordinated structures. This constraint prevents extraction of the lower DP out of the higher DP in which it is included as in (2b), but allows the more inclusive DP to be fronted as in (2c).

(2) a. We have to read [$_{DP}$ [$_{DP}$ some books] and [$_{DP}$ some papers]].
b. *Which books$_1$ do we have to read [$_{DP}$ [$_{DP}$ t_1] and [$_{DP}$ some papers]]?
c. [$_{DP}$ [$_{DP}$ Which books] and [$_{DP}$ which papers]]$_1$ do we have to read t_1?

But the following sentences are grammatical although they violate the A-over-A Constraint:

(3) a. Who$_1$ would you approve of [$_{DP}$ my seeing [$_{DP}$ t_1]]?
b. What$_1$ are you certain about [$_{DP}$ giving [$_{DP}$ t_1] to Ross]?
c. What$_1$ would you be surprised by [$_{DP}$ his reading [$_{DP}$ t_1]]?

Ross's (1967) islands are a description or a stipulation of the displacement effect in natural language.

In what follows, we will examine three ways to generalize the constraints on wh-movement: Chomsky's (1973) Subjacency, Chomsky's (1981) Empty Category Principle (ECP), and Rizzi's (1990) Relativized Minimality.

11.2 Subjacency

The following is an example of long-distance wh-movement:

(4) What did he say that he was selling?

We consider two possible derivations for long-distance wh-movement.

◀ Option 1 ▶

The wh-element moves in one fell swoop. This movement is called a non-cyclic movement.

(5) [The irrelevant parts are suppressed.]

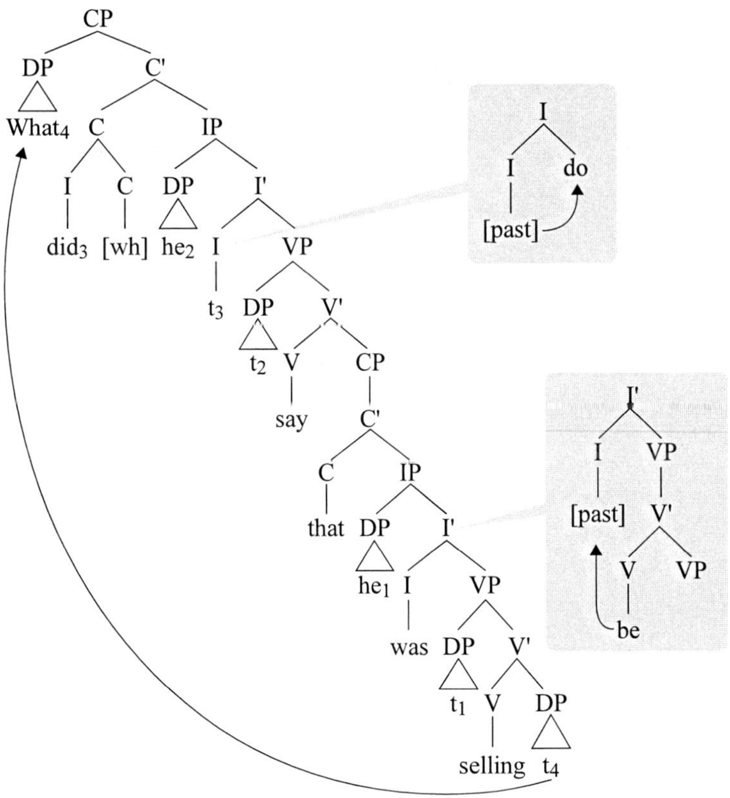

《 Option 2 》

The wh-element moves to the nearest Spec of CP and then to the next higher Spec of CP. This movement is called a cyclic movement.

(6) [The irrelevant parts are suppressed.]

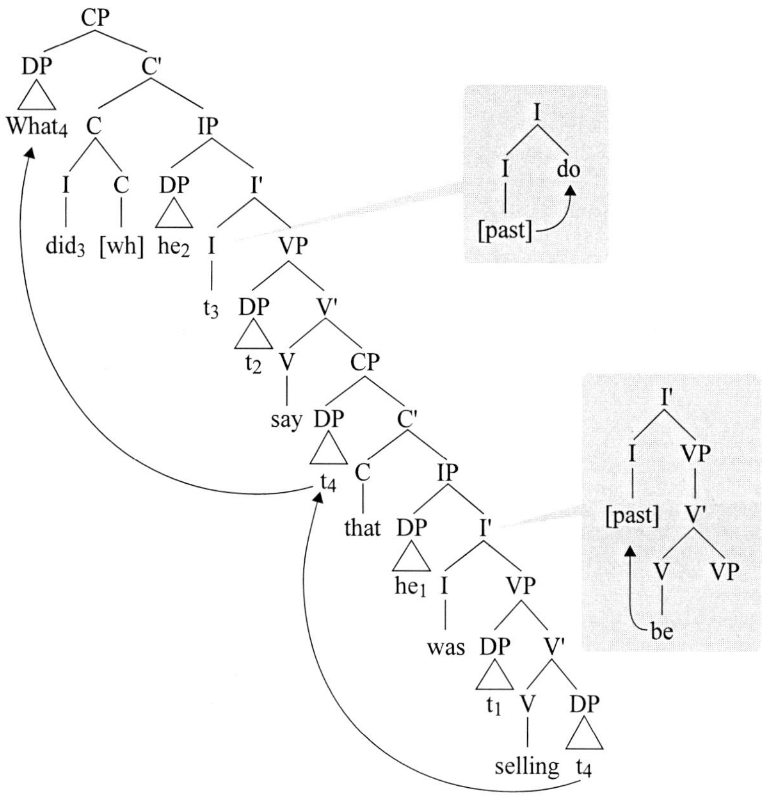

Considering well-formed constructions, we could not choose which option is preferred.

(7) a. What$_1$ did he say [(t$_1$) that he was selling t$_1$]?

b. What$_1$ does she assume [(t$_1$) that he said [(t$_1$) that he was selling t$_1$]]?

c. What$_1$ are they claiming [(t_1) that she assumes [(t_1) that he said [(t_1) that he was selling t_1]]]?

d. What$_1$ do you think [(t_1) that they are claiming [(t_1) that she assumes [(t_1) that he said [(t_1) that he was selling t_1]]]]?

But given the contrast of well-formed (7) and ill-formed (8a), we can choose the cyclic approach to long-distance wh-movement. Why is (8a) ill-formed? It violates the Wh-island Constraint in that *when* cannot stop by the embedded Spec of CP that is occupied by *which one*.

(8) a. *When$_2$ has she realized [which one$_1$ she could trust t_1 t_2]?

b. [The irrelevant parts are suppressed.]

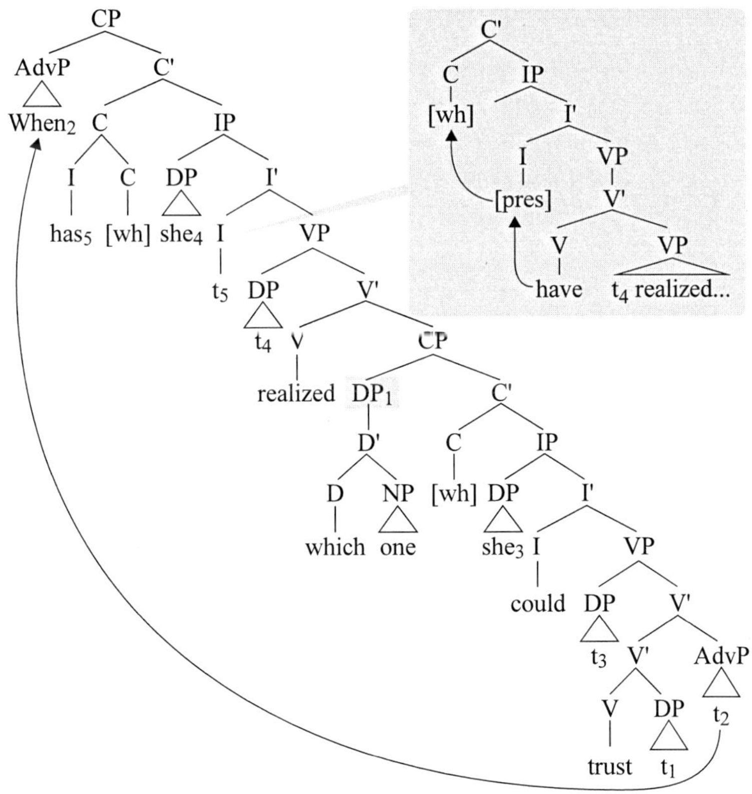

We assume that wh-movement observes (9).

(9) The Subjacency Condition (Chomsky 1973)
In a chain formed by movement, the path of branches connecting two neighboring links in the chain must contain at most one bounding node.♣

Note that (8a) is ungrammatical so there should be no good derivation.

◀ Question ▶

How can we rule out the following alternative derivation in (10)? (10) seems to observe (9).

(10) a. $[_{IP}$ she has realized $[_{CP}$ $when_1$ $[_{\text{(IP)}}$ she could trust which one $t_1]]]$

b. $[_{CP}$ $when_1$ has $[_{\text{(IP)}}$ she realized $[_{CP}$ t_1 $[_{\text{(IP)}}$ she could trust which one $t_1]]]]$

c. *$[_{CP}$ $when_1$ has $[_{\text{(IP)}}$ she realized $[_{CP}$ which one_2 t_1 $[_{\text{(IP)}}$ she could trust t_2 $t_1]]]]$

In (10a) *when* moves to the embedded Spec of CP (crossing over one bounding node). In (10b) *when* moves further to the matrix Spec of CP (crossing over one bounding node). In (10c) *which one* moves to the embedded Spec of CP (crossing over one bounding node). What is wrong with this derivation?

◀ Answer 1 ▶

In (10c) the trace of *when* in the embedded Spec of CP blocks the movement of *which one*.

♣ Bounding nodes = {S, NP}, where S = IP, NP = DP.

Answer 2

We can rule out the derivation in (10) via the notion of cycle. In (10b) when *when* moves to the matrix Spec of CP, the domain (i.e., cycle) of operations is expanded up to the matrix clause. Right this time, for the computational reason, operations cannot go back to the previous cycle, roughly speaking, the embedded clause.

Question

Why should *which one* move in (8a)?

Answer

Wh-elements must move in order for the sentence to be interpreted as *indirect question.*

(11) a. She has realized which one she could trust.
b. *She has realized she could trust which one.

(12a) violates the CNPC. (12b) violates the LBC. But if an IP is the sole bounding node, (12) cannot be explained by Subjacency.

(12) a. *Who$_1$ did [$_{IP}$ he make [$_{DP}$ these tabloid allegations [$_{CP}$ t'$_1$ that [$_{IP}$ Jimmy actually threatened t$_1$]]]]?
b. *Whose$_1$ did [$_{IP}$ she like [$_{DP}$ t$_1$ top-siders]]?

The DP should be a bounding node. In (13a) the movement from the original position (t$_1$) to the embedded Spec of CP (t'$_1$) does not violate the Subjacency Condition, crossing over one bounding node, while the subsequent movement from the embedded Spec of CP to the matrix Spec of CP violates the Subjacency Condition, crossing over two bounding nodes.

(13) a. *Who$_1$ did [$_{IP}$ he make [$_{DP}$ these tabloid allegations [$_{CP}$ t'_1 that [$_{IP}$ Jimmy actually threatened t_1]]]]?

b. *Whose$_1$ did [$_{IP}$ she like [$_{DP}$ t_1 top-siders]]?

Normally, the movement out of a DP is ungrammatical.

(14) a. He wrote an essay about the importance of concerted cooperation.

b. *What$_1$ did [$_{IP}$ he write [$_{DP}$ an essay about t_1]]?

(15) *[About what]$_1$ did [$_{IP}$ he write [$_{DP}$ an essay t_1]]?

The following illustrates the violation of the CSC:

(16) a. *Which fruit$_1$ did Lori want me to buy [t_1 and mango]?

b. *Which car$_1$ did Keith own [Porsche 911 and t_1]?

The following is the partial structure of (16a):

(17) [$_{DP}$ [$_{DP}$ banana] and [$_{DP}$ mango]]

(18) a. symmetric view

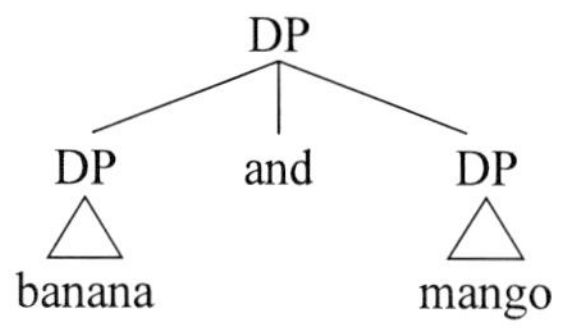

b. asymmetric view

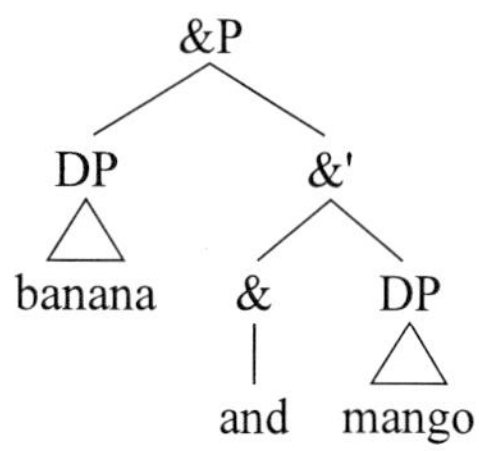

There is evidence that the asymmetric view of coordination is preferred over the symmetric view of coordination. (19) indicates that the first conjunct is higher than the second conjunct. That is, the asymmetric structure in (18b) captures the hierarchical difference between the first conjunct and the second conjunct in (19). However, we adopt (18a) for ease of exposition.

(19) a. Dan gave [Serena$_1$ and her$_1$ boyfriend] a book.
b. *Dan gave [her$_1$ boyfriend and Serena$_1$] a book.

Then, we can rule out (16) by Subjacency, as shown below:

(20) a. *Which fruit$_1$ did $[_{IP}$ Lori want me to buy $[_{DP}$ t_1 and mango]]?
b. *Which car$_1$ did $[_{IP}$ Keith own $[_{DP}$ Porsche 911 and t_1]]?

What about (21) and (22)? We cannot explain the ungrammaticality of (21) and (22) via Subjacency.

(21) a. $[_{PP}$ In which chapter and in which section]$_1$ is $[_{IP}$ the book worth reading $[_{PP}$ t_1]]?
b. *$[_{PP}$ In which section]$_1$ is $[_{IP}$ the book worth reading $[_{PP}$ t_1 and in which chapter]]?
c. *$[_{PP}$ In which chapter]$_1$ is $[_{IP}$ the book worth reading $[_{PP}$ in which section and t_1]]?

(22) He said the tax-cut for the rich would wreak havoc and create turmoil, and ...
a. $[_{VP}$ wreak havoc and create turmoil]$_1$, $[_{IP}$ he did $[_{VP}$ t_1]].
b. *$[_{VP}$ wreak havoc]$_1$, $[_{IP}$ he did $[_{VP}$ t_1 and create turmoil]].
c. *$[_{VP}$ create turmoil]$_1$, $[_{IP}$ he did $[_{VP}$ wreak havoc and t_1]].

Let us consider the following contrast. (23) violates the CSC according to which extraction out of the coordinated site is not allowed unless that extraction affects all conjuncts, as shown in (24). That is, (23) violates the ATB requirement, a sort of the Parallelism Constraint.

(23) *[Which pants]$_1$ have [$_{IP}$ they [$_{VP}$ [$_{VP}$ sewn up t$_1$] and [$_{VP}$ patched the jean]]]?

(24) [Which pants]$_1$ have [$_{IP}$ they [$_{VP}$ [$_{VP}$ sewn up t$_1$] and [$_{VP}$ patched t$_1$]]]?

The following shows the structure of (24):

(25) [The irrelevant parts are suppressed.]

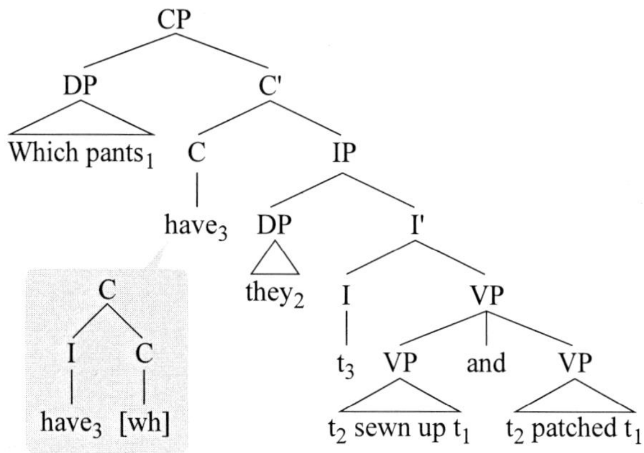

The CSC is elusive. It is not easily generalized with other island constraints.

11.3 The Empty Category Principle (ECP)

Ross observes that it is more acceptable to move complements than adjuncts out of indirect questions. Subjects behave like adjuncts. This is the so-called complement (object) vs. non-complement (subject, adjunct) asymmetry. Although all the examples in (26) violate the Wh-island Constraint, there is a contrast. Why?

(26) a. ?Which one$_1$ has she realized [when$_2$ she could trust t_1 t_2]?
b. *When$_2$ has she realized [which one$_1$ she could trust t_1 t_2]?
c. *Which one$_1$ has she realized [when$_2$ t'_1 could be trusted t_1 t_2]?

The following shows the *that*-t effect (Chomsky and Lasnik 1977). Movement from the object position is easier than that from the subject position.

(27) a. What$_1$ did Mom say (that) Lori wanted t_1?
b. Who$_1$ did Mom say (*that) t_1 wanted a mango?

The Empty Category Principle (ECP) is motivated to explain the complement vs. non-complement asymmetry. Proper government is a more restrictive version of government. Lexical heads (e.g., V, P, N, A) are proper governors, but functional heads (e.g., C, I ,D) are not.

(28) The Empty Category Principle (Chomsky 1981, 1986b)
Traces must be properly governed.

(29) Proper government
α properly governs β iff
a. α lexically governs β, or
b. α antecedent-governs β.

(30) α lexically governs β iff
a. α is a lexical head,
b. β is a maximal projection, and
c. α m-commands β.

(31) α antecedent-governs β iff
  a. α governs β, and
  b. α is co-indexed with β.

In (32a) the intermediate trace (t') properly governs the subject trace (t). In (32b) the intermediate trace (t') does not properly govern the subject trace (t) because of the presence of *that*.

(32) a. [$_{CP}$ Who$_1$ did [$_{IP}$ Mom say [$_{CP}$ t'$_1$ [$_{IP}$ t$_1$ wanted a mango]]]]?
  b. *[$_{CP}$ Who$_1$ did [$_{IP}$ Mom say [$_{CP}$ t'$_1$ that [$_{IP}$ t$_1$ wanted a mango]]]]?

In (33) the intermediate trace (t') is properly governed by *what*, and the lowest trace (t) is properly governed by both the intermediate trace (t') and the lexical verb.

(33) What$_1$ did Mom say [$_{CP}$ t'$_1$ [$_{IP}$ Lori wanted t$_1$]]?

In sum, a trace can be licensed by either a lexical head or an antecedent. The object trace is always licensed because it is always governed by a local head. On the other hand, the subject trace is never lexically head-governed. Hence, it should be antecedent-governed. This gives rise to the so-called *that*-t effect in that antecedent government is blocked by the overt complementizer *that*.

Let us return to (26). In (26a) t$_1$ is lexically governed by *trust*, and t$_2$ is antecedent-governed by *when*$_2$. Thus, both traces are properly governed. In (26b) t$_1$ is lexically governed by *trust* and antecedent-governed by *which one*$_1$, but t$_2$ is not properly (i.e., antecedent-) governed. In (26c) t$_1$ is lexically governed by *trusted* and antecedent-governed by t'$_1$, and t$_2$ is antecedent-governed by *when*$_2$. However, t'$_1$ is neither lexically governed nor antecedent-governed.

11.4 Relativized Minimality

Rizzi's (1990) Relativized Minimality approach to movement phenomena does not set up absolute bounding nodes for movement.

With respect to head movement, a head cannot cross over another head. (34b) violates the Head Movement Constraint (HMC).

(34) a. $[_{CP}$ Could$_1$ $[_{IP}$ he t_1 $[_{VP}$ have given me a heads-up]]]?

b. *$[_{CP}$ Have$_1$ $[_{IP}$ he could $[_{VP}$ t_1 given me a heads-up]]]?

c. $[_{CP}$ Had$_1$ $[_{IP}$ he t_1 $[_{VP}$ t_1 given me a heads-up]]]?

As a case of A'-movement, a wh-element cannot cross over another wh-movement.♣ (35b) violates the Wh-island Constraint.

(35) a. $[_{CP}$ What$_1$ do $[_{IP}$ you think $[_{CP}$ t_1 $[_{IP}$ he stuttered out t_1]]]]?

b. *$[_{CP}$ What$_1$ do $[_{IP}$ you ask $[_{CP}$ where $[_{IP}$ he stuttered out t_1]]]]?

Regarding A(rgument)-movement, an A-element cannot cross over another A-element. (36b) is a case of Superraising.

(36) a. $[_{IP}$ He$_1$ seemed $[_{IP}$ t_1 to be likely $[_{IP}$ t_1 to leave]]].

b. *$[_{IP}$ He$_1$ seemed $[_{IP}$ it is likely $[_{IP}$ t_1 to leave]]].

In this light, Rizzi (1990) proposes the principle of Relativized Minimality.

♣ A'-movement = non-Argument movement

(37) Relativized Minimality

No X can move over another X, where X is either a head, an argument or a wh-element.

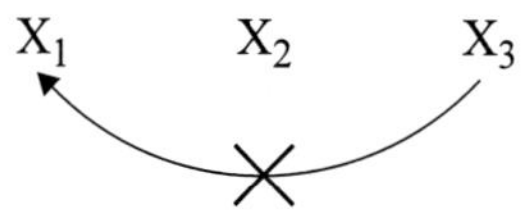

Exercise 11

11-1

Explain the following terms:

(38) a. Bounding Theory
b. Head Movement, A-Movement, A'-Movement
c. A-over-A Constraint
d. Island Constraints
e. Subjacency Condition, Bounding Node
f. Empty Category Principle (ECP)
g. Government, Proper Government, M-command
h. Proper Governor, Lexical Head, Functional Head
i. Complement vs. Non-Complement Asymmetry
j. *That*-t Effect
k. Relativized Minimality
l. One Fell Swoop Movement, Non-Cyclic Movement, Cyclic Movement, Cycle
m. Parallelism Constraint, ATB Movement
n. Superraising

11-2

Draw the trees of the following:

(39) Ross gave Rachel and her mother a book.

(40) Who did he say wanted a beer?

◀ 11-3 ▶

Explain the contrast of the following:

(41) a. Who did you take a picture of?
b. *Who was a picture of taken?

◀ 11-4 ▶

In (42) a wh-phrase cannot be extracted from the first DP, but it can from the second DP. Discuss the theoretical implication of the following paradigm:

(42) a. [$_{DP}$ A picture of the wall] was [$_{DP}$ the cause of the riot].
b. *Which wall$_1$ was [a picture of t$_1$] [the cause of the riot]?
c. Which riot$_1$ was [a picture of the wall] [the cause of t$_1$]?

◀ 11-5 ▶

The sentences in (43) start from the same underlying structure in (44). Given the Predicate-internal Subject Hypothesis, it amounts to saying that there are two options of the subject movement: *all the students* and *the students*. This phenomenon is called Quantifier Floating in that the quantifier *all* seems to have floated away from the DP it modifies. Discuss a theoretical implication of Quantifier Floating with respect to the A-over-A Constraint.

(43) a. All the students should take the exam.
b. The students should all take the exam.

(44) should [$_{VP}$ all the students take the exam]

12 Binding

Binding theory has a set of conditions on the structural relations between nominals such as anaphors, pronominals, and r-expressions. These nominals are semantically distinct, but they also have different syntactic distributions.

(1) a. Anaphors = reflexive pronouns (e.g., *himself, herself, themselves*, etc.) + reciprocal pronouns (e.g., *each other, one another*)
    b. Pronominals (e.g., *he, she, it, his, one, they, them, him*, etc.)
    c. R(eferential)-expressions (e.g., proper names, common nouns)

Anaphora comes from Greek *anaphorá*, 'carrying back', and means 'repetition'. An anaphor is a DP that obligatorily gets its meaning from other DP in the sentence.

(2) Mike could defend himself.
(3) Armand and Fiona would go out with each other.

Cataphora comes from Greek *kataphorá,* which means 'carrying forward'. A cataphor is a pronoun that refers forward to a constituent introduced later on in discourse.♣

(4) When he took a roll, Professor Kim recognized that Rene was absent.

(5) When he reached the checkpoint, Frank realized that there was an engine problem.

Pronominals are DPs that may (but need not) get their meaning from other words in the sentence. They can also get their meaning from DPs previously mentioned in the discourse or by context.

(6) Ross said that he played basketball.
  a. 'Ross said that Ross played basketball.'
  b. 'Ross said that Chandler played basketball.'

R-expressions express content. They are DPs that get their meaning by referring to entities in the world.

(7) a. Ki-moon Ban, Kofi Annan, Tim Cook, Steve Jobs, chair, desk, etc.
  b. the current Secretary General of the United Nations, the CEO of Apple, a snow globe, etc.

An antecedent is a DP that gives its meaning to a pronoun or an anaphor.

(8) Mike shaved himself.

Indexing is a means of representing the meaning of a DP. Each index represents a different reference.♣♣

(9) $[\text{Mike}]_i$ left $[\text{Sam}]_j$ $[\text{a note}]_k$.

♣ In the text, anaphora is used as a cover term for both anaphora and cataphora.

♣♣ We assume that there is no difference between indices (i.e., i, j, k) and numbers (i.e., 1, 2, 3) with respect to the co-reference relation.

Let us consider the concept of co-indexing and co-reference.

(10) a. Two DPs that have the same index are said to be co-indexed.
b. Two DPs that are co-indexed are said to co-refer (that is, refer to the same entity in the world).

(11) a. [Frank]$_i$ believed that [he]$_i$ could catch up [the leading one]$_k$ in [the corner]$_l$.
b. [Frank]$_i$ believed that [he]$_j$ could catch up [the leading one]$_k$ in [the corner]$_l$.

Now, let us consider the relations of referential dependencies among DPs.

(12) a. Liam said Noel criticized <u>him</u>. [Liam ← him]
b. Liam criticized <u>him</u>. [*Liam ← him]
c. Liam criticized <u>himself</u>. [Liam ← himself]

(13) a. <u>He</u> said a fan blackmailed Noel. [*he → Noel]
b. After <u>he</u> left the room, Noel pulled out a cigarette. [he → Noel]
c. <u>His</u> brother criticized Noel. [his → Noel]

Based on the data in (12) and (13), we can make the generalization in (14).♣

(14) A pronoun cannot take an element of its c-command domain as its antecedent.

What is the c-command domain of *he* or *his*?

♣ The c-command domain of an item is everything that the item c-commands. An element c-commands its sister and everything dominated by its sister. More precisely, α c-commands β iff α and β do not dominate each other, and the first branching node dominating α dominates β.

(15) He said a fan blackmailed Noel.

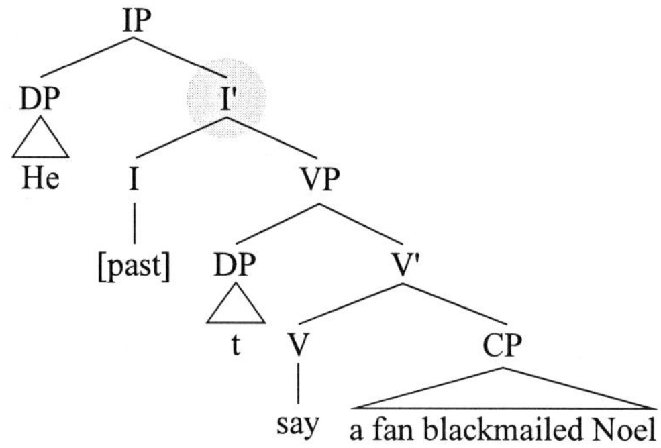

(16) After he left the room, Noel pulled out a cigarette.

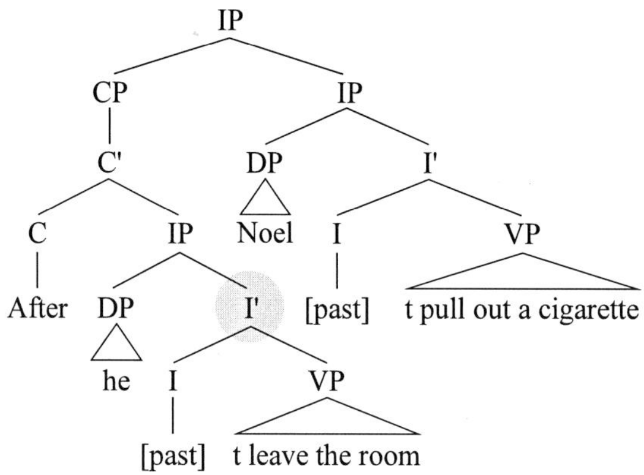

(17) His brother criticized Noel.

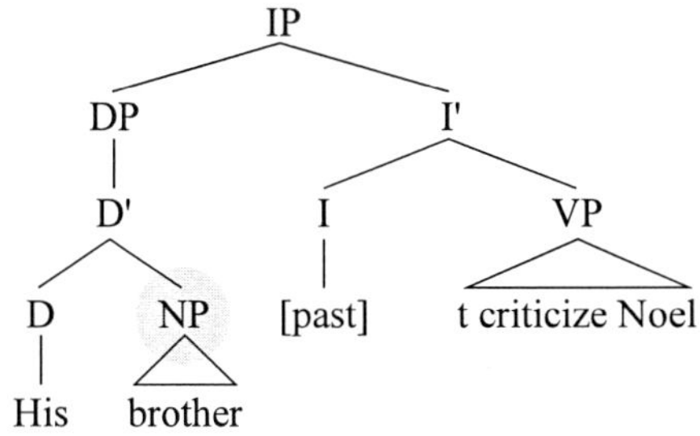

The core of (14) is provided below:

(18) α binds β if (i) α c-commands β, and (ii) α and β are co-indexed.

(19) If β is not bound, then β is free.

(20) A pronominal must be free locally.

Let us consider the co-reference relation of the following:

(21) *He_1 said a fan blackmailed $Noel_1$.

(22) He_1 said a fan blackmailed $Noel_2$.

(23) After he_1 left the room, $Noel_1$ pulled out a cigarette.

(24) His_1 brother criticized $Noel_1$.

If the index of α is distinct from that of β, then one cannot be the antecedent of the other. If the index of α is identical to that of β, then one can be the antecedent of the other.

(25) $Liam_1$ criticized him_2.

(26) *$Liam_1$ criticized him_1.

An anaphor must be bound in a local domain (LD).

(27) [$_{LD}$ Liam$_1$ criticized himself$_1$].

(28) *He$_1$ said [$_{LD}$ a fan blackmailed himself$_1$].

A pronoun must be free in a local domain.

(29) Noel$_1$ said [$_{LD}$ a fan blackmailed him$_1$].

(30) [$_{LD}$ Noel$_1$'s brother criticized him$_1$].

Anaphors and pronominals have a complementary distribution with each other.♣

(31) a. Sam$_1$ believes Mike$_2$ can defend him$_1$/himself$_{*1}$.
b. Sam$_1$ believes Mike$_2$ can defend him$_{*2}$/himself$_2$.
c. Sam$_1$ believes Mike$_2$ can defend him$_3$/himself$_{*3}$.

It is possible for references to overlap or for one reference to be included in the other.

(32) a. High school students like to talk about TV idols.
b. I think we must give it a second thought.

In the following, the contrast comes from the structure, not from the linear order, of the antecedent:

(33) a. *Jessie$_1$'s mother loved himself$_1$.
b. Jessie$_1$'s mother loved him$_1$.

In short, Binding theory has three principles.

(34) a. Principle A: An anaphor must be bound locally.

♣
However, complementarity collapses with respect to binding across DP boundaries, as follows:
(i) They$_1$ never discuss [$_{DP}$ {each other's$_1$, their$_1$} work].

The above example suggests that the local domain of Principle A may be different from that of Principle B (Chomsky 1986a).

b. Principle B: A pronominal must be free locally.

c. Principle C: An r-expression must be free everywhere.

Some nonfinite clause does not count as a local domain.

(35) [$_{LD}$ Sam$_1$ believes [himself$_1$ to be skillful]].

Finite clauses are always local domains.

(36) *Sam$_1$ believes [$_{LD}$ himself$_1$ is skillful].

Some nonfinite clause is a local domain.

(37) *Sam$_1$ believes [$_{LD}$ Madeline to support himself$_1$].

The local domain is often defined as *governing category*.

(38) Governing category (tentative)

β is a governing category for α if β is the smallest clause which contains α and the governor γ of α.♣

(39)

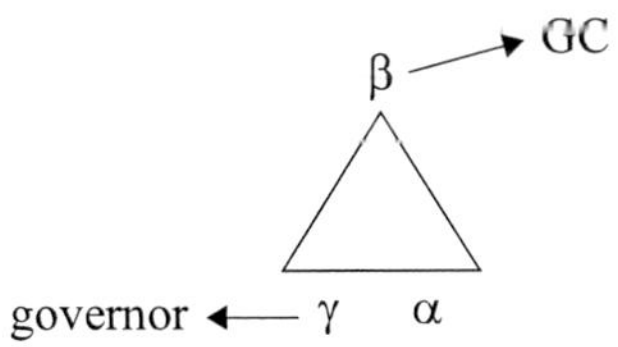

Then, (34) is revised as follows:

(40) a. Principle A: An anaphor must be bound within its governing category.

b. Principle B: A pronominal must be free within its governing category.

♣ γ is a governor if γ = X^0 (not nonfinite INFL).

c. Principle C: An r-expression must be free everywhere.

Below, the DP is a governing category.

(41) *Noel$_1$ found [$_{DP}$ Liam's picture of himself$_1$].

Below, the DP is not a governing category.

(42) Noel$_1$ found [$_{DP}$ a picture of himself$_1$].

The possessor of the DP plays the role of a subject.

(43) a. *The facility* had emitted a large amount of toxic gases.
b. *the facility's* emission of a large amount of toxic gases

Then, (38) is revised as follows:

(44) Governing category (final)
β is a governing category for α if β is the smallest IP or DP with a subject which contains α and the governor γ of α.♣

With respect to binding, some covert DPs pattern together with some overt DPs.

DP traces are anaphors.

(45) a. Jessie$_1$ hurt himself$_1$.
b. *Jessie$_1$ believed Fiona likes himself$_1$.
c. Jessie$_1$ believed himself$_1$ to be screwed.
d. *Jessie$_1$ believed himself$_1$ is screwed.

♣
[$_β$ ... SU ... γ α ...]

(46) a. Jessie$_1$ was hurt t$_1$.
b. *Jessie$_1$ was believed Fiona likes t$_1$.
c. Jessie$_1$ was believed t$_1$ to be screwed.♣
d. *Jessie$_1$ was believed t$_1$ likes Fiona.

(Some) wh-traces are r-expressions. (48b) violates Principle C in that the trace of a wh-argument cannot be bound from an A(rgument)-position.♣♣ That is, in (48b) an A-element (*he*) binds the wh-trace (t$_1$), which is a variable.

(47) a. Who$_1$ did Ross think [$_{CP}$ t$_1$ [$_{IP}$ Rachel liked t$_1$]]?
b. Who$_1$ did Ross think [$_{CP}$ t$_1$ [$_{IP}$ t$_1$ liked Rachel]]?

(48) a. Who$_1$ [$_{IP}$ t$_1$ thinks [$_{IP}$ he$_1$ should win]]?
b. *Who$_1$ does [$_{IP}$ he$_1$ think [$_{IP}$ t$_1$ should win]]?

English allows a PRO subject in nonfinite clauses. Since PRO is a pronominal anaphor, it is subject to Principle A and Principle B of Binding theory, from which it follows that PRO lacks a governing category and is therefore ungoverned (Chomsky 1982: 21).♣♣♣ It is not subject to the Case Filter because it is a covert DP.

(49) a. I tried [PRO to go].
b. Ross ordered Rachel [PRO to go].
c. [PRO to be late in class] is likely to make your professor upset.

Some binding facts seem to be established before movement. In (50a) the anaphor is bound at DS. In (50b) the anaphor is bound at surface structure (SS). It thus seems that Principle A is a derivational constraint.

♣
More precisely, (46c) has the following chain headed by *Jessie*.
(i) Jessie$_1$ was believed t'$_1$ to be screwed t$_1$.

For the sake of comparison, (46c) is used in the text. Note that in (i) both t'$_1$ and t$_1$ are DP traces.

♣♣
Postal (1971) observes that (48b) is an instance of *Strong Crossover* violation.

♣♣♣
The PRO Theorem: PRO must be ungoverned.

(50) a. [Which picture of $himself_2]_1$ did $Ross_2$ display t_1?

b. The men_1 seem to each $other_1$ t_1 to be smart.

A logophor is an anaphor with no proper antecedent in the sentence, but rather with a discourse antecedent. In the following, the reflexive pronouns are logophors:

(51) Rene Russo thinks that there is a picture of herself in Mel Gibson's House.

(52) John was going to get even with Mary. That picture of himself in the paper would really annoy her, as would the other stunts he had planned.

Exercise 12

⟨ 12-1 ⟩

Explain the following terms:

(52) a. Anaphor, Pronominal, R-expression
b. Anaphora, Cataphora
c. Antecedent
d. Indexing, Co-indexing, Co-reference
e. Referential Dependency
f. C-command Domain
g. Binding Theory, Principle A, Principle B, Principle C
h. Local Domain, Governing Category
i. PRO Theorem
j. Derivational Constraint
k. Logophor

⟨ 12-2 ⟩

Discuss the binding relations in the following:

(53) a. Ross_2 said that Joey_1 admires $\text{himself}_{1/*2}$.
b. Ross_2 said that Joey_1 admires $\text{him}_{2/3/*1}$.
c. He_3 said that $\text{Joey}_{1/*3}$ admires $\text{Ross}_{2/*3}$.

⟨ 12-3 ⟩

In (54a) the anaphor is bound by an antecedent, but in (54b) it is not. Explain the contrast. What is the difference between the two examples?

(54) a. Perry proved [Jill and Tony]$_1$ to have lied during [each other]$_1$'s trials.

b. *Perry proved that [Jill and Tony]$_1$ lied during [each other]$_1$'s trials.

《 12-4 》

The following sentence is ambiguous. Discuss the binding facts involved.

(55) Ross$_1$ wondered which picture of himself$_{1/2}$ Fred$_2$ liked.

13 Logical Form

The *Principles and Parameters* (also called *Government and Binding*) theory of Grammar assumes the following model. In this model, there are four significant levels of representation:

(1)

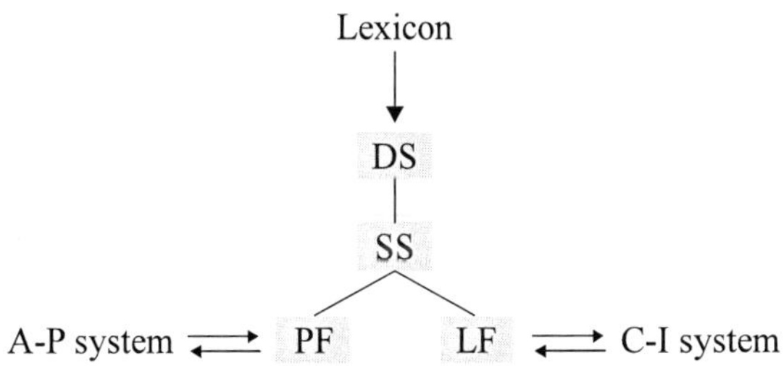

D-structure (DS) is the level of the projection of lexical properties, including θ-role assignment and subcategorization. According to Chomsky (1965), DS is the locus of all lexical insertions as well as the input to the transformational component.

S-structure (SS) is the enriched DS derived by transformations, involving traces.

Logical Form (LF) is the syntax-semantics interface with the *Conceptual-Intentional* (C-I) system of the mind. LF interfaces with a speaker's general knowledge and with extralinguistic cognitive systems.

Phonetic Form (PF) is the interface with the *Articulatory-Perceptual* (A-P) system. PF is the structure that interfaces with the perceptual system in speech recognition and with the articulatory system in speech production.

The portion of the derivation between DS and SS is called *overt syntax*. The portion of the derivation between SS and LF is called *covert syntax*.

The A-P and C-I systems are *Performance systems*. They are also called *Grammar-external systems*.

In fact, LF is ambiguous:

(2) a. The LF *component* of a Grammar is the component which converts the syntactic structures produced by operations into LF representation.

b. LF is a *level* of representation relevant to semantic interpretation. In Chomsky's theory, this is the initial representation of sentence meaning, which results from the interpretation of SS. It is complemented in the semantic component by a further level of semantic representation.

In this chapter, we focus on the second meaning of LF as in (2).

Languages may differ as to where certain movements take place: at SS or at LF. If a language opts for the former, then the movement will be visible. If a language opts for the latter, then the movement will be invisible.

Let us consider the following fronting possibility of interrogative wh-words. In Chinese, the wh-element does not move overtly, whereas in English the wh-element does:

(3)	[ni	renwei	[ta	weishenme	meiyou	lai]]?
	you	think	he	why	not	come

(4) Why do you think [he didn't come t]?

In (3) *weishenme* seems to be in-situ. However, the interrogative reading of (3) suggests that *weishenme* has moved. Of particular interest is that *weishenme* inside a complex DP cannot be interpreted out of the island, triggering the Complex DP Constraint (CDPC, i.e., CNPC) effect, as shown below:

(5)	*ni	xiangxin	$[_{DP}$ $[_{IP}$	Lisi	weishenme	lai]	de shuofa]?
	you	believe		Lisi	why	come	claim

(6) *Why do you believe $[_{DP}$ the claim $[_{IP}$ that Rachel came t]]?

It has been argued that (3) and (5) may involve movement, though they involve a kind of movement that has no effects on the phonetic form of the utterances. The model of the Grammar in (1) allows for the possibility of abstract movement that does not feed into PF.

In short, we assume that wh-phrases move overtly in English between DS and SS, but move covertly in Chinese between SS and LF (Huang 1982).

Thus, language variation can be stated as a parameter. This parameter distinguishes the languages at the level of SS.

Let us consider another piece of evidence for LF. It has been argued that the quantificational scope is decided by an LF operation called *Quantifier Raising* (QR).♣ By way of QR, a quantificational expression may adjoin to IP, leaving behind a trace. The SS of (7) is then mapped onto an LF like (8).♣♣

(7) Rachel likes someone. SS

(8) $[_{IP}$ someone $[_{IP}$ Rachel likes t]] LF

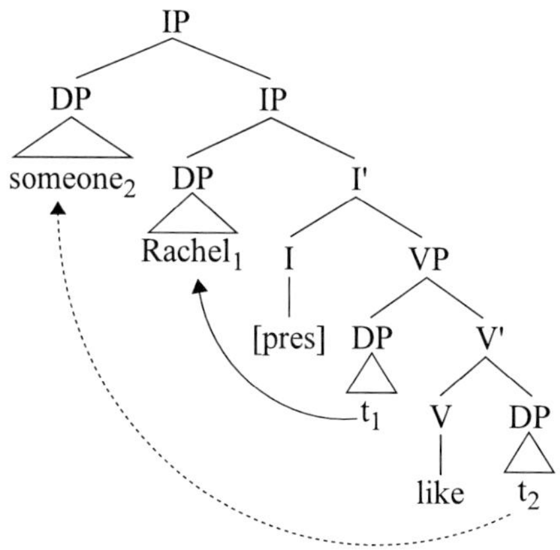

The interpretation of (7) is given below:

(9) For some x, x a person, Rachel likes x.

♣
Scope is a semantic notion which is structurally instantiated by c-command.

♣♣
In this chapter, a solid arrow indicates overt movement, and a dotted arrow covert movement.

Given this story, the scope ambiguity in (10) can receive a straightforward explanation:

(10) Every man likes some woman.

We assume that there are height effects at LF which disambiguate the scope ambiguity regarding quantifiers. If QR first raises the existential quantifier (∃) and then the universal quantifier (∀) in LF, (11) is derived. It represents the reading where every man likes some woman or other.

(11) $[_{IP}$ every man_1 $[_{IP}$ some $woman_2$ $[_{IP}$ t_1 likes $t_2]]]$

$\forall x \exists y$, x likes y

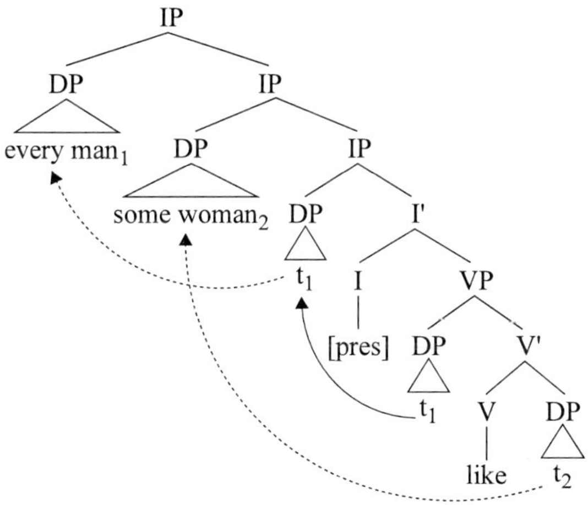

If QR first raises the universal quantifier and then the existential quantifier, (12) is derived. It represents the reading where there is a single particular woman that every man likes.

(12) [$_{IP}$ some woman$_2$ [$_{IP}$ every man$_1$ [$_{IP}$ t_1 likes t_2]]]
$\exists y \forall x$, x likes y

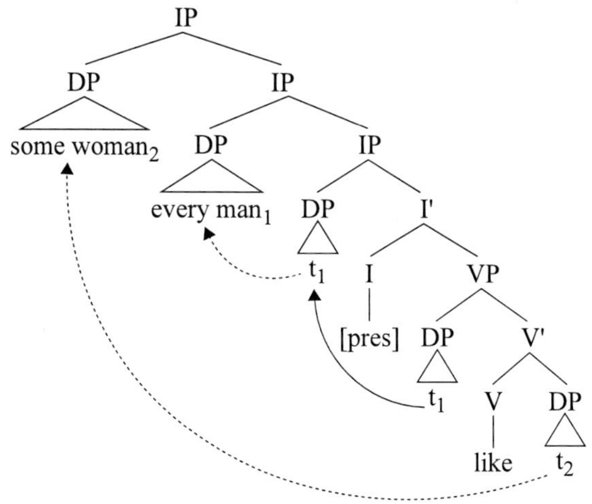

In short, following Chomsky (1973), May (1977), and Huang (1982), we assume that every wh-phrase and quantifier phrase must undergo movement to an operator position in order to bind its trace as a variable at the level of LF. We assume further that wh-phrases appear in Spec of CP, whereas other quantifiers taking clausal scope are adjoined to IP.

Exercise 13

◀ 13-1 ▶

Explain the following terms:

(13) a. Principles and Parameters Theory
b. Government and Binding Theory
c. Level, Level of Representation, Representation, Derivation, Component
d. D-structure (DS), S-structure (SS), Logical Form (LF), Phonetic Form (PF)
e. Interface
f. Overt Syntax, Covert Syntax
g. Performance System, Grammar-external System
h. Quantifier Raising (QR)
i. Scope, Scope Ambiguity
j. Existential Quantifier, Universal Quantifier
k. Variable

◀ 13-2 ▶

As discussed above, scope phenomena are not solely semantic in nature. They should be represented syntactically as well. Provide the two different meanings of the following:

(14) Every performer sang a song.
(15) A girl reads every book.
(16) Some professor believes every student to have failed.

◀ 13-3 ▶

The following sentence is not ambiguous. Discuss the difference between (16) and (17).

(17) Some professor believes every student has failed.

◀ 13-4 ▶

The apparently unmoved wh-elements undergo covert movement at LF, just like Chinese wh-elements. Draw the trees of (18b) and (18c).

(18) a. DS: Who saw what?
b. SS: Who_1 [t_1 saw what]?
c. LF: $What_2$ who_1 [t_1 saw t_2]?

◀ 13-5 ▶

Provide the LF forms of the following:

(19) No man should mistreat his friends.

(20) The fact that he_2 owned a gun implicated $everyone_1$.

14 Minimalism

Since the mid-1950s, Noam Chomsky has endeavored to develop Universal Grammar in a more optimal way, arguing that an innate linguistic knowledge exists.

That is, Chomsky argues that children are born with a genetically encoded language faculty, thus enabling children to acquire a given language relatively easily in an impoverished environment.

For the past few decades, it has been believed that Universal Grammar is composed of a few universal principles (that restrict the class of attainable grammars and constrain their form) and language-specific parameters (that have to be fixed by experience) and that the interaction of these principles and parameters is responsible for different manifestations of each language.

Economy considerations have always played a role in the tradition of Generative Grammar. Recently, Chomsky has increasingly focused on developing the concept of Economy in linguistic theory.

The Economy principles, some general considerations of simplicity, play a crucial role in the minimalist program of Chomsky (1991, 1993, 1994, 1995, 2000, 2001, 2004, 2005) and Chomsky and Lasnik (1993).

The minimalist program is based on the notion of conceptual necessity.

Within this model, the independent levels of D-structure and S-structure, which are postulated in the pre-minimalist framework (Chomsky 1981, 1986a, 1986b), do not have any linguistic significance. The basic model of the system is illustrated below:

(1) Lexicon → Numeration → Spell-Out ⟨ PF ↔ A-P system ; LF ↔ C-I system

Language is believed to consist of the Lexicon and the computational system.

The Lexicon lists all the lexical items of a language including their idiosyncratic properties. Lexical items are selected from the Lexicon by the Numeration, and are then inserted into the computational system.

The computational system, which generates each linguistic expression, consists of the derivation from the Numeration to the LF interface.

More precisely, the derivation from the Numeration to Spell-Out (= a point in the derivation where splitting occurs, leading to the two interface levels, PF and LF) is called *overt syntax*, and the derivation from Spell-Out to the LF interface is called *covert syntax*.

PF is the interface between the language faculty and the Articulatory-Perceptual system. LF is the interface between the language faculty and the Conceptual-Intentional system.

The operations of the computational system that produce linguistic expressions must be optimal; superfluous steps in a derivation are prohibited (Derivational Economy). Similarly, unnecessary symbols are not allowed at interface levels, leaving only legitimate PF and LF objects (Representational Economy).

Since the mid-1980s, it has been argued that every movement operation must be motivated by some requirement (the Last Resort view of movement). In the minimalist framework, the requirement is regulated by a feature checking mechanism.

Specifically, Chomsky (1993) proposes that the morphological features of a linguistic expression must be checked by functional head morphemes with the matching features. If all the relevant features are checked, the derivation converges; otherwise, it crashes.

These features are subdivided into two groups, depending on whether they are strong or weak. According to Chomsky (1993), an unchecked strong feature is an ill-formed object in PF, causing a PF crash.♣ As a result, it must be checked off before it reaches PF. On the other hand,

♣ Several different views have been advanced on the technical aspects of strong feature checking. As opposed to Chomsky (1993), Chomsky (1994) argues that failure to check a strong feature before Spell-Out leads to an LF crash. In an analysis of English Pseudogapping, Lasnik (1995) suggests that an unchecked strong feature may cause both PF and LF crashes. Instead of regarding a strong feature as an ill-formed object at the interface levels, Chomsky (1995) defines strong features derivationally. More precisely, he defines strong features as objects that are not tolerated by the derivation and thus must be checked off immediately upon insertion into the derivation.

a weak feature is assumed not to cause a PF crash. Thus, it need not be checked off in overt syntax. Consequently, it is not allowed to be checked off earlier in the derivation by Chomsky's (1993) Procrastinate, which favors covert over overt operations.

Chomsky (1995) further argues that since movement is always triggered by the need for formal features to be checked, all else being equal, only formal features move. When movement is overtly triggered by a strong feature, the considerations of PF interpretability require that entire categories move via a type of pied-piping since lexical items with scattered features cannot be interpreted or pronounced at PF. However, when movement is covert, PF requirements are inoperative so that in LF the operation Move applies only to formal features.♣

♣ Procrastinate was postulated in Chomsky (1993) to ensure that operations are delayed as late as possible. However, this principle is derivable from Move-F. In Chomsky's (1995) Move-F, LF movement is always cheaper than overt movement in that it affects less material. In other words, since covert movement is more economical than overt movement, the former should be preferred to the latter.

Appendix: Drawing Trees

Draw the trees of the following, assuming the DP structure and the Predicate-internal Subject Hypothesis. You are allowed to use the dummy symbol (Δ) for your benefit.

(1) A vegetarian would never eat a hamburger.

a. [Good]♣

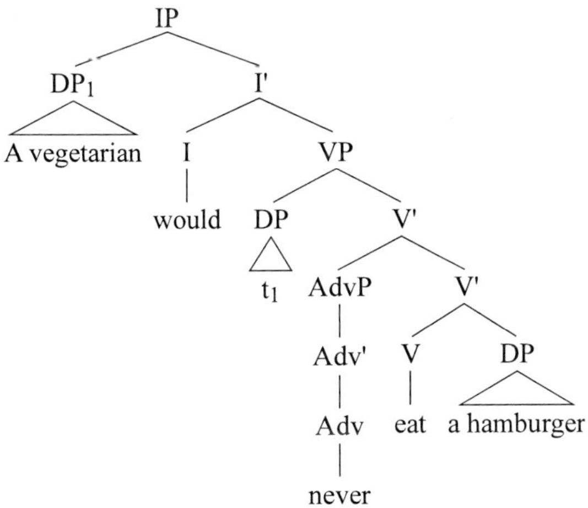

♣ This text assumes that *never* is a V'-adjunct. Modal auxiliaries like *would* are directly inserted in INFL since they carry tense as part of their morphology.

b. [Acceptable]♣

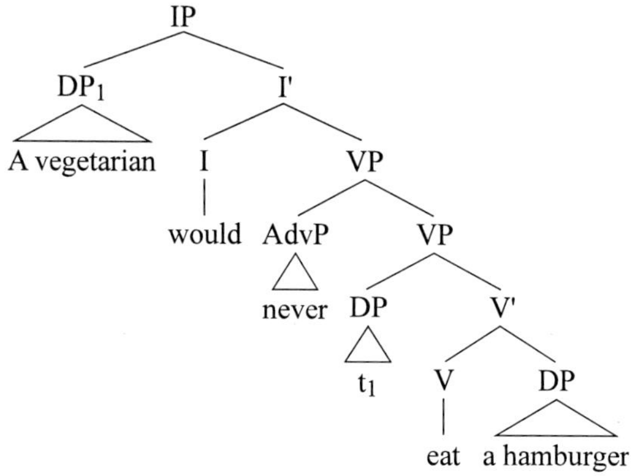

(2) We opened the door for Andy with a crowbar.♣♣

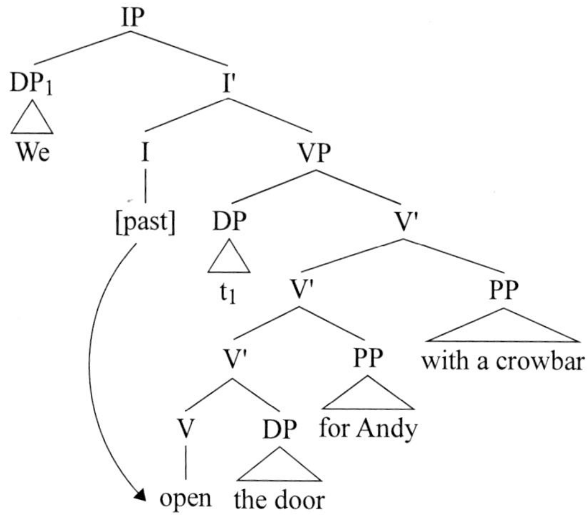

♣
This tree is acceptable if *never* is a VP adjunct. In fact, a later development of syntactic theory assumes that *never* is an XP adjunct.

♣♣
The door is a complement. *For Andy* and *a crowbar* are adjuncts.

(3) The coach knows whether the team will win.

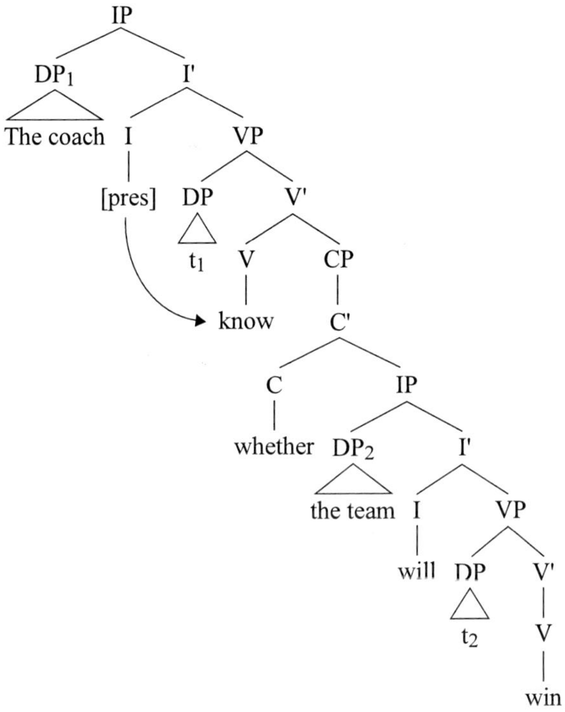

(4) Should that guy go?

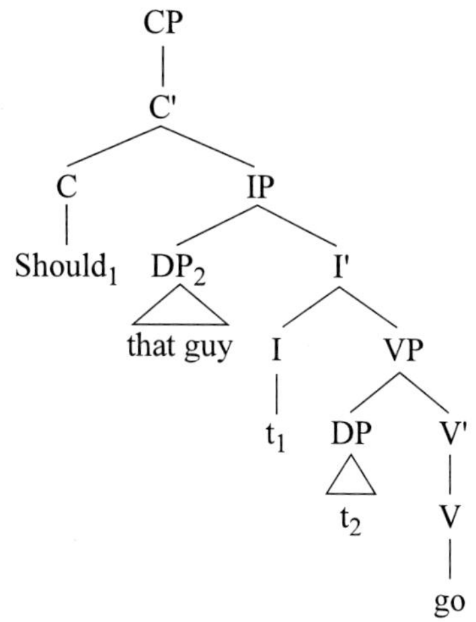

(5) Do those birds sing?

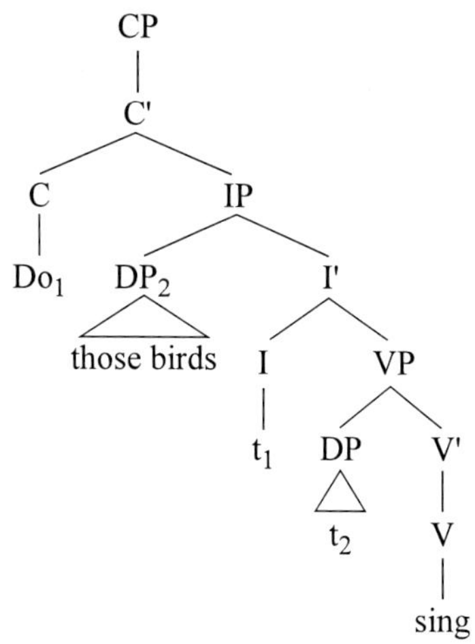

(6) The children have waited.♣

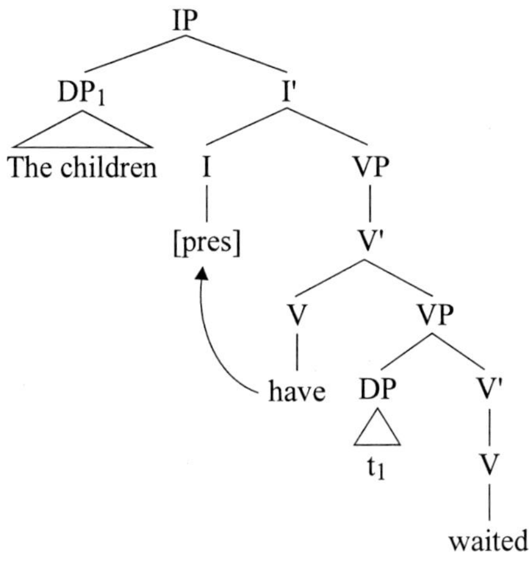

(7) The children should have waited.

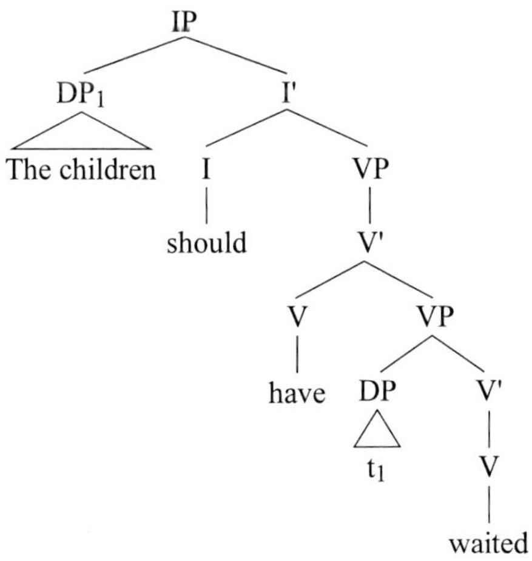

♣ The text assumes that aspectual auxiliaries like *have* originate in a higher V position. According to the PISH, the subject should originate in Spec of the lower VP since *waited* assigns the subject Θ-role.

(8) The car which Mary bought was a lemon.♣

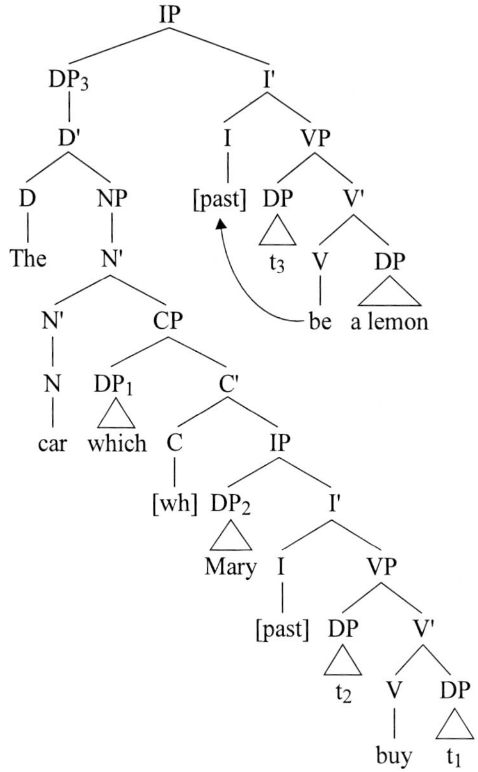

♣
Which Mary bought is an adjunct clause.

(9) Harry visited the village which Sue walked to.

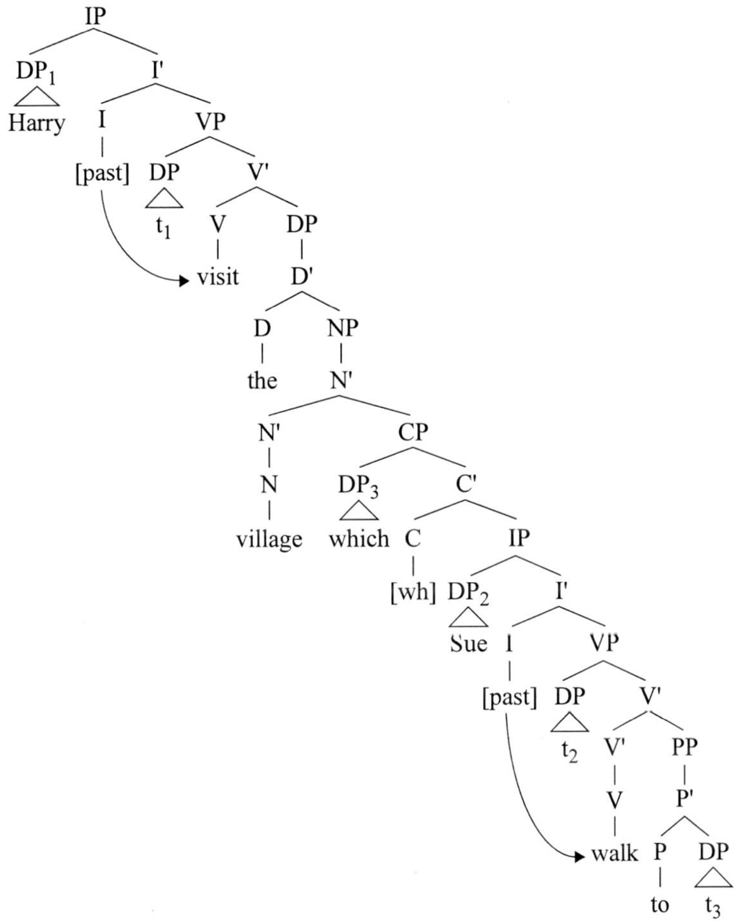

(10) John slept very soundly in his bed all night dreaming beautiful dreams.♣

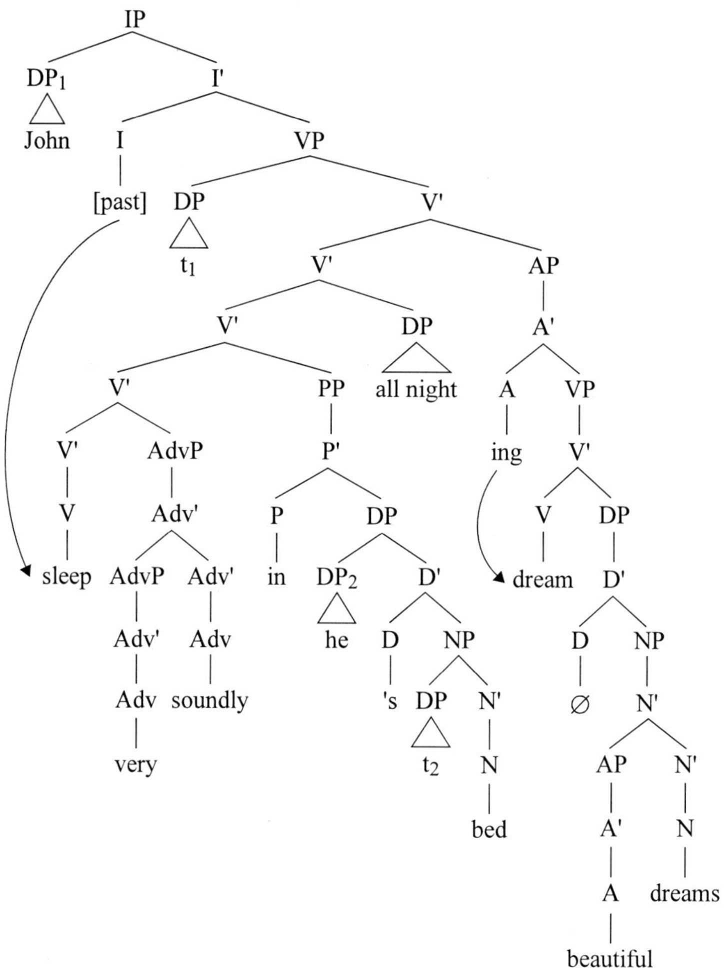

♣
There are four adjuncts: *very soundly, in his bed, all night, dreaming beautiful dreams.*

(11) his jump over the fence [assuming Abney's (1987) DP structure]♣

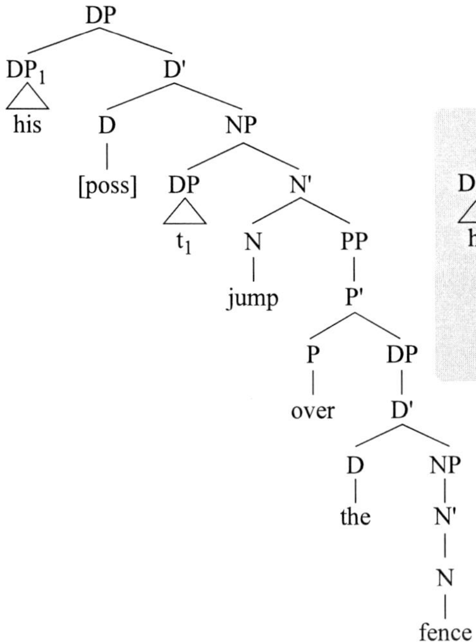

[Alternative]

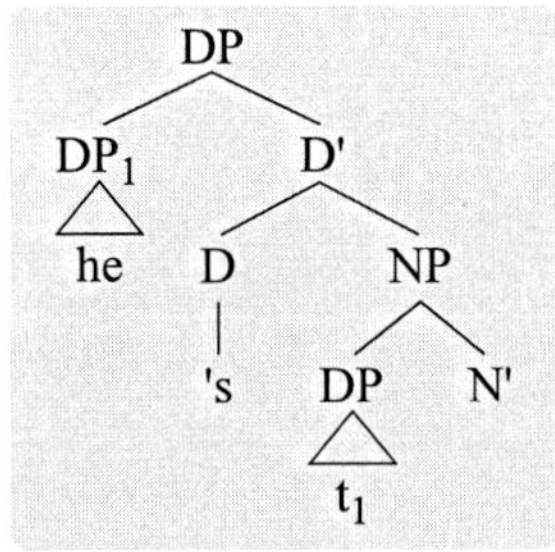

(12) John gave Mary a book. [assuming Larson's (1988) VP shcll]♣♣

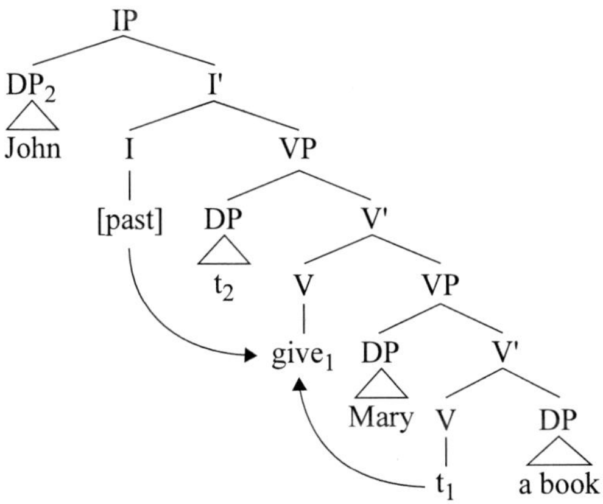

♣
In the tree, *over the fence* is drawn as a complement. It may be an adjunct. *His* may be drawn either *his* + [*poss*] or *he* + *'s*.

♣♣
Larson (1988) argues that some verbs have two VPs as in (i). The empty head is a place holder and has no independent thematic requirement. The thematic verb moves to the position of the empty verb in order to discharge the external Θ-role.

(i) $[_{VP}$ SU $[_{V'}$ e $[_{VP}$ DO $[_{V'}$ V IO$]]]]$

(13) Which contract has the lawyer amended?

a. [Unacceptable]♣

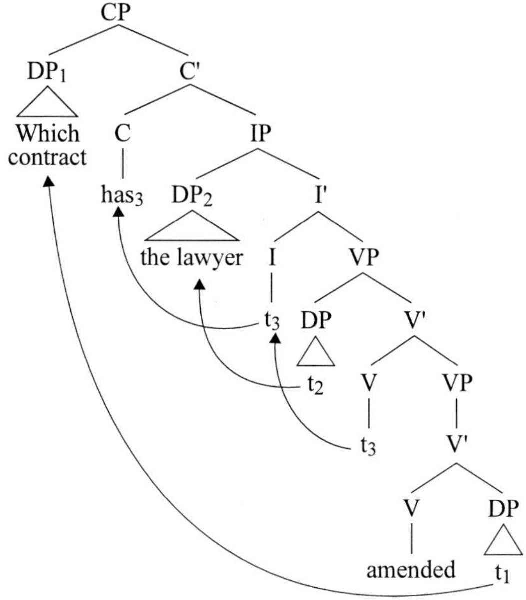

♣
Has occupies the final landing site of head movement, C. This is OK. But the subject should be generated in Spec of the lower VP, considering the PISH and the Θ-role assignment.

b. [Good]♣

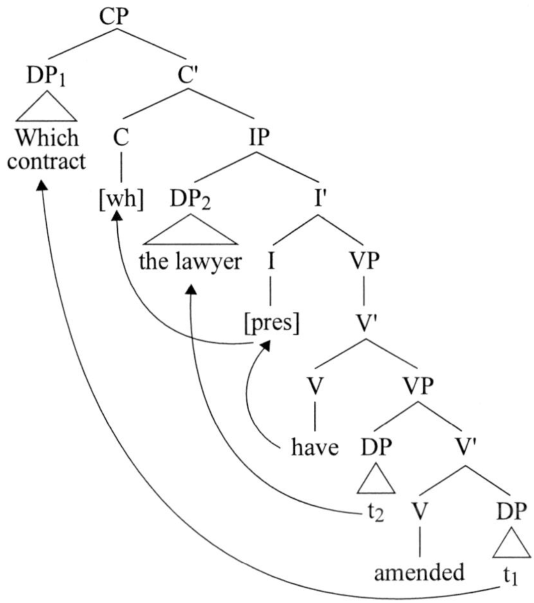

♣
Although *have* occupies the underlying position, the arrows indicate the final landing site of head movement, C. The original subject position is correctly marked as t_2 in Spec of the lower VP.

(14) Never again would I fly to KAL.

[if *I would fly to KAL never again* is the non-inverted word order]

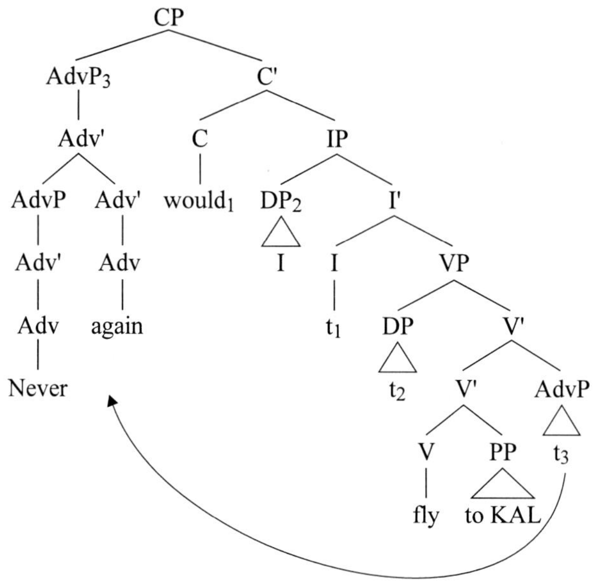

(15) Who does he think she likes?
[The irrelevant parts are suppressed.]

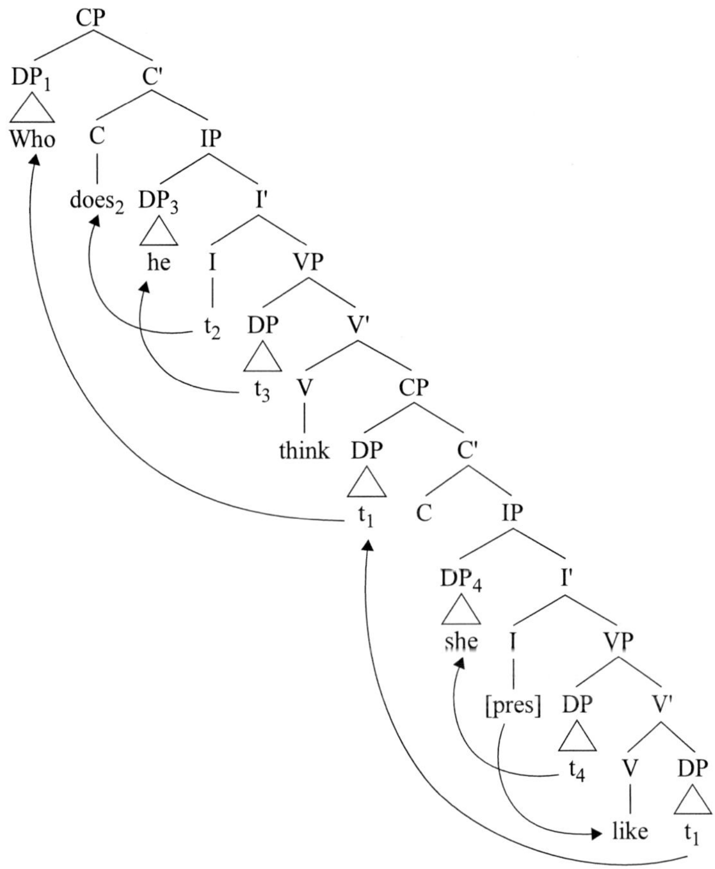

(16) Tim thought that Kate believed the story.

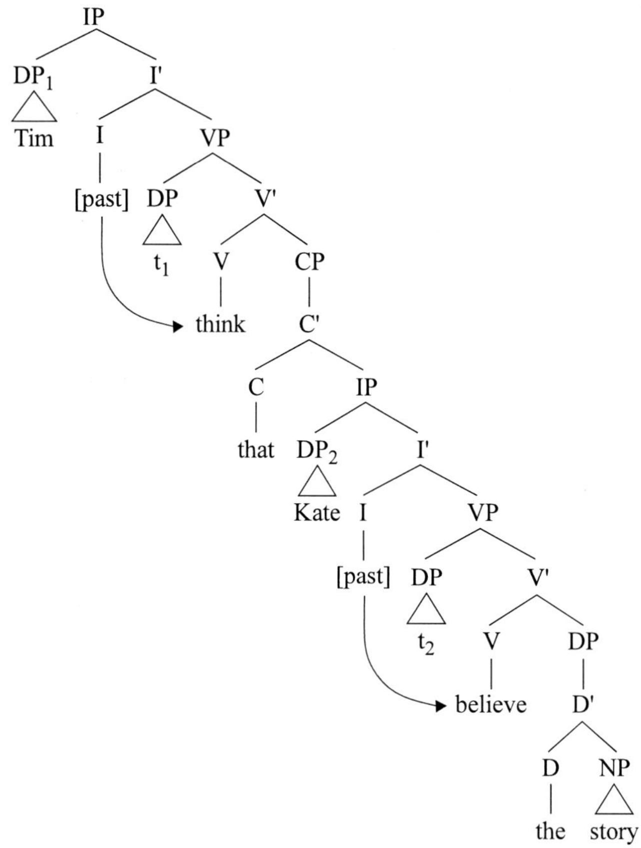

(17) Tim thought that Kate believed that Greg is a liar.

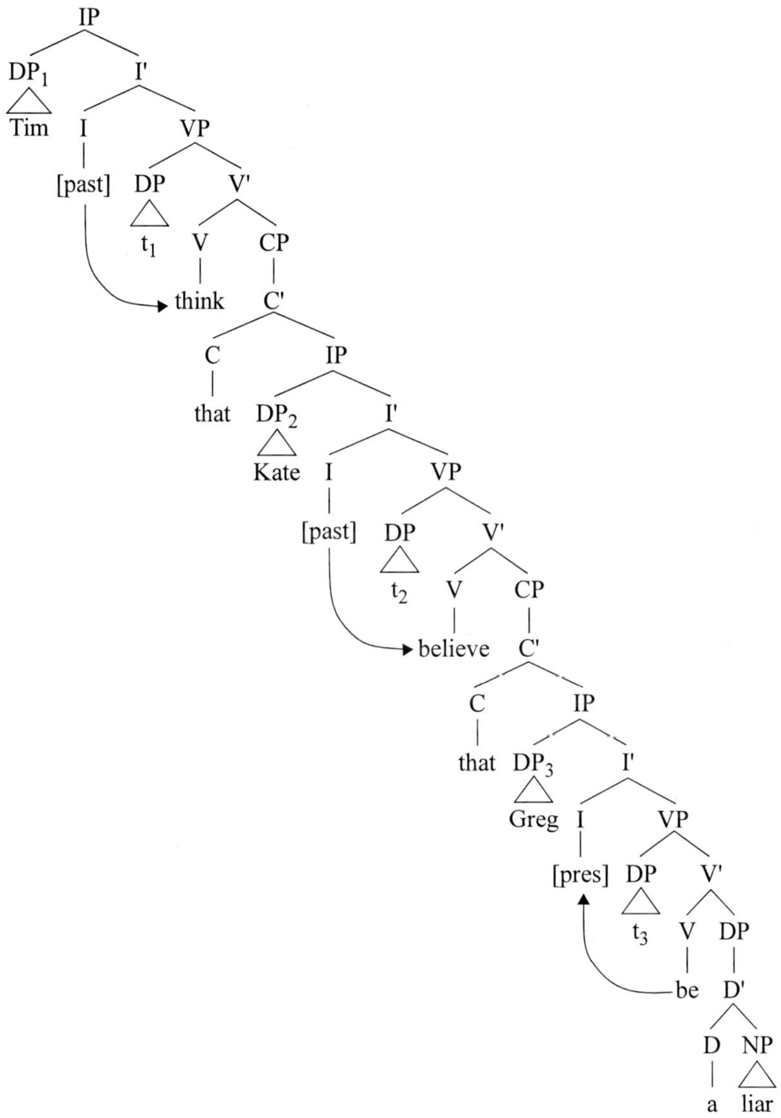

(18) an analysis of the sentence

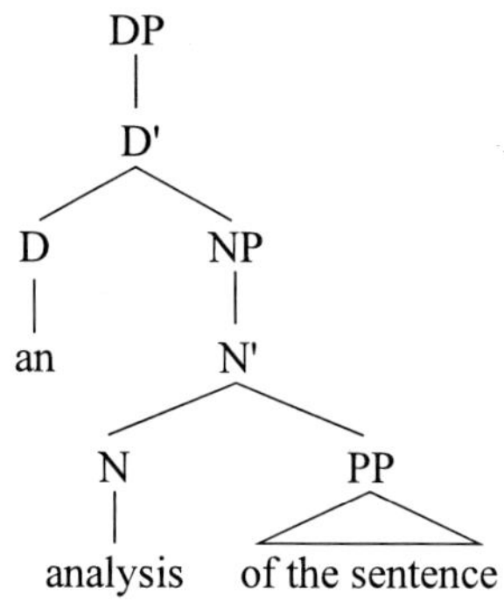

(19) a silly analysis of the sentence

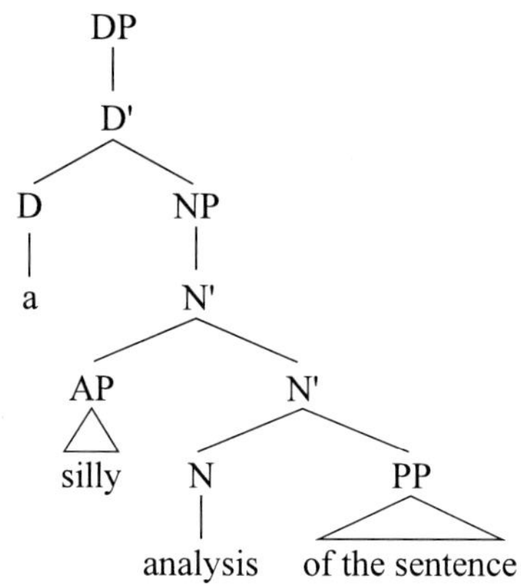

(20) an analysis of the sentence with tree diagrams

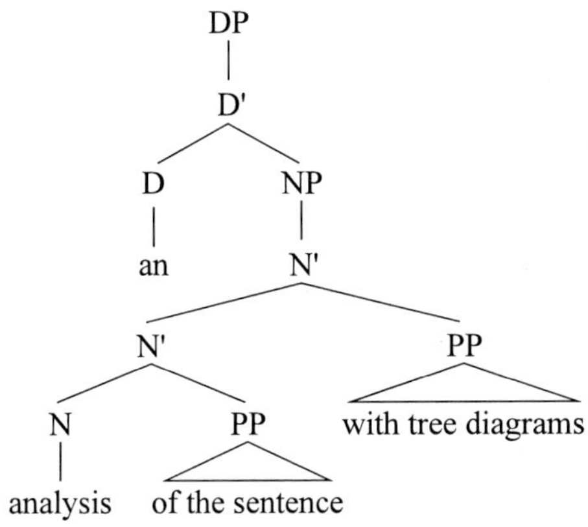

(21) a silly preposterous analysis of the sentence

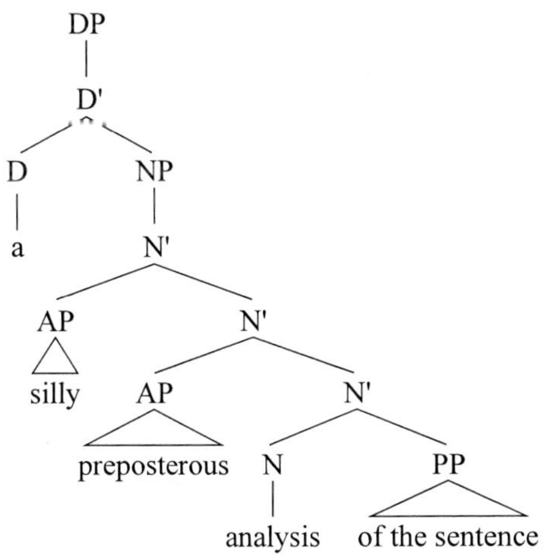

(22) a silly analysis of the sentence with tree diagrams♣

a. [Good]

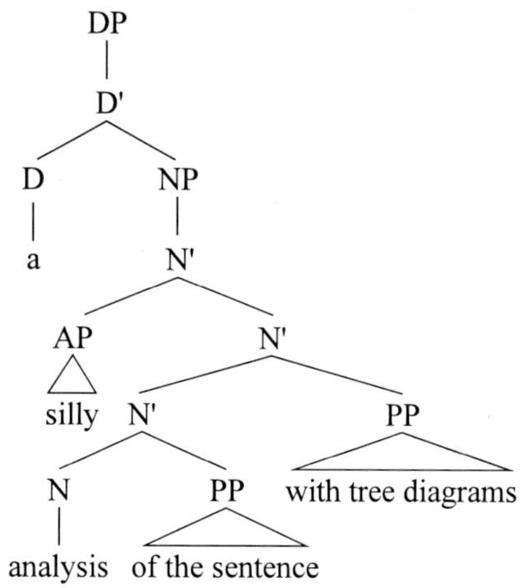

b. [Acceptable]

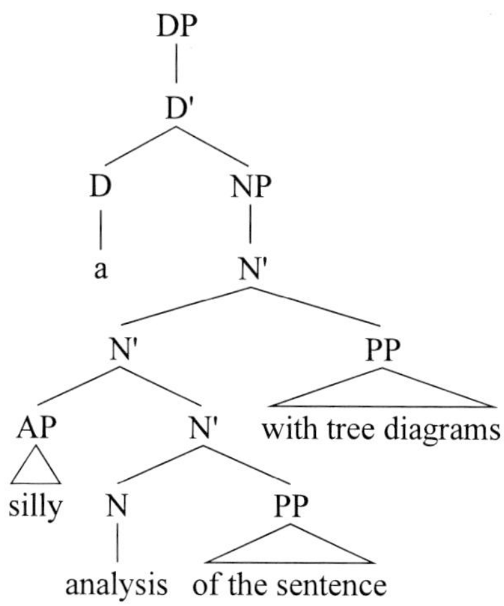

♣ There are two adjuncts. In (22a) the AP adjunct is higher than the PP adjunct. Considering the dominant reading in (22), (22a) is better than (22b): *an analysis of the sentence with tree diagrams, which is silly*. In (22b) the PP adjunct is higher than the AP adjunct: *a silly analysis of the sentence, which is made with tree diagrams*.

(23) not unthinkingly deliberately destroy the garden

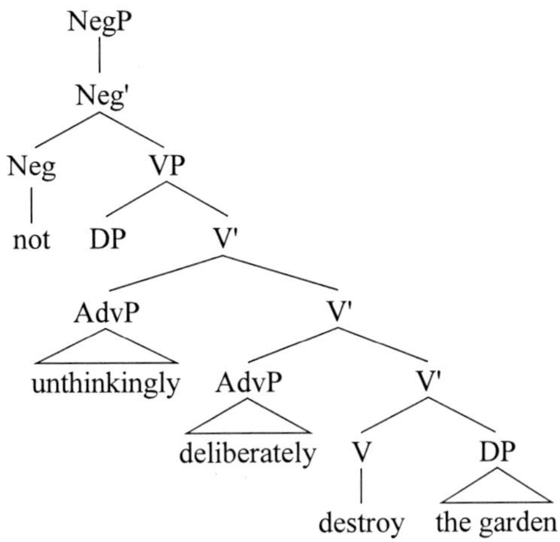

(24) not destroy the garden deliberately

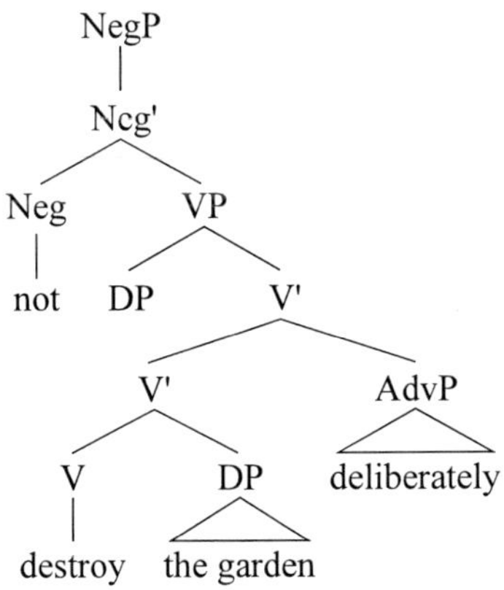

(25) not deliberately destroy the garden

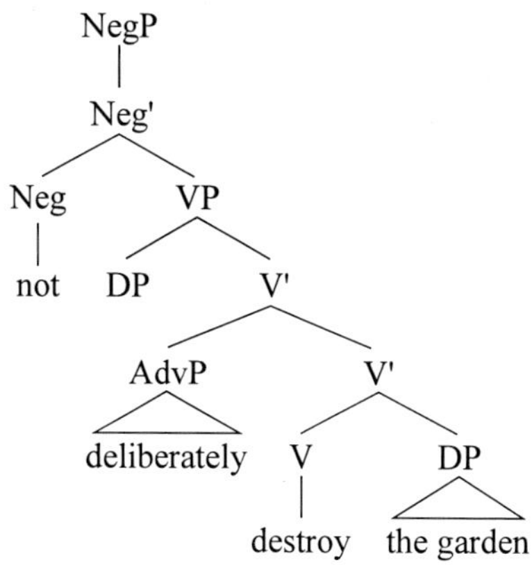

(26) so fond of coffee♣

a. [Acceptable]

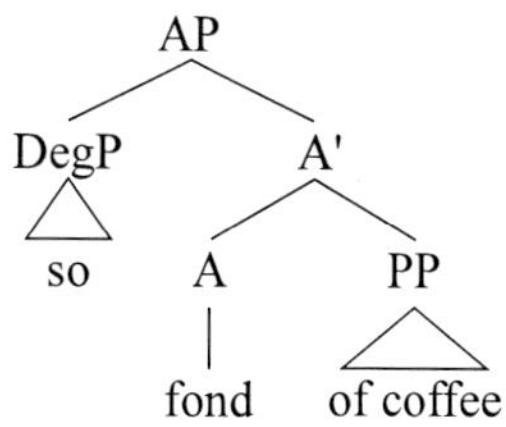

b. [Good]

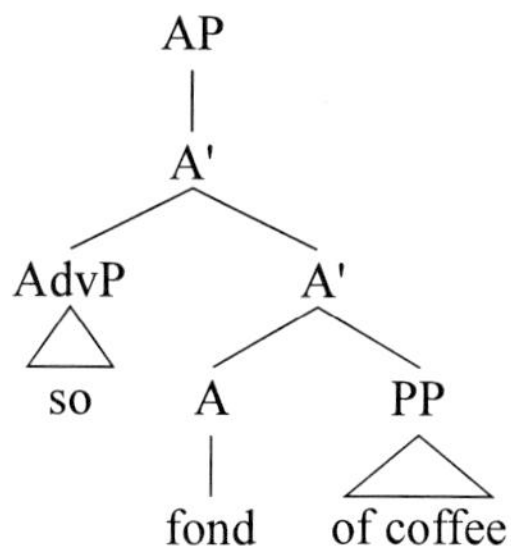

♣
According to the text, *so* is analyzed as an adjunct as in (26b). There is an alternative view that *so* projects to Degree Phrase (DegP), occupying Spec of AP.

(27) so fond of coffee after dinner

a. [Acceptable]

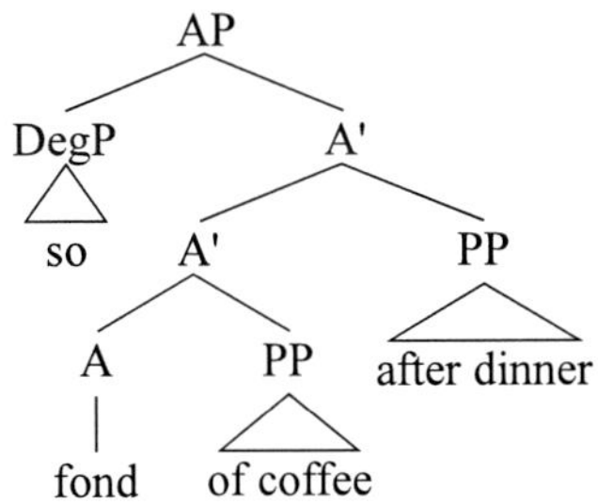

b. [Good]

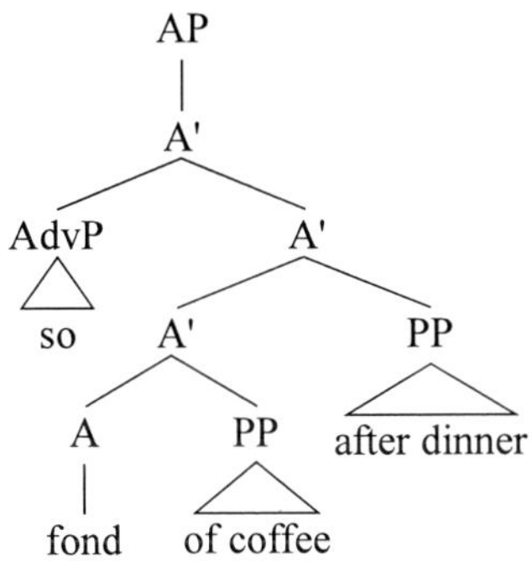

(28) so terribly fond of coffee♣

a. [Acceptable]

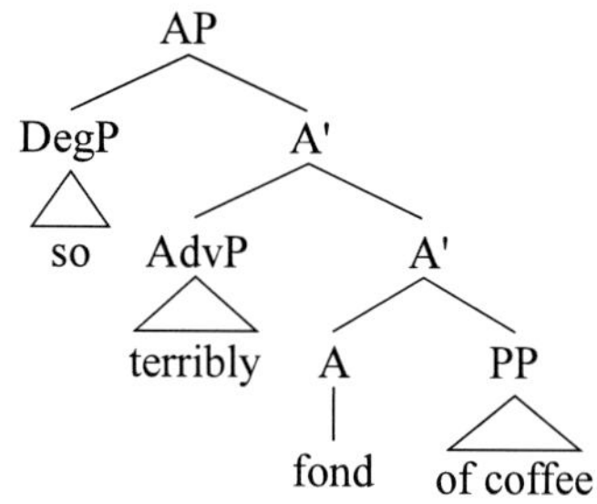

b. [Good]

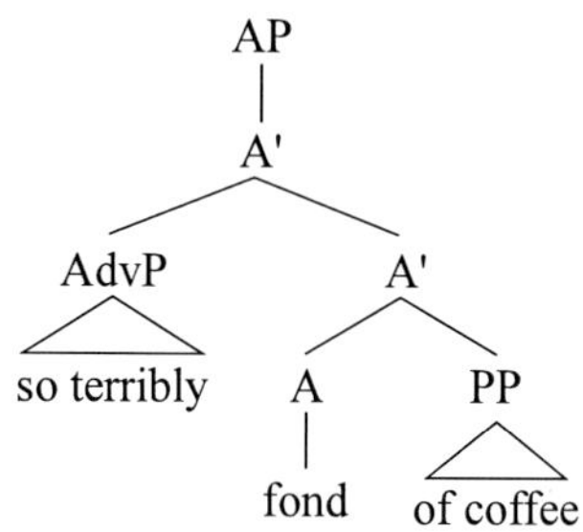

♣ The point is whether *so terribly* is a constituent.

(29) so terribly fond of coffee after dinner

a. [Acceptable]

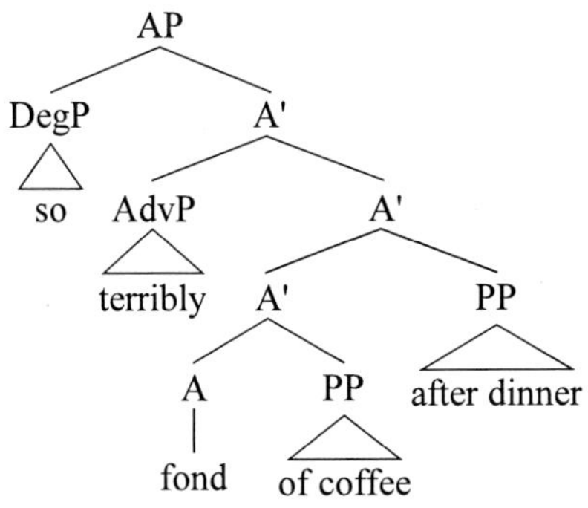

b. [Good]

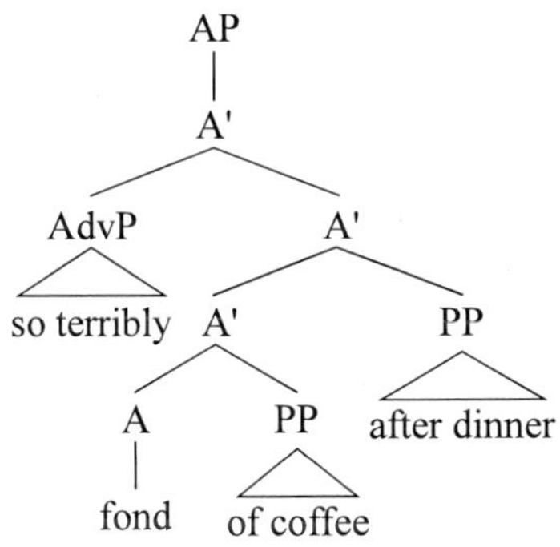

(30) so eager to work with you

a. [Acceptable]

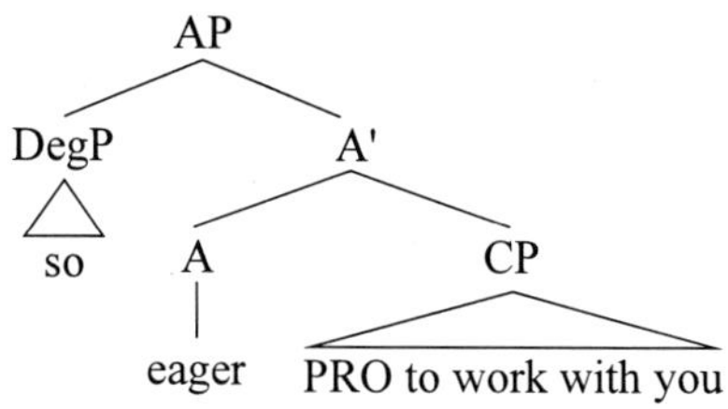

b. [Good]

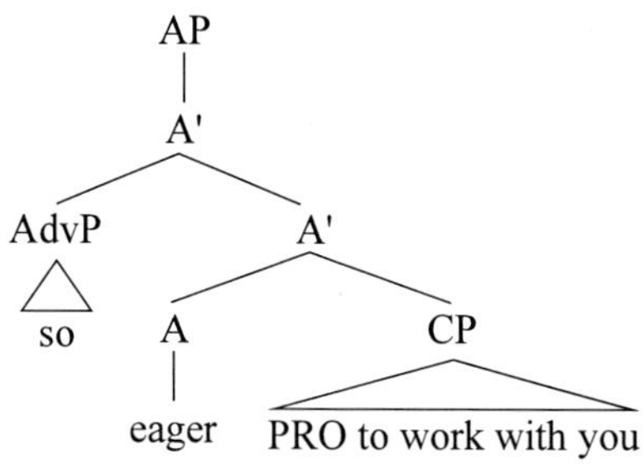

(31) quite in agreement♣

a. [Acceptable]

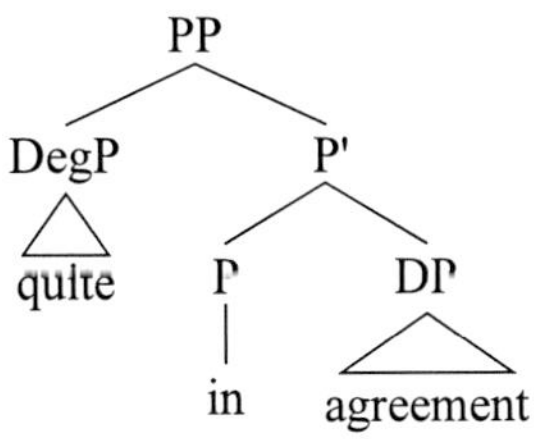

b. [Good]

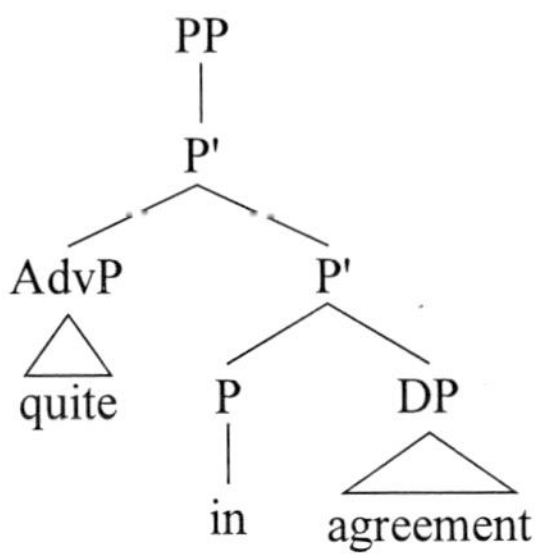

♣ According to the text, *quite* is analyzed as an adjunct as in (31b). There is an alternative view that *quite* projects to DegP, occupying Spec of PP.

(32) quite in agreement about this

a. [Acceptable]

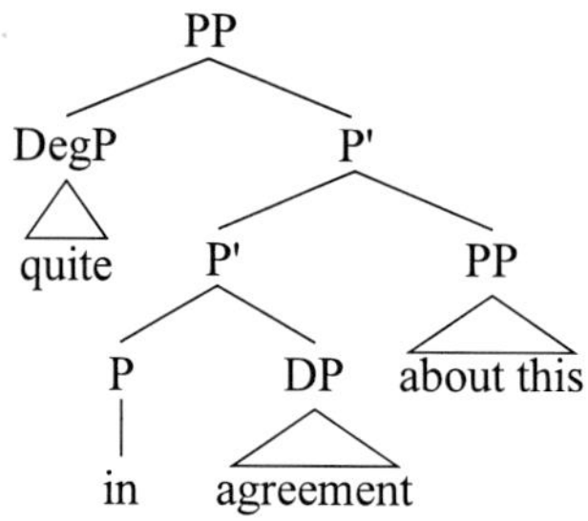

b. [Good]

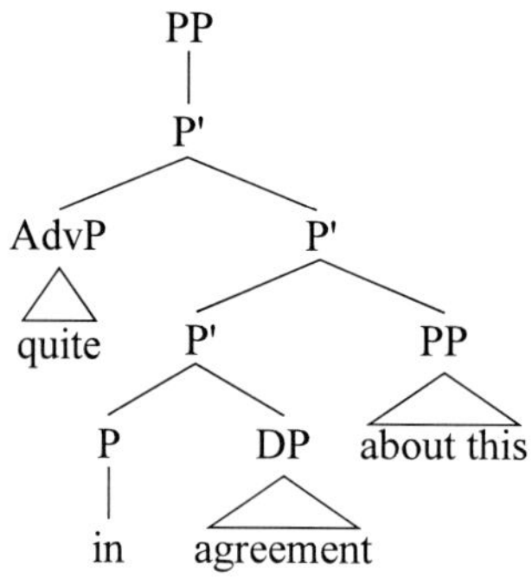

(33) quite unhesitatingly in agreement♣

a. [Acceptable]

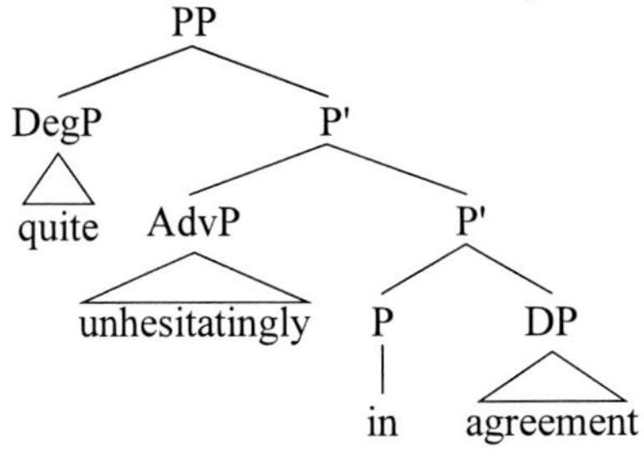

b. [Good]

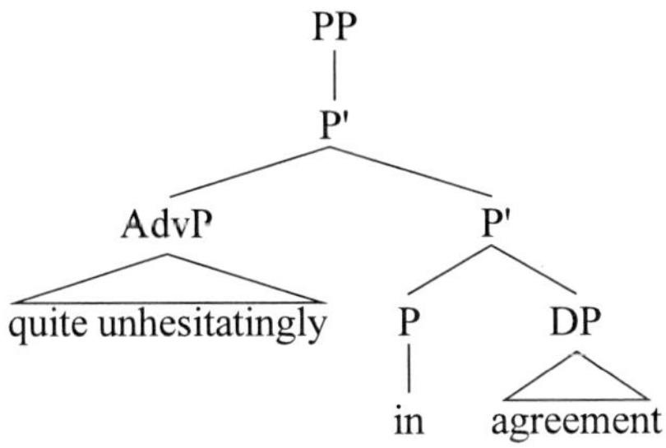

♣ The point is whether *quite unhesitatingly* is a constituent.

(34) quite unhesitatingly in agreement with each other

a. [Acceptable]

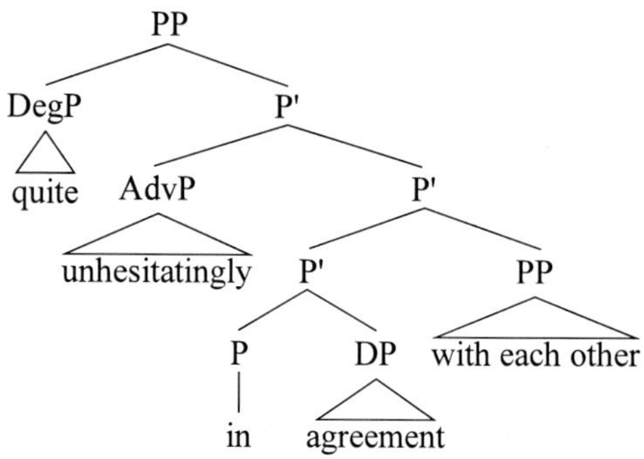

b. [Good]

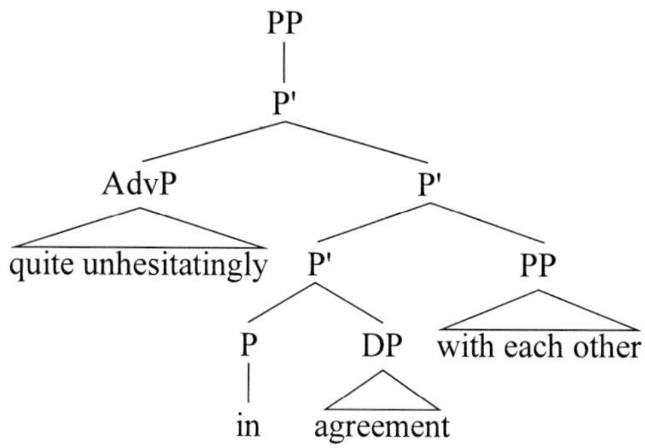

(35) the destruction of Carthage

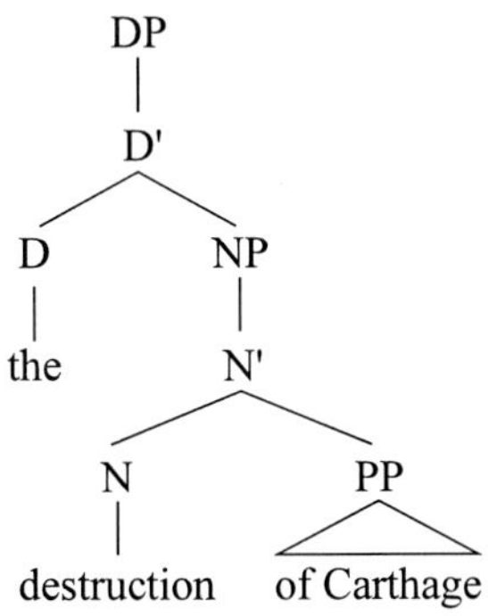

(36) their realization that all is lost

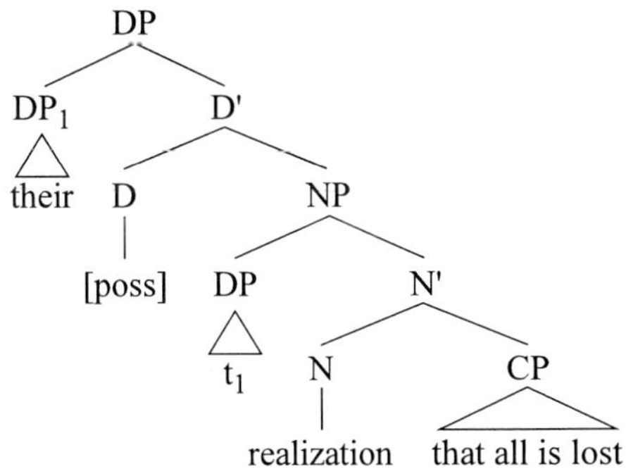

(37) about what you said to me

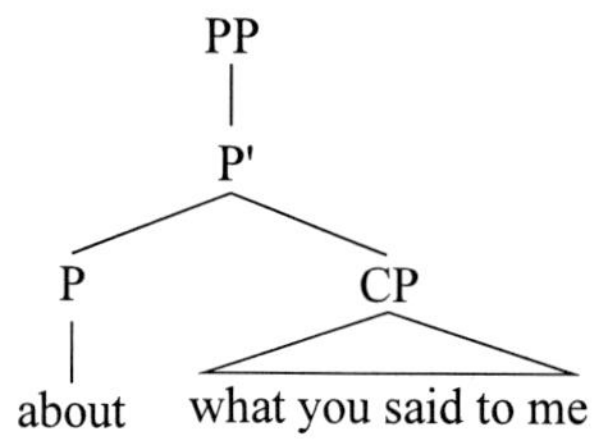

(38) that summer which was so sunny

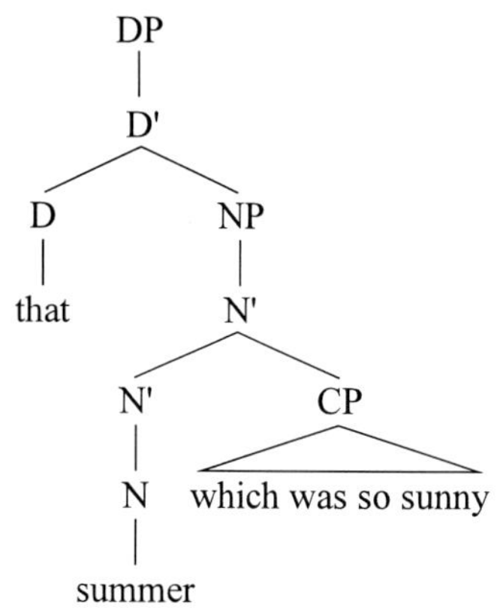

(39) the watch that was stolen

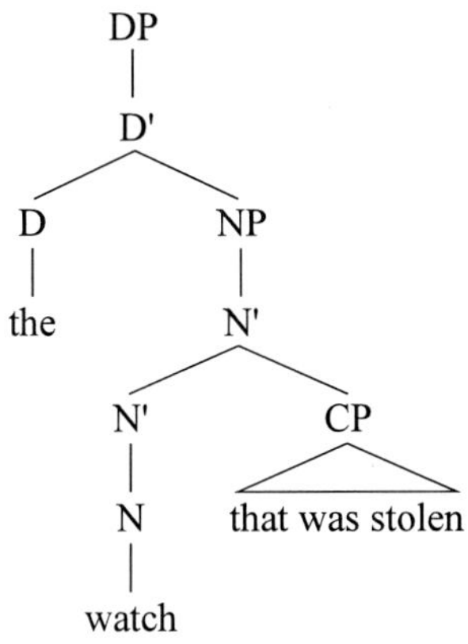

(40) He has broken the mirror.

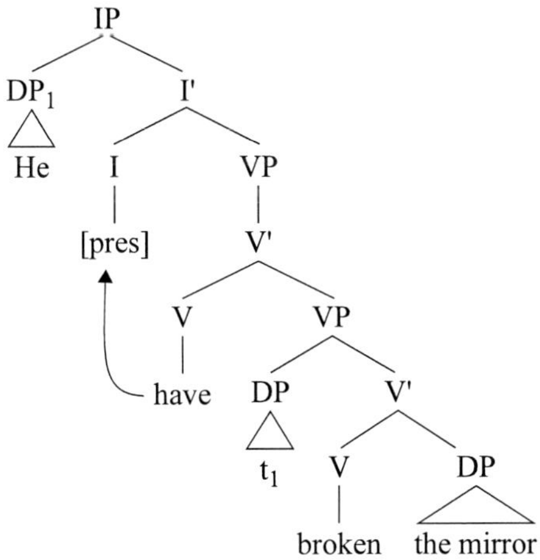

(41) I am dreaming.

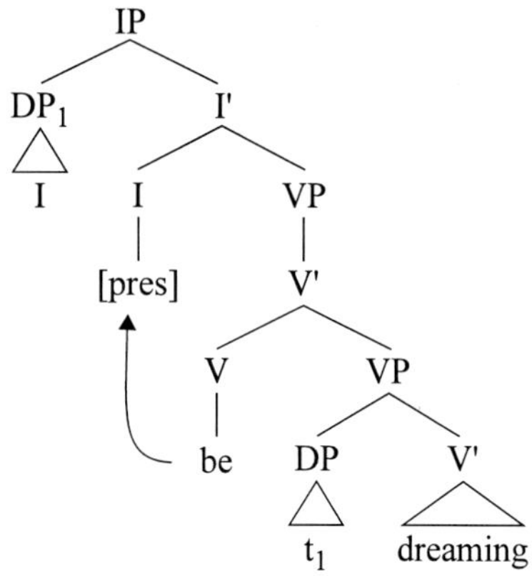

(42) He has not broken the mirror.

a. [Unacceptable]♣

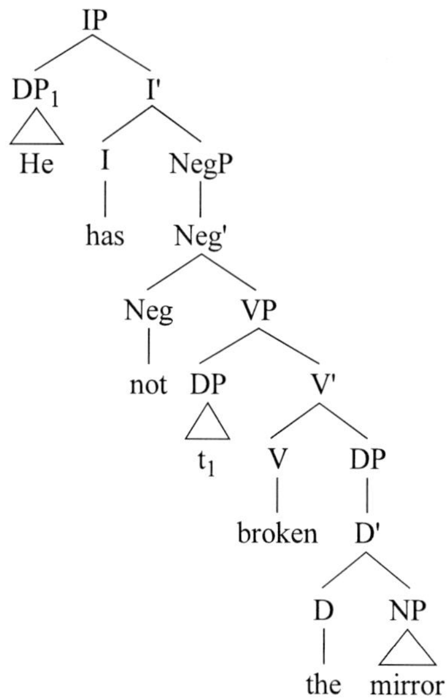

♣
(42a) is unacceptable. In English, an aspectual Aux like *have* cannot be directly inserted in INFL.

b. [Good]♣

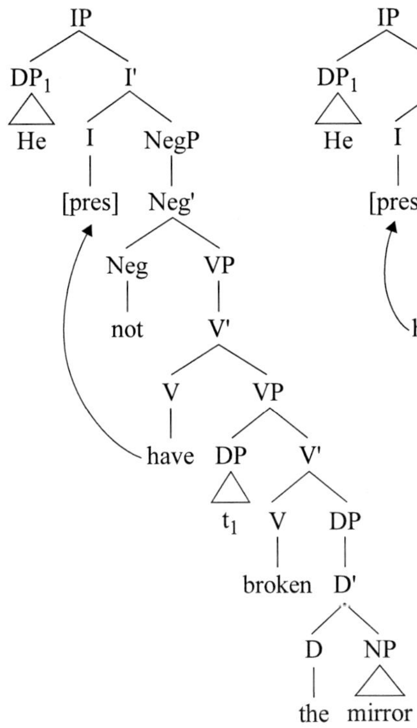

c. [Good]♣♣

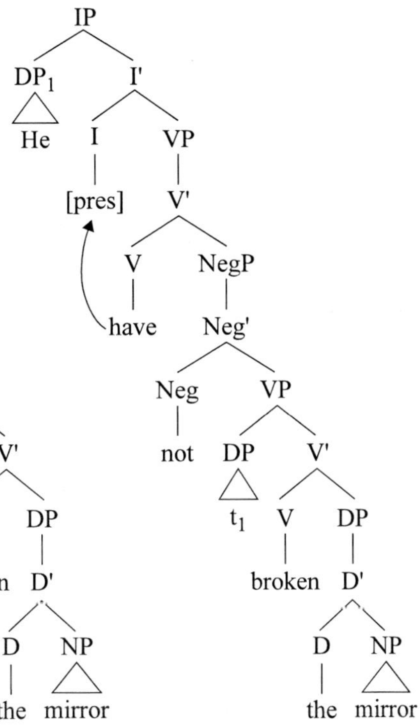

♣
(42b) is good. NegP is placed between IP and VP. VP can be iterative. An aspectual Aux like *have* is generated in a higher VP. The subject is generated in Spec of a thematic V.

♣♣
(42c) is good. NegP is placed between two VPs.

(43) I am not dreaming.♣

a.

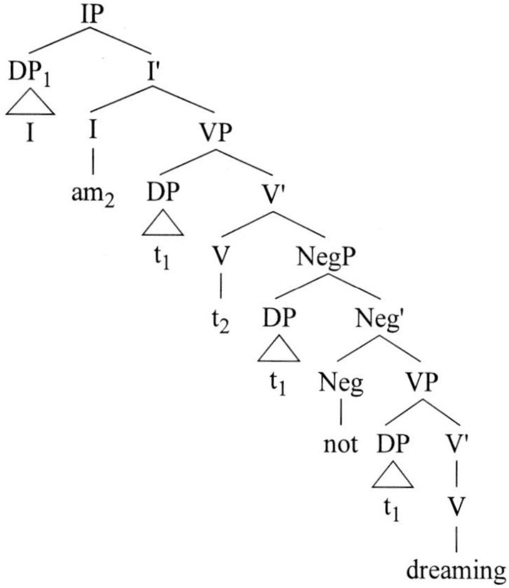

b.

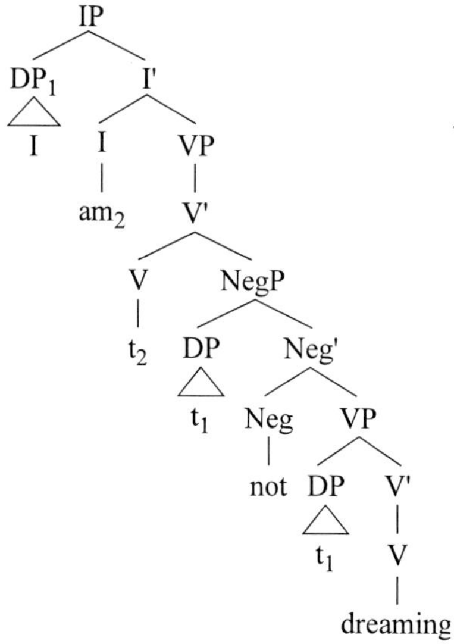

c. [Good]

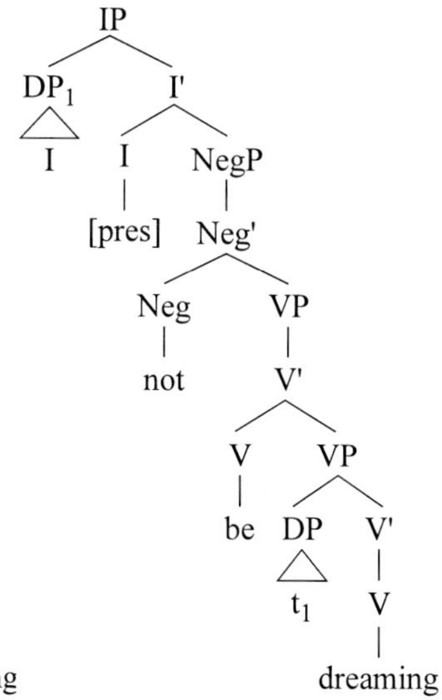

♣

(43a) is unacceptable. Spec of the higher VP and Spec of NegP are not required to be projected. Note that *am* in INFL shows the amalgamated SS form of [*pres*] + [*be*].

(43b) is unacceptable. Spec of NegP is not required to be projected. Note that *am* in INFL shows the amalgamated SS form of [*pres*] + [*be*].

(43c) is good. Note that *be* in the higher V moves to [*pres*] in INFL at SS.

(44) He has probably not broken the mirror.

a. [Unacceptable]♣

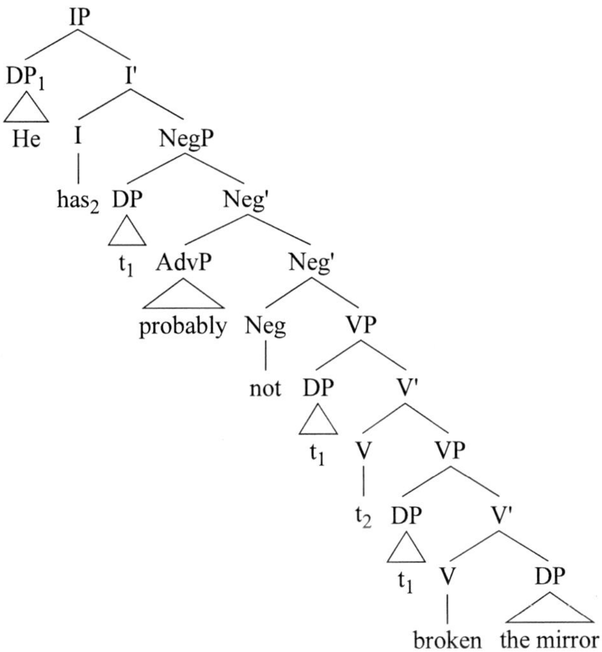

♣

(44a) is unacceptable. Spec of NegP and Spec of the higher VP are not required to be projected. *Probably* is not likely to be a Neg'-adjunct. It is better to be treated as a V' or VP adjunct.

b. [Unacceptable]♣

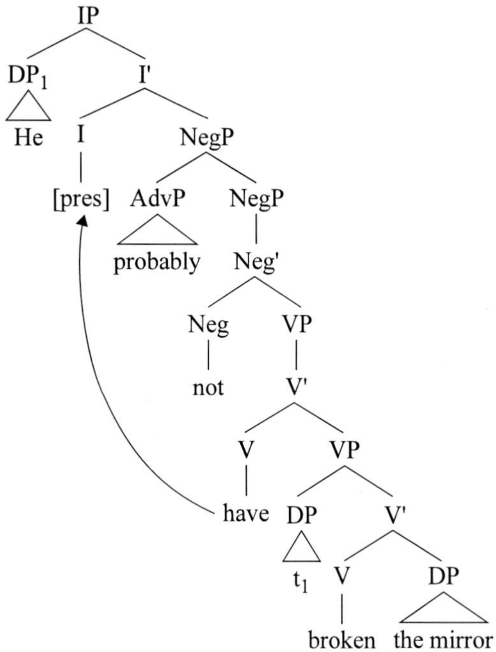

♣
(44b) is unacceptable. *Probably* is not likely to occupy Spec of NegP.

c. [Unacceptable]♣

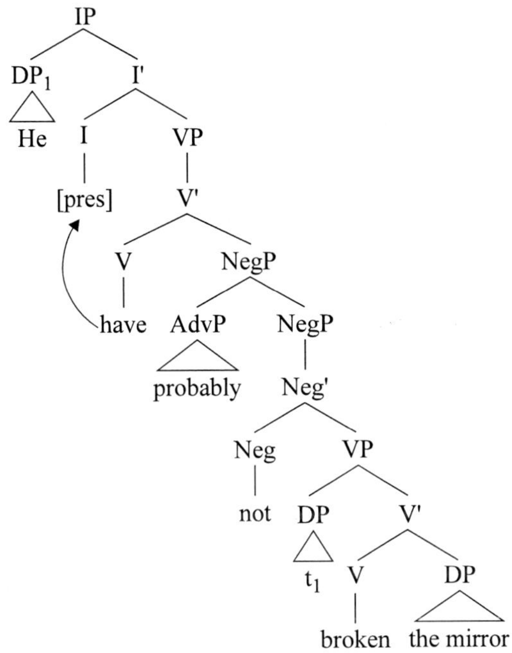

♣
(44c) is unacceptable. *Probably* is not likely to occupy Spec of NegP. Note that NegP is placed between VPs.

d. [Good]♣

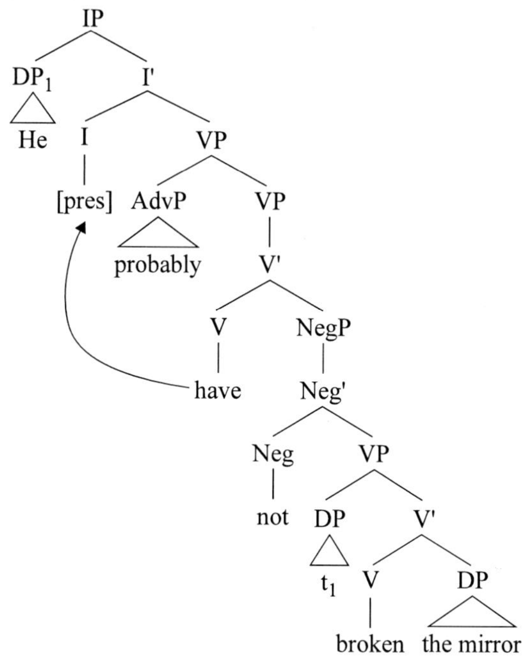

♣
(44d) is good. *Probably* is treated as a VP adjunct. Considering the word order, NegP is placed between VPs.

(45) I am probably not dreaming.♣

a.

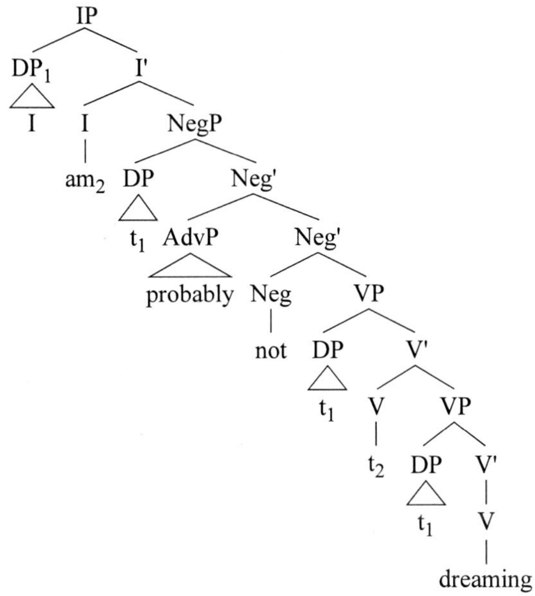

b.

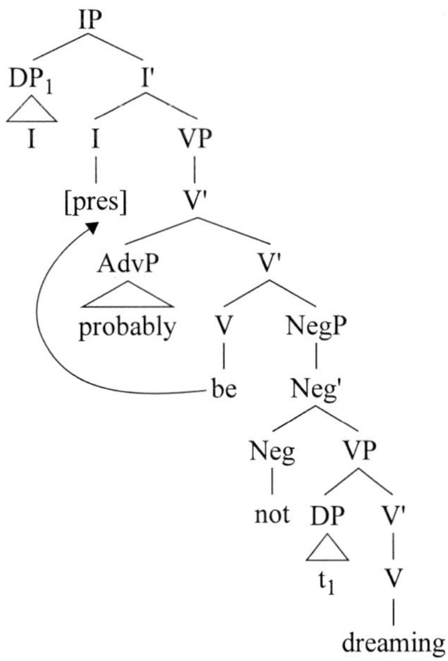

♣

(45a) is unacceptable. Note that *am* in INFL shows the amalgamated SS form of [*pres*] + [*be*]. Spec of NegP and Spec of the higher VP are not required to be projected. *Probably* is not likely to be a Neg'-adjunct.

(45b) is good. Note that NegP is placed between VPs.

(46) He will not have broken the mirror.♣

a.

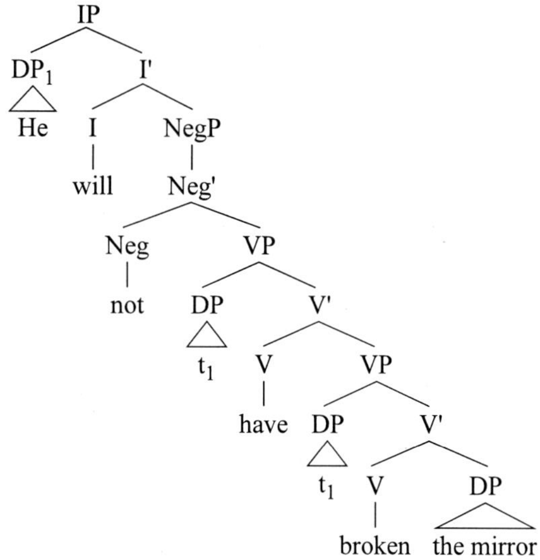

b.

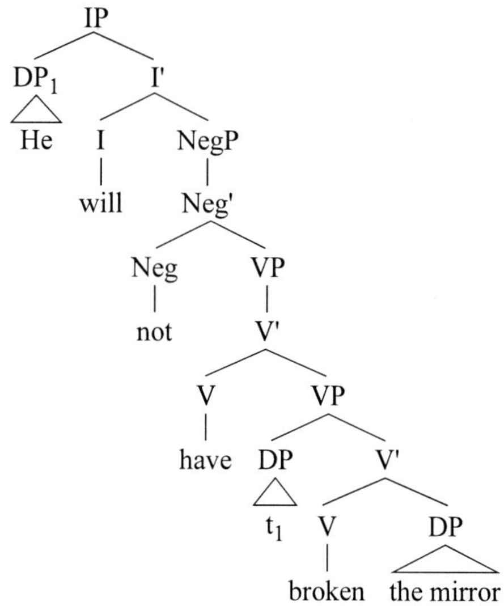

♣
(46a) is unacceptable. Spec of the higher VP is not required to be projected.

(46b) is good.

(47) Filthy fumes are produced by lorries.

a. [Unacceptable]♣

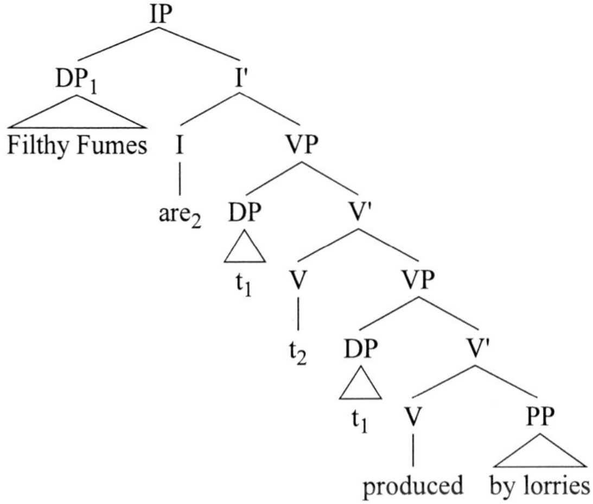

b. [Acceptable]♣♣

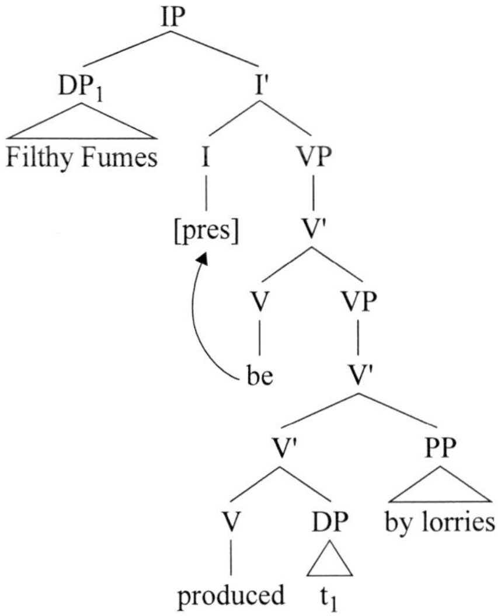

♣
(47a) is unacceptable. *Are* in INFL shows the amalgamated SS form of [*pres*] + [*be*]. Spec of the higher VP and Spec of the lower VP are not required to be projected. Although a passivized verb like *produced* is analyzed as A in the text, it has been often analyzed as V. The analysis of a passivized verb as V is OK.

♣♣
(47b) is acceptable. The analysis of a passivized verb as V is OK. The Agent PP is treated as a V'-adjunct.

c. [Acceptable]♣

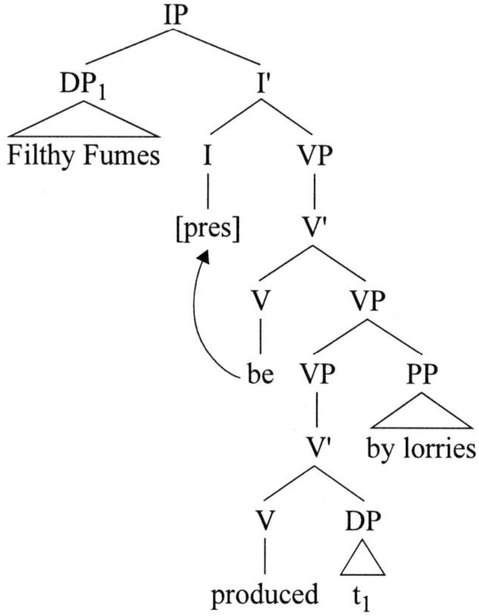

(48) This student must write two essays.

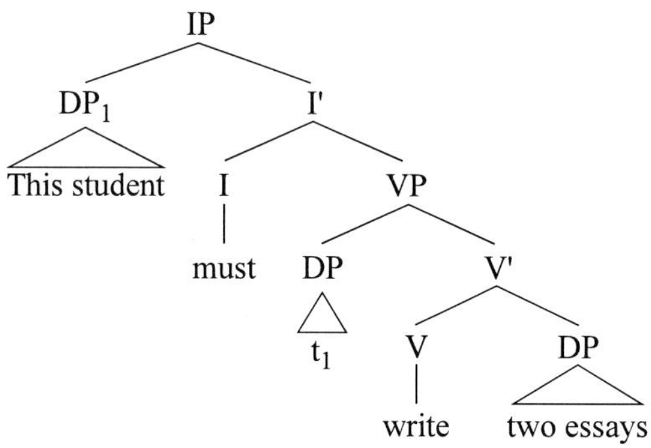

♣
(47c) is acceptable. The analysis of a passivized verb as V is OK. The Agent PP is treated as a VP-adjunct.

(49) This student has written two essays.

a. [Unacceptable][♣]

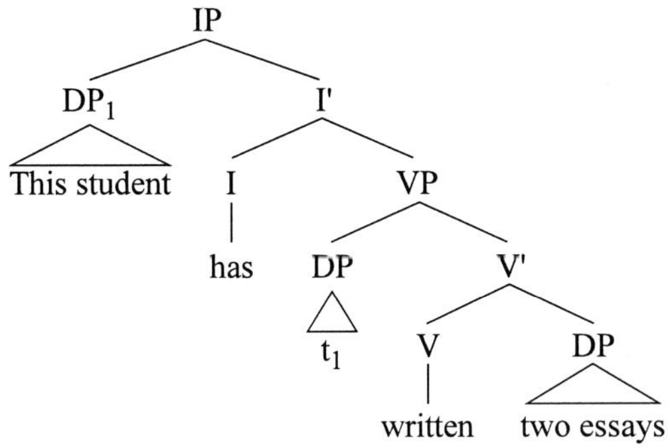

b. [Good]

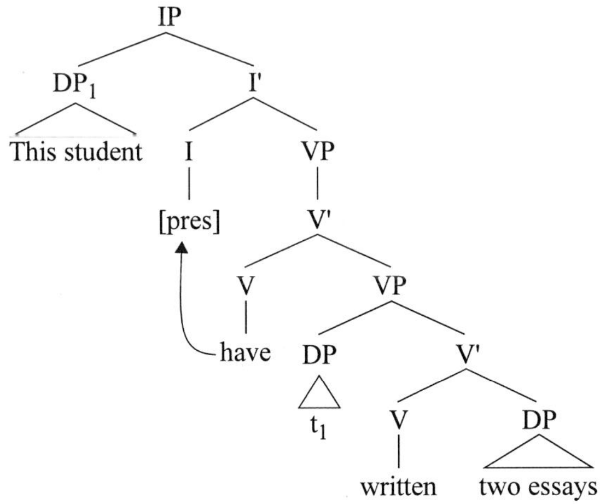

♣ *Has* cannot be directly inserted in INFL.

(50) This student is writing two essays.

a. [Unacceptable][♣]

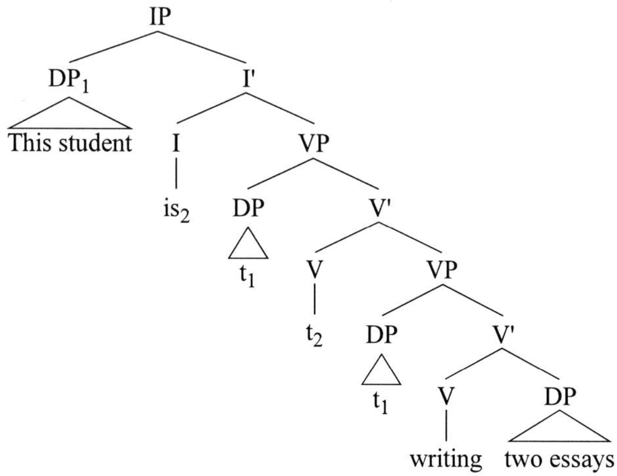

b. [Good]

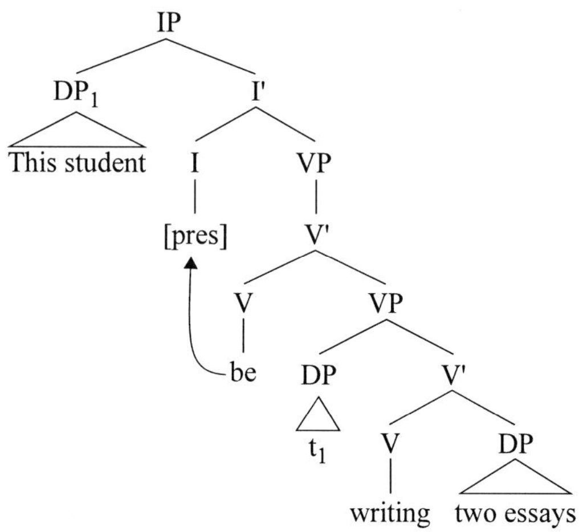

♣
Is cannot be directly inserted in INFL. Spec of the higher VP is not required to be projected.

(51) Two essays were written by this student.

a. [Unacceptable]♣

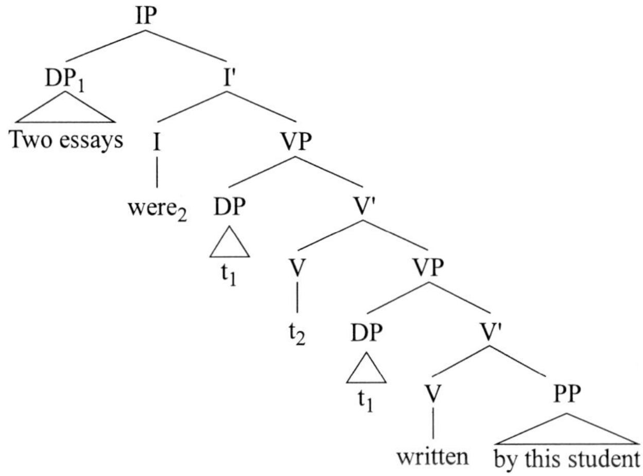

b. [Good]

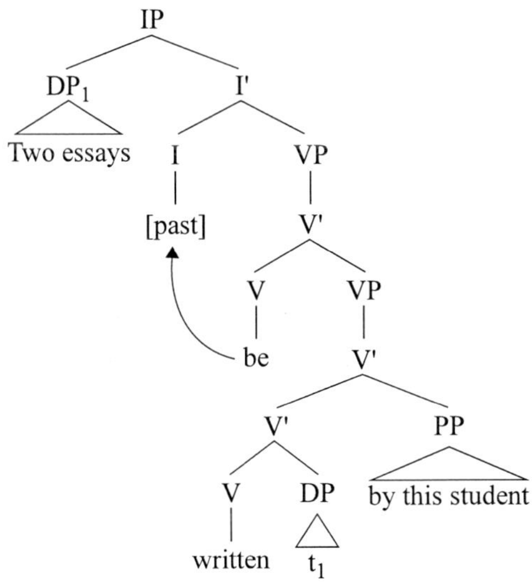

♣
(51a) is unacceptable. *Were* cannot be directly inserted in INFL. Spec of the higher VP and Spec of the lower VP are not required to be projected. The analysis of a passivized verb as V is OK. The Agent PP is treated as a complement.

(52) Danny seems to be working.♣

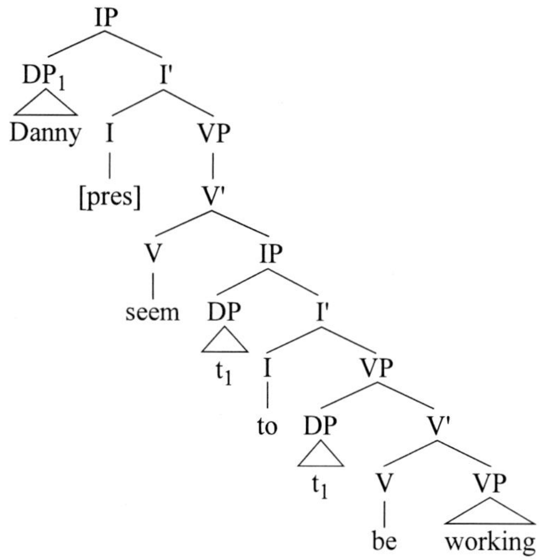

(53) Phil appears to be singing.♣♣

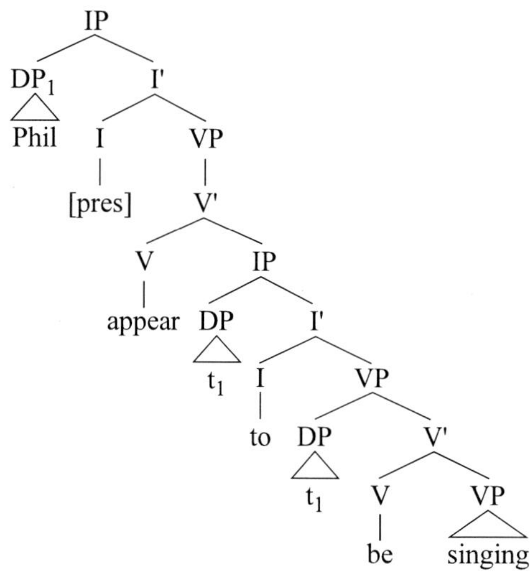

♣
(52) is acceptable. It would be better if the subject were generated within the lower VP.

♣♣
(53) is acceptable. It would be better if the subject were generated within the lower VP.

(54) Is Neil playing squash?

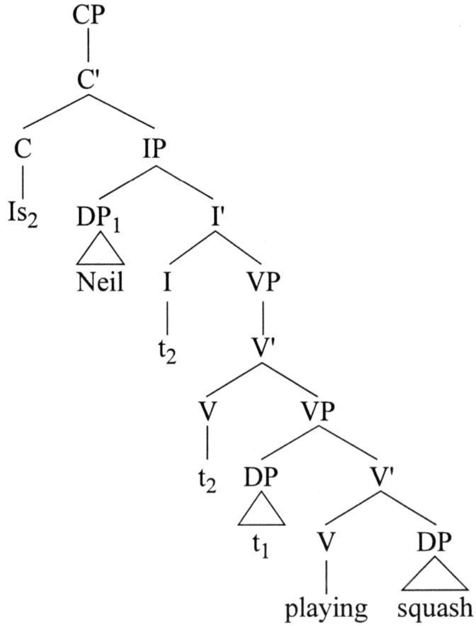

(55) What will you buy?

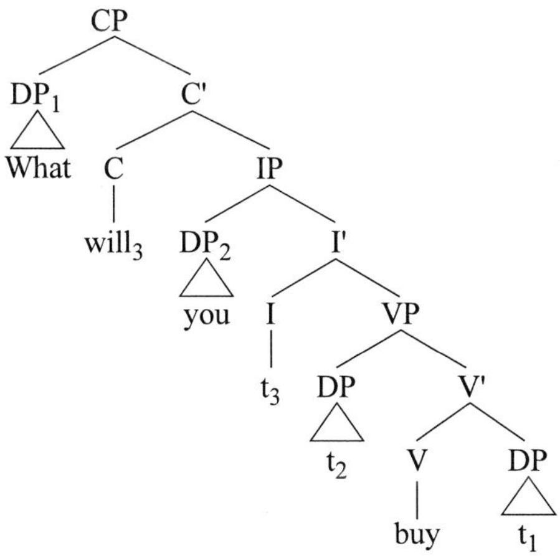

(56) Which book did you read?

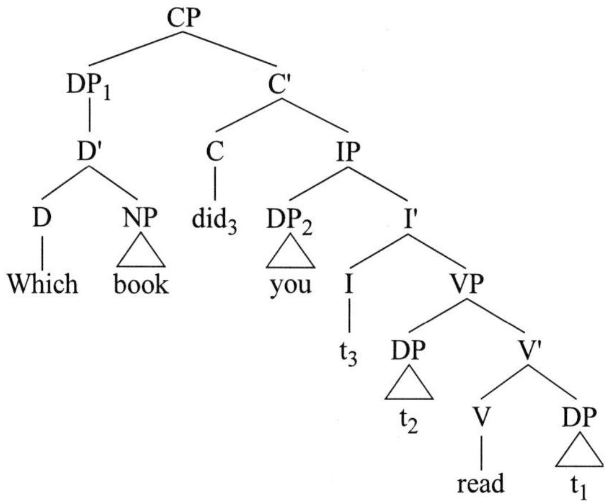

(57) Who did you see?

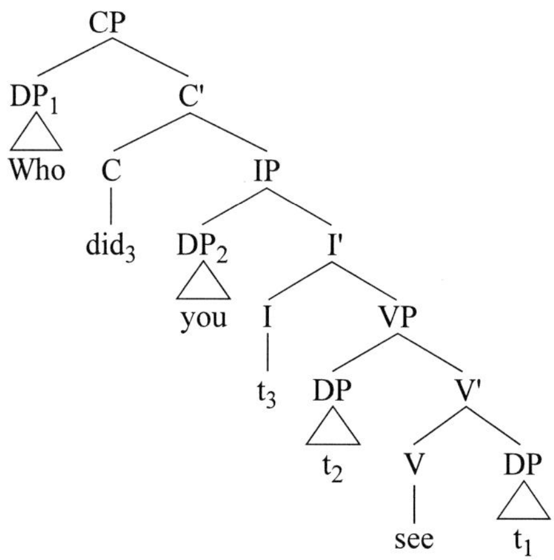

(58) What did Sally give James?♣

a.

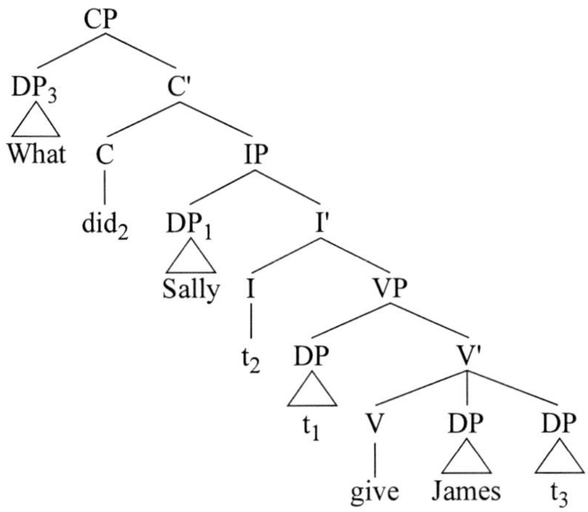

b. [Larson's (1988) VP-shell structure]

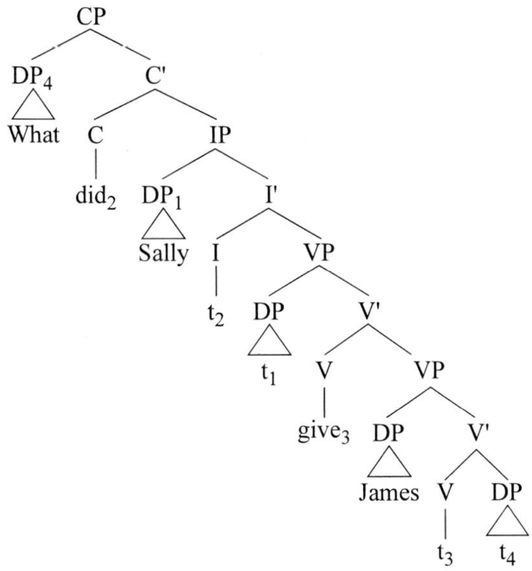

♣ (58a) is acceptable although it has a three-way branching.

(58b) is good. It observes the Binary Branching Condition of X'-theory.

(59) Which film did you like?

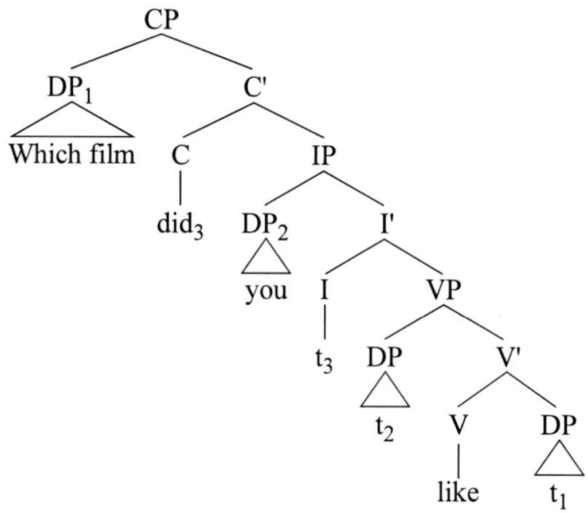

(60) The artist has painted two portraits.

a. [Unacceptable]♣

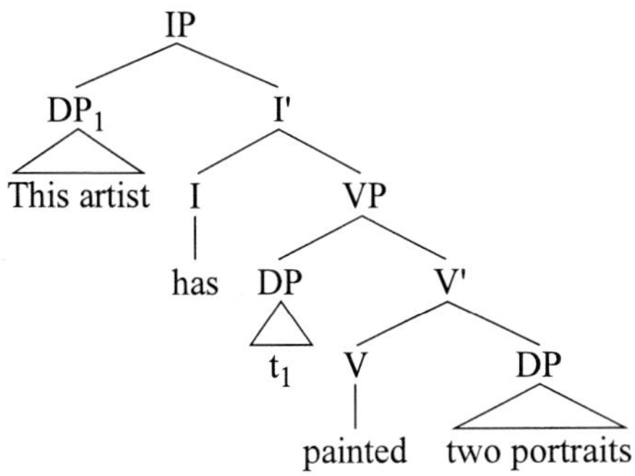

b. [Good]

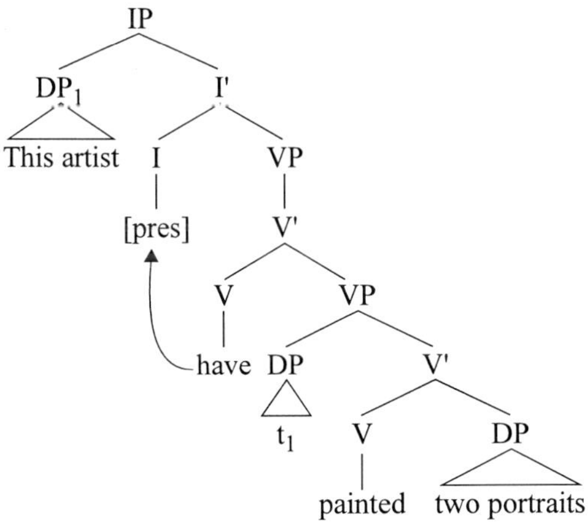

♣ (60a) is unacceptable. *Has* cannot be directly inserted in INFL.

(61) This artist will have painted two portraits.

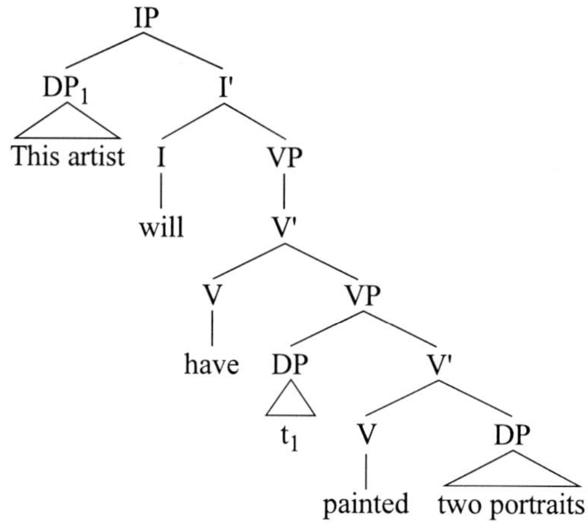

(62) This artist will have been painting two portraits.

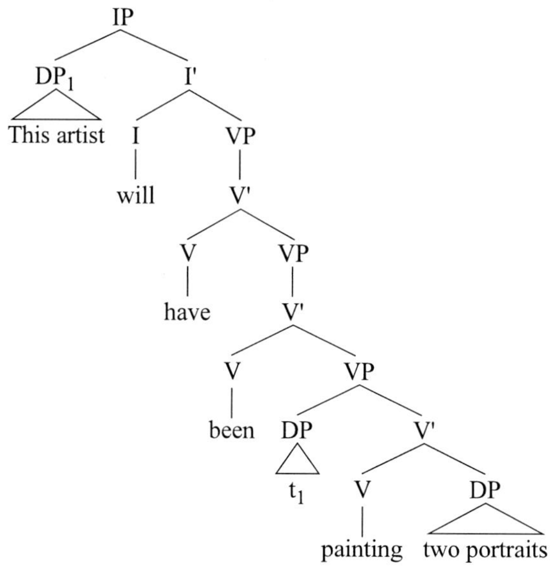

(63) Two portraits will have been being painted by this artist.♣

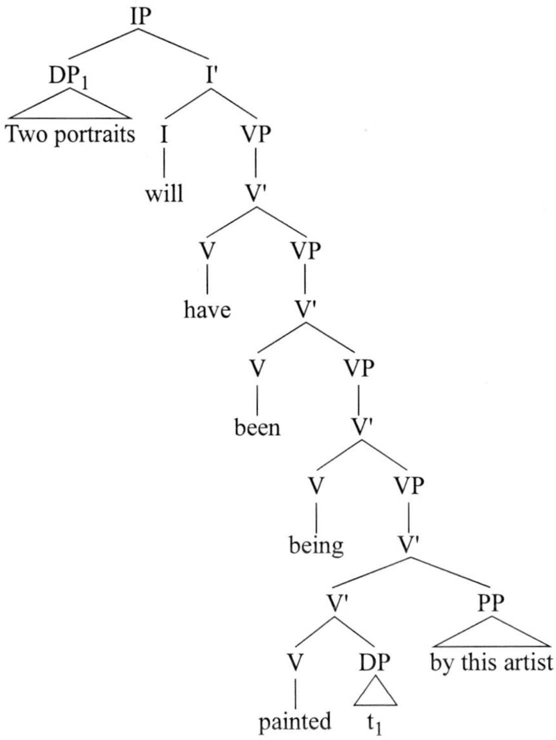

♣
(63) is acceptable. The analysis of a passivized verb as V is OK. The Agent PP is treated as a V'-adjunct.

(64) clean his room meticulously

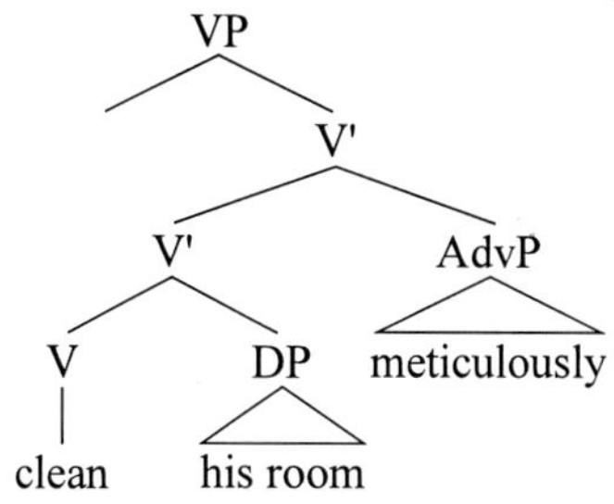

(65) carefully clean his room

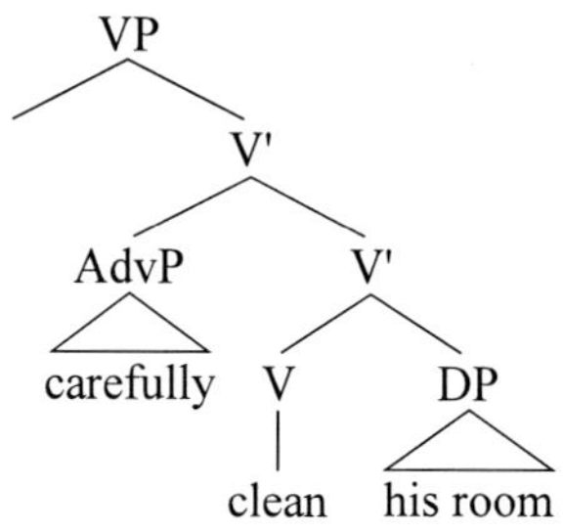

(66) with yellow hats on their heads♣

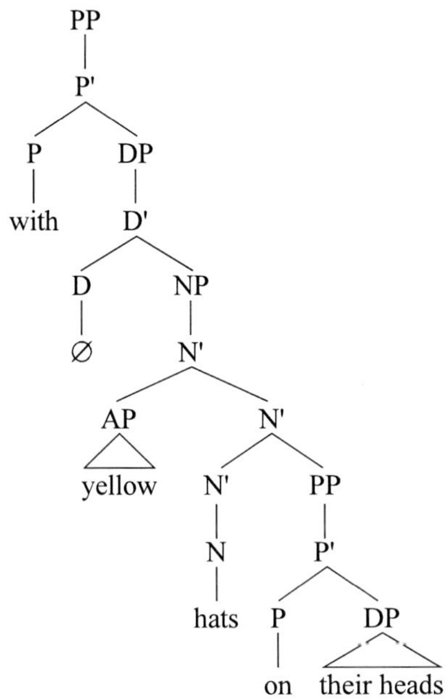

♣
(66) is acceptable. *On their heads* is treated as an adjunct. It could be a complement.

(67) a dedicated teacher of language

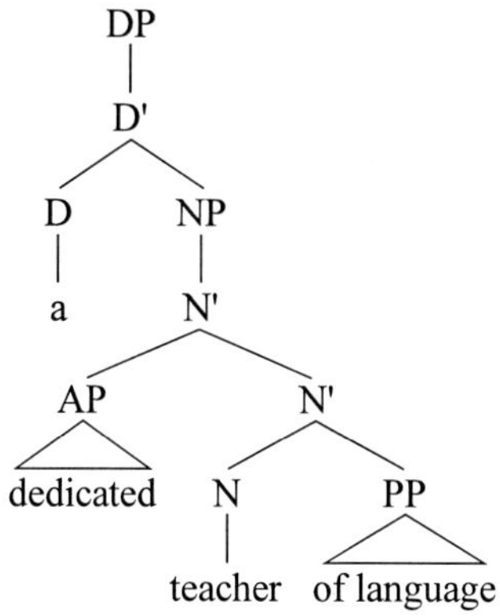

(68) an indifferent one

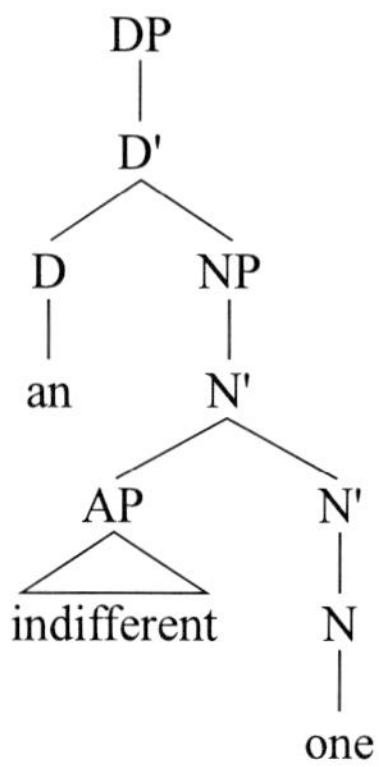

(69) a student of English

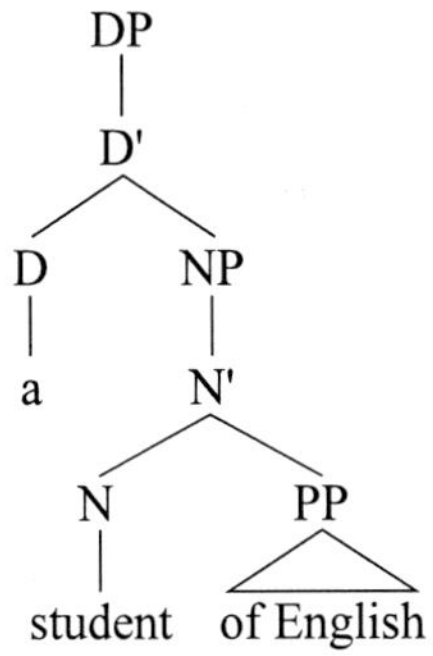

(70) a clever Italian student of English

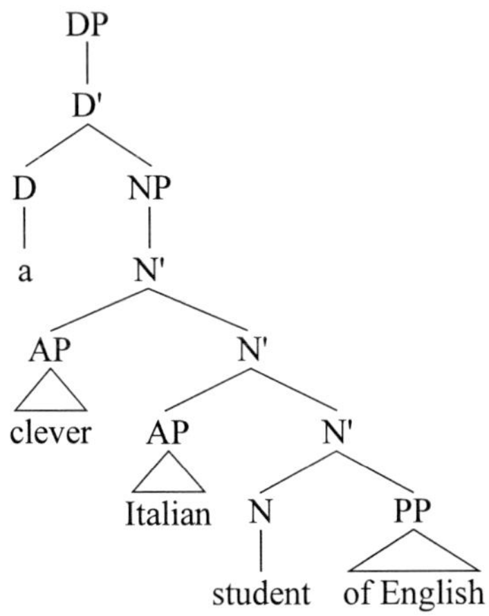

(71) rudely interrupt the speaker

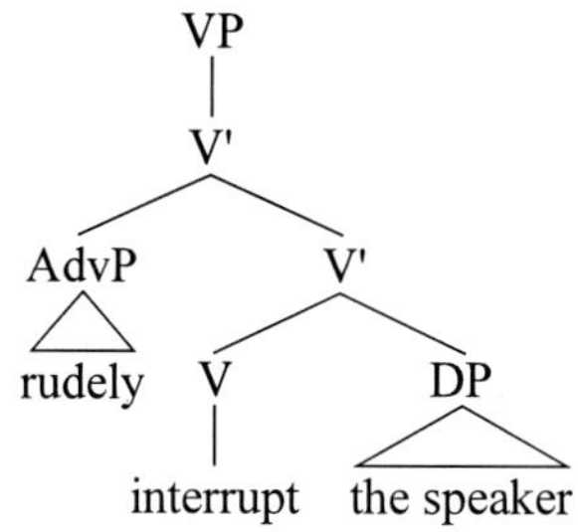

(72) Frank washed his shirts yesterday.

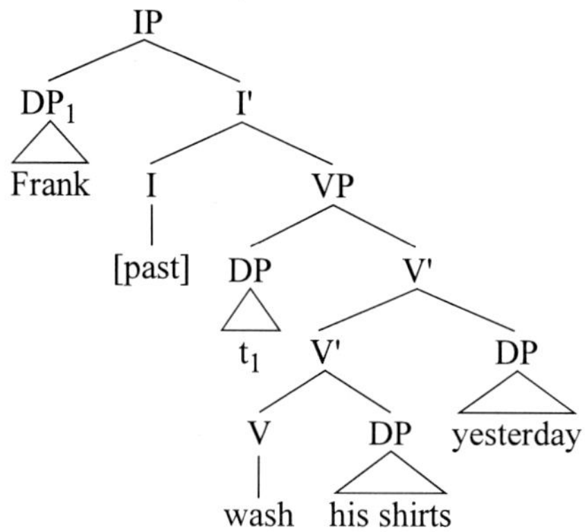

(73) eat the pizza naked

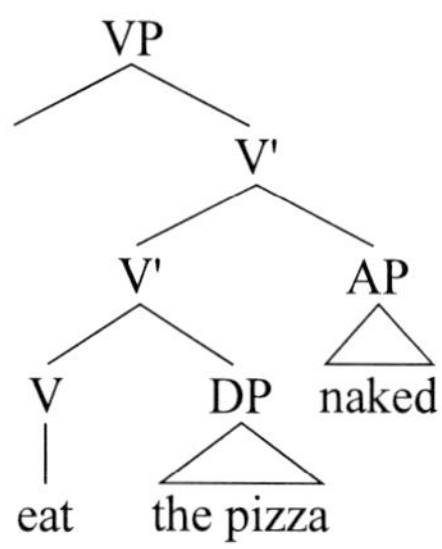

References

Abney, Steven. 1987. *The English noun phrase in its sentential aspect.* Doctoral dissertation, MIT.

Burzio, Luigi. 1986. *Italian syntax*. Dordrecht: Reidel.

Carnie, Andrew. 2007. *Syntax: A generative introduction* (*2nd edition*). Oxford: Blackwell Publishers.

Chomsky, Noam. 1964. *Current issues in linguistic theory*. The Hague: Mouton.

Chomsky, Noam. 1965. *Aspects of the theory of syntax*. Cambridge, Mass.: MIT Press.

Chomsky, Noam. 1977. On wh-movement. In *Formal syntax*, ed. Peter W. Cole, Thomas Wasow, and Adrian Akmajian, 71-132. New York: Academic Press

Chomsky, Noam. 1981. *Lectures on government and binding*. Dordrecht: Foris.

Chomsky, Noam. 1982. *Some concepts and consequences of the theory of government and binding*. Cambridge, Mass.: MIT Press.

Chomsky, Noam. 1986a. *Knowledge of language: Its nature, origin, and use*. New York: Praeger.

Chomsky, Noam. 1986b. *Barriers*. Cambridge, Mass.: MIT Press.

Chomsky, Noam. 1991. Some notes on economy of derivation and representation. In *Principles and parameters in comparative grammar*, ed. Robert Freidin, 417-454. Cambridge, Mass.: MIT Press.

Chomsky, Noam. 1993. A minimalist program for linguistic theory. *The view from Building* 20, ed. Ken Hale and Samuel J. Keyser, 1-52. Cambridge, Mass.: MIT Press.

Chomsky, Noam. 1994. *Bare phrase structure*. *MIT Occasional Papers in Linguistics* 5.

Chomsky, Noam. 1995. Categories and transformations. In *The minimalist program*, 219-394. Cambridge, Mass.: MIT Press.

Chomsky, Noam. 2000. Minimalist inquiries: The framework. In *Step by step: Essays on minimalist syntax in honor of Howard Lasnik*, ed. Roger Martin, David Michaels, and Juan Uriagereka, 89-155. Cambridge, Mass.: MIT Press.

Chomsky, Noam. 2001. Derivation by phase. In *Ken Hale: A life in language*, ed. Michael Kenstowicz, 1-52. Cambridge, Mass.: MIT Press.

Chomsky, Noam. 2004. Beyond explanatory adequacy. In *Structures and beyond: The cartography of syntactic structures* 3, ed. Adriana Belletti, 104-131. Oxford: Oxford University Press.

Chomsky, Noam. 2005. Three factors in language design. *Linguistic Inquiry* 36, 1-22.

Gruber, J. S. 1976. *Lexical structures in syntax and semantics*. Amsterdam: North-Holland.

Huang, C.-T. James. 1982. *Logical relations in Chinese and the theory of grammar*. Doctoral dissertation, MIT.

Koopman, Hilda, Dominique Sportiche, and Edward Stabler. 2003. *An introduction to syntactic analysis and theory*. Ms., UCLA.

Larson, Richard. 1988. On the double object construction. *Linguistic Inquiry* 19, 335-391.

Lasnik, Howard. 1995. A note on pseudogapping. In *Papers on minimalist syntax, MIT Working Papers in Linguistics* 27, 143-163. [Reprinted, with minor revisions, in Lasnik. 1999. *Minimalist Analysis*.]

May, Robert. 1985. *Logical form: Its structure and derivation.* Cambridge, Mass.: MIT Press.

Postal, Paul. 1971. *Cross-over phenomena*. New York, NY: Holt, Rinehart and Winston.

Radford, Andrew. 2004. *Minimalist syntax: Exploring the structure of English*. Cambridge, UK: Cambridge University Press.

Rizzi, Luigi. 1990. *Relativized minimality*. Cambridge, Mass.: MIT Press.

Ross, John Robert. 1967. *Constraints on variables in syntax*. Doctoral dissertation, MIT.

Williams, Edwin. 1978. Across-the-board rule application. *Linguistic Inquiry* 9, 31-43.

Index

Syntactic Analysis
A First Course

지은이 | Jeong-Seok Kim

초판 1쇄 발행 | 2012년 3월 02일
초판 3쇄 인쇄 | 2015년 2월 25일

펴낸곳 | 세진
주　소 | 12284 경기도 남양주시 다산지금로 202 현대테라타워 DIMC A동 79호
전　화 | 031-554-2118, 9
팩　스 | 031-554-2116
전자우편 | sejintrc@hanafos.com

가　격 | 20,000원
ISBN 978-89-956507-3-8 (93740)